G000154647

Let's Bake

Carmen Niehaus

First edition 2010
by Human & Rousseau
an imprint of NB Publishers
40 Heerengracht, Cape Town 8000

© published edition Human & Rousseau (2010)
© text Carmen Niehaus (2010)

No part of this book may be reproduced or transmitted in any form or by any
electronic or mechanical means, including photocopying and recording, or by
any other information storage or retrieval system, without written
permission from the publisher.
.

Commissioning Editor: Daleen van der Merwe
Translation: Celia van Zyl
Design: PETALDESIGN
Photography: David Briers
Food preparation: Christine Capendale
Proofreader and index: Joy Clack

Reproduction by Resolution Colour Pty (Ltd) Cape Town
Printed and bound in China through Colorcraft Ltd., Hong Kong

ISBN 978-0-7981-5125-2

Accessories courtesy of
Koöperasiestories, Simondium
and The Perfect Place, Wellington.

contents

acknowledgements

Without the support of Media24 Family Magazines, publisher Willem Breytenbach and **YOU** editor Esmaré Weideman, another **Let's Cook** would never have seen the light of day. Thank you also, Esmaré, for writing the foreword to this special baking book.

As with all the other **Let's Cook** books, Magda Herbst of Human & Rousseau typed in all the recipes before I finalised them. Human & Rousseau editor Daleen van der Merwe not only fine-tuned the concept for this book but also tweaked many of the recipes while still at **YOU** and coordinated the production logistics. Our photographer, David Briers, is such an old hand when it comes to **YOU** food photography we nearly take his stunning pictures for granted. David, thank you not only for your eagle eye but also for being willing to sacrifice seaside holidays and weekends to work from early morning until late at night. Christine and Robyn Capendale of Delici Studio in Langebaan agreed to bake the cakes and tarts over New Year so we could photograph them. Besides the fact that the goods were always on time and perfect, it was also wonderful to work in such beautiful surroundings and to break for a delicious light lunch specially prepared for us by Robyn every day. To my children, HW and Hanje, thank you for your help.

You can't take pictures without props. To Henri Droomer of Koöporasiestories, Simondium R45, thank you for letting me pop in at all hours to borrow odds and ends. Thank you also Susan van Rensburg of The Perfect Place, Church Street, Wellington, where I found the most wonderful antiques and silverware, and Isabella Niehaus of Langebaan, who gladly lent me her most precious pieces. To each and everyone who helped to make this book a success, a big thank you.

Carmen Niehaus

foreword

YOU Let's Bake is the eighteenth title in the **Let's Cook** series of bestselling cookery books, which have become indispensable aids in thousands of South African kitchens.

Like me, many of you probably learnt to cook with **YOU's** fantastic **Let's Cook** recipe books. They are practical books that are meant to be used instead of merely gracing coffee tables. **YOU Let's Bake** is a proud addition to this national treasure and contains the cream of our readers' most-prized recipes from the past 10 years, plus popular **YOU** food editor Camen Niehaus' own recipes for delicious cakes, tarts and cookies.

There are recipes for old favourites and new creations; for cakes laden with kilojoules but also for healthier cakes that contain less butter and sugar and more veggies, fruit, fibre and nuts. In typical **YOU** style the recipes are straightforward, easy and (hopefully) flop-proof. Carmen has also added loads of invaluable tips and information for both experienced and novice bakers.

Enjoy!

Esmaré Weideman
Editor **YOU, Huisgenoot** and **DRUM**

Facts at your fingertips

It's worthwhile getting to grips with the finer details of the ingredients and utensils you need for baking; it will ensure perfect results.

Flour, leavening agents, liquid, sugar and **shortening** are the basic ingredients for baking. The proportions in which they are used, measuring and mixing methods, baking tins and oven temperature play a role in the success of the end product, which is why it's important to understand the finer details of each to achieve perfect results every time.

The gluten in **flour** ensures the baked product has a good texture and retains its volume.

Leavening agents give the product a light, porous texture while the amount of **liquid** determines how smooth the batter is.

Sugar not only provides sweetness but also ensures the baked product turns golden brown.

Eggs act as a rising agent and also help to emulsify (mix) water and shortening in, for instance, choux pastry.

Shortening helps to give the product a soft texture and rich taste and improves its ability to keep because it stays moist for longer.

ALWAYS KEEP THE FOLLOWING IN MIND

- The longer you handle the batter or dough the more gluten development takes place. For instance, the longer you knead bread dough the more elastic it becomes and the better the texture of the bread. Too much gluten development can spoil the end product, for instance it results in tunnels forming in muffins, scones and cakes.

- The proportion rising agent (for instance baking powder) to flour for most baked products is 5 ml (1 t) baking powder for every 250 ml (1 c) flour.
- Bicarbonate of soda (an alkali) must always be used with an acidic ingredient such as buttermilk, molasses, brown sugar, citrus juice, vinegar, syrup or apricot jam when using it as a rising agent. Cream of tartar is the ideal acidic ingredient – use one part bicarbonate of soda for every two parts cream of tartar.
- Only use as much liquid as needed. The quantity given in the recipe may be either too little or too much.
- If using very large eggs use a little less liquid as eggs also form part of the liquid in the mixture.

EGGS
HOW TO WHISK EGG YOLKS
Egg yolks must be whisked until they form a fine, fairly stable foam with big volume and pale yellow colour. This can take a few minutes. If adding sugar don't add it when you start whisking; add it only once the egg yolks are fairly frothy.

HOW TO WHISK EGG WHITES
Egg whites mainly consist of protein parts dissolved in water. When they are whisked, air is captured and they become frothy.

It's important to whisk egg whites to the right stage – beating them too much or too little could cause the product to flop. See table below.

WHISKING EGG WHITES AND THEIR USES

STAGE	DESCRIPTION	USE
Beginning stage	Egg whites transparent and slightly yellow	
Foam stage	Frothy with large air bubbles, transparent, liquid, bigger in volume (Salt and cream of tartar are added at this stage to help stabilise the foam)	To glaze baked products Addition to choux pastry
Soft-peak stage	Less frothy and air bubbles become smaller, egg whites thicken Egg whites becomes whiter and opaque Very glossy and moist The egg whites slide out slowly when the bowl is tipped When lifting the beater, soft round peaks form (When making meringue, sugar is added at this stage)	Soft meringue, for instance topping for tarts
Stiff-peak stage	No longer frothy Very white, glossy and moist Maximum volume and stiffness are obtained Slides from the bowl only slightly when it's tipped Stiff peaks form when the beater is lifted	Cakes
Unusable stage (dry)	Very white and no longer glossy Stiff, dry and flaky The egg whites draw water and air bubbles burst Volume decreases	

FACTORS THAT AFFECT THE FORMING OF EGG WHITE FOAM

- Use a deep, clean, fat-free bowl and fine wire beater.
- To improve the volume, egg whites must be at room temperature.
- Separate the egg whites and yolks carefully – there must be no egg yolk in the whites as the fat in the egg yolks will prevent the egg whites beating to a foam.
- An acidic ingredient, such as cream of tartar, and salt slow down the foam process but ensure a more stable foam, provided it is added at the frothy stage and not when you start beating.
- Adding sugar results in a fine but stable foam with a fine texture; add sugar only at the soft-peak stage.
- It's important to use egg whites immediately after whisking them or they will draw water and become stiffer and less elastic. The cells will also break down if they are mixed with other ingredients.

SUBSTITUTING INGREDIENTS

Don't substitute baking ingredients willy-nilly as each ingredient has a specific function. Here are basic guidelines in case you don't have an ingredient on hand.

INGREDIENT	QUANTITY	SUBSTITUTE
baking powder	20 ml	10 ml cream of tartar and 5 ml bicarbonate of soda
butter	120 g	120 g margarine or 120 ml oil
self-raising flour	250 ml	250 ml cake flour less 10 ml + 7 ml baking powder and 2 ml salt
egg	1 whole	30 ml water + 2 ml baking powder OR 1 egg white + 10 ml oil
yoghurt	250 ml	250 ml sour milk or buttermilk
buttermilk or sour milk	250 ml	250 ml less 15 ml full-cream milk + 15 ml lemon juice or vinegar (leave to stand for 5–10 minutes) OR 250 ml full-cream milk + 7 ml cream of tartar OR 250 ml less 15 ml evaporated milk + 15 ml vinegar
cream of tartar	5 ml	15 ml lemon juice or vinegar OR 2 ml tartaric acid
cornflour	15 ml	30 ml cake flour (as thickener)
corn syrup	250 ml	250 ml honey
cream, thick	250 ml	170 ml buttermilk + 80 ml oil
cream, thin	250 ml	250 ml undiluted evaporated milk
chocolate, unsweetened	30 g	50–60 ml cocoa + 10 ml butter
shortening, melted	250 ml	250 ml oil
lemon juice	5 ml	2 ml vinegar
sour cream	250 ml	210 ml buttermilk + 40 ml butter
vanilla essence	5 ml	1 vanilla pod or 1 ml vanilla extract
allspice, ground	5 ml	2 ml ground cinnamon + 1 ml ground cloves

HOW TO MEASURE INGREDIENTS

- The volume (ml) and mass (gram) of ingredients are not the same, for instance 250 ml sugar = 200 g sugar and 250 ml bran = 30 g bran. So you cannot randomly convert the measures.
- Dry ingredients must preferably be weighed. Before weighing ingredients ensure the scale is set on 0 after putting the weighing bowl on top.
- Alternatively use measuring cups in different sizes, such as 50 ml, 60 ml, 125 ml and 250 ml to measure sugar or flour, instead of using a measuring jug with a spout. Spoon the flour or sugar into the measuring cup until it is overfull and level the excess flour or sugar with a spatula. Do not press it into the measuring cup or level it with a spoon or your hand.

- For small quantities, such as leavening agents and essences, use 15 ml, 12 ml, 5 ml, 2 ml and 1 ml measuring spoons. Level dry ingredients with a spatula.
- Shortening should preferably be weighed. A whole brick of margarine or butter can first be lightly marked at the halfway mark before dividing it into quarters.
- Water, oil, milk or syrup is measured in a calibrated measuring jug, preferably with a spout. Fill it to the desired level, checking that it's correct by looking at the jug from the side. If you look from the top an error of parallax is made.
- We used only extra-large eggs in our recipes. For difficult recipes, such as a sponge cake where the number of eggs is important, the volume of eggs is given. This can be measured by first beating the eggs gently and then measuring them.

carmen says
Take out all the ingredients before you start baking. Weigh and measure exactly.

MIXING THE BATTER

When baking, ingredients aren't simply thrown together and mixed. Various techniques are used to obtain a specific result so it's important to understand the terminology.

TECHNIQUE	DEFINITION	PURPOSE	EQUIPMENT
Beating	Use rapid, smooth circular movements, lifting the mixture each time.	To evenly distribute the ingredients To incorporate air	Wooden spoon
Stirring	Use circular movements. Not as rapid and vigorous as beating.	To evenly distribute ingredients	Wooden spoon
Whisking	Faster than beating, using a specific utensil/appliance.	To mix ingredients To incorporate air	Wire whisk Egg whisk Electric beater
Kneading	Fold and press dough without stretching it.	To develop gluten	Hand, or electric mixer
Creaming	Shortening is beaten or whisked until soft. Add sugar and beat or whisk until smooth and creamy.	To emulsify shortening, sugar and egg	Wooden spoon Electric beater
Cutting/ rubbing in	Hard pieces of shortening are rubbed into dry ingredients. Liquid is mixed into dry ingredients using cutting movements.	To distribute shortening particles in the dry ingredients To mix the ingredients	Table knife Shortening cutter Fingertips to rub in shortening
Folding in	Flour or whisked egg white is gently folded into the mixture using circular movements and a specific utensil.	To mix ingredients without losing air	Spatula Table knife

Carmen says
Only start mixing once everything has been measured. Also remember to prepare the tins and switch on the oven.

BAKING
The effect of height above sea level

A recipe developed at sea level often flops at altitudes higher than 900 m above sea level because the atmospheric pressure is lower at higher altitudes.

Gases expand more readily at higher levels, causing cells in baked products to stretch and break. Steam is also formed sooner during the baking process because water boils at a lower temperature, causing the cake to rise before the heat can set the protein and gelatinise the starch to provide a sturdy structure to the baking. The result is a cake that collapses.

Adjustments to allow for height above sea level

- For pastry, choux pastry or yeast batters simply set the temperature higher, usually by about 10 °C.
- For muffins and scones, using a little less baking powder should do the trick.
- Cakes are more delicate and require more adjustments:
  Reduce the rising agent so less gas forms.
  Reduce the sugar and sometimes shortening so the gluten doesn't become too soft; this will ensure a sturdier structure.
  Increase the liquid to compensate for its rapid condensation.

SUGGESTED ADJUSTMENTS TO RECIPES DEVELOPED AT SEA LEVEL			
	900 M	1 500 M	2 100 M
Reduce baking powder For every 5 ml in recipe reduce	0.5 ml to 1 ml	1 ml	1 ml
Reduce sugar Reduce every 200 g (250 ml) in recipe by	15 ml	15–30 ml	15–45 ml
Increase liquid Increase every 250 ml in recipe by	15–30 ml	30–60 ml	45–60 ml
Increase the oven temperature by	10 °C	10 °C	10 °C
For rich mixtures reduce the shortening by	⅙	⅙	⅙

EQUIPMENT
Tins

Different kinds of baked goods required different tins.
The material used to make the tin will affect the baking time and result.

Dark metal tins with a matt finish

Cakes bake faster because the dark surface absorbs the heat well, resulting in a product with more volume but that's inclined to rise with a slight point.

Shiny metal tins

Cakes bake slower as the shiny surface reflects the heat.

Glass dishes

Cakes bake even slower than in shiny tins and produce a result that's flat on top and with a weaker crumb than if baked in metal tins.

Shape of cake tins

■ Besides specific tins for a specific product such as bread, Swiss rolls and sponge cakes, cakes can also be baked in ring, springform, square or sandwich tins.

■ Sandwich cake tins must have straight not slanted sides.

■ The volume of a 20 cm square cake tin is larger than that of a 20 cm round cake tin, which means the same amount of batter will form a shallower layer in the square tin.

Size and depth of tins

■ A shallow sandwich cake tin (30 mm deep) results in a larger, softer cake with a flatter crust than if the cake was baked in a deeper tin.

■ A deep sandwich cake tin (50-90 mm deep) results in a more rounded top crust. It could even cause the crust to crack because the sides bake more rapidly than the centre, which is still soft and in the process of rising.

■ The larger the tin, the shallower the layer of batter in the tin and the more rapidly it will bake.

■ Baking sheets with shallow sides are used for cookies.

■ Pie tins and dishes must conduct heat rapidly and should preferably be made of aluminium. Ovenproof glass, ceramic and stainless steel are not good heat conductors and could result in the bottom crust not baking through.

How to prepare tins

Prepare the tins before mixing the ingredients. For most cakes, at least the bottom of the tin must be greased. In some instances the bottom must be lined with greased baking paper. You can also dust the tin with flour to prevent the cake sticking. It's unnecessary to grease the sides; leaving the sides ungreased makes it easier for the batter to cling to the sides of the tin as it rises.

For cakes such as a sponge cake use a clean, ungreased ring tin.

Swiss rolls are also a kind of sponge cake and the bottom must be lined with baking paper.

Line the bottom of microwave tins with paper towels to help absorb moisture or the batter will form a thick, solid layer in the bottom of the tin.

Nonstick tins and silicone moulds require no preparation.

OVEN TEMPERATURES

The right oven temperature plays a very important role in baking: it's the first thing to check if the result is not perfect.

Temperature too low

Slows down the setting of protein and gelatinising of starch, causing:

- Loss of gas.
- Enlarging of remaining cells.
- Thickening of cell walls.
- Loss in volume and weakening of texture.
- Collapse in the centre and stodgy texture.
- Formation of white flecks on the crust caused by expelled gas that dries out.
- The product to stick to the tin.

Temperature too high

- Causes the upper and side crusts to form before the batter has risen properly.
- Causes the soft part in the middle to continue rising, form a bulge and even crack through the upper crust.

How to use the oven

Preheat the oven to the right temperature before putting the cake in the oven.

Don't put the cake in the oven while the oven is still heating up. Ensure the oven is preheated well in advance as leaving the batter to stand while you wait for the oven to heat up will affect the result.

Put the tin on the middle shelf of the oven. If using a convection oven you can use all the shelves, but ensure the solid plates are all in position for optimum air circulation.

If baking more than one product at a time in a conventional oven ensure that the tins standing on one shelf don't touch. If using more than one shelf, don't put the tins directly above each other.

The baking time in the recipe is merely a guideline as several factors determine if the cake should stay in the oven for a longer or shorter time.

You can determine if a cake is done by merely looking at it or touching it: a cake is done if the edges shrink slightly away from the sides of the tin and the cake is springy to the touch.

How to turn out a cake

All cakes, except sponge and chiffon cakes, are left in the tin on a wire rack to cool slightly. This allows the cake to become firmer and helps to ensure it won't break or stick when turned out. If necessary the sides can be carefully loosened with a knife.

When cooled, turn out the cake on a wire rack.

To prevent deep marks forming on the top of the cake, cover the rack with a thin layer of cheesecloth or a clean tea towel.

Remove the baking paper and using a second rack to turn the cake the right way up.

A sponge or chiffon cake must be turned out on a wire rack as soon as it comes out of the oven as the tin is not greased and the cake sticks to the sides.

Leave a Swiss roll to cool on a wire rack for about 30 seconds before turning it out on a damp tea towel. Remove the paper and roll it up, using the cloth to help you. Leave to cool while rolled up.

To give the Swiss roll a nice round shape, wedge the sides of the tea towel in a closed drawer so the cake hangs over the edge.

The best way to master baking is to start with tried and trusted standard recipes. Once you've grasped the various methods you can start experimenting and be assured of a perfect result each time.

When I did domestic science at university our baking bible was **Food and Cookery,** which we dubbed **The Green Book.** To this day I rely on **The Green Book's** instructions and tips.

CAKE CATEGORIES

Cakes are categorised according to their ingredients and mixing method.

A. INGREDIENTS

1. Cakes that don't contain shortening or leavening agent. Example: sponge cake.

2. Cakes that contain shortening or oil and chemical leavening agent (such as baking powder).
   Examples: butter cake, Madeira cake, feather cake, chiffon cake.

B. MIXING METHOD

1. Sponge-cake method
Examples: sponge cake, Swiss roll.
Separate the eggs and whisk the whites and yolks. The whites must be stiff but not dry. Add part of the sugar to both the whites and yolks and beat well (meringue method). Fold the two mixtures into each other. Sift the dry ingredients over the mixture in layers and carefully fold in.
OR
Whisk the whole eggs until pale yellow and frothy. Gradually whisk in the sugar, sift the dry ingredients over the egg mixture and carefully fold in.

2. Cream or rub-and-beat method
Examples: Madeira cake, fruitcake.
Beat together the softened butter and sugar until light and creamy. Gradually add the whisked egg to form an emulsion. Fold in the dry ingredients, alternating with the liquid.

3. Melting method
Examples: ginger loaf, brandy snaps.
Heat together the shortening, liquid and sugar or syrup until melted and leave to cool slightly. Stir the sifted dry ingredients into the cooled shortening mixture. Add the whisked eggs and mix until smooth.

4. Instant or one-bowl method
Example: instant cakes.
Sift together the dry ingredients. Mix the remaining ingredients, which must be at room temperature, with the dry ingredients, blending until smooth.

5. Combination of melting and sponge-cake methods
Example: feather cake.
Heat the shortening in the liquid and leave to cool slightly. Whisk together the eggs and sugar until well blended. Add the shortening mixture to the egg mixture and mix well.

6. Combination of instant and sponge-cake methods
Examples: chiffon cake, oil cake.
Sift together the dry ingredients. Add the oil, egg yolks and liquid and beat until smooth. Whisk the egg whites until stiff with or without part of the sugar. Fold the stiffly whisked egg whites/meringue into the batter.

WHAT IS THE DIFFERENCE BETWEEN A BATTER AND A DOUGH?

A batter is runny and is classified into runny and drop batter, the former being much thinner than the latter. A dough is thick enough to be handled and is classified into soft or stiff dough.

SPONGE CAKE (ANGEL FOOD CAKE)

Traditionally the classic American angel food cake, which is based on whisked egg white and is snowy white, is baked in an ungreased ring tin.

Baking a perfect sponge cake the first time round is rare but once you've grasped the technique you'll be home and away!

It's important to weigh the flour, as a volume measure is not reliable. No chemical leavening agent is added and the sides of the tins are not greased. This ensures the batter sticks to the sides and rises to perfection.

Sponge cake

CAKE
5 extra-large eggs, separated
200 ml (160 g) sugar
12 ml (1½ t) lemon juice or
    5 ml (1 t) cream of tartar dissolved in
    10 ml (2 t) water
120 g cake flour
pinch salt

ICING
200 ml lemon curd (see p. 206)
icing sugar

Preheat the oven to 160 °C. Line the bottoms of two 20 cm sandwich cake tins with greased baking paper. Sprinkle a small spoonful of caster sugar over the paper and knock out the excess sugar. Dust with a little flour and knock out the excess flour. Do not grease the sides of the tins.

CAKE Whisk the egg whites until stiff peaks begin to form.
Gradually whisk in 125 ml (½ c) of the sugar and the lemon juice or dissolved cream of tartar. Without rinsing the beater, whisk the egg yolks until thick and pale yellow.
Gradually add the remaining sugar, beating until dissolved (ribbon stage). Using a metal spoon, fold the whisked egg yolks into the whisked egg whites.
Sift the flour and salt together three times, then sift layers of the mixture over the egg mixture, folding in each layer with a spatula. Repeat until all the flour has been folded in but do not overmix or the air will escape.
Turn the batter into the prepared tins. Tap the tins gently to remove any large air bubbles.
Bake for 35–45 minutes or until golden brown on top and the cakes have shrunk slightly from the inside of the tins and are springy to the touch. Cool the cakes in the tins for 15 minutes before turning them out onto a wire rack to cool

completely. Carefully loosen the cakes when nearly cold so they can slide out.

ICING Sandwich the cake layers together with lemon curd and dust with icing sugar.

MAKES 1 MEDIUM-SIZED CAKE.

VARIATION

Sandwich the cake layers together with caramel cream icing (see p. 205) and serve with fresh fruit compote (see p. 211).

Carmen says
- Adding cream of tartar helps to stabilise the egg whites so they can retain more air, reduces shrinking during the baking process and helps to ensure a finer, whiter sponge cake. Lemon juice also acts as a stabiliser and reduces the eggy taste.
- Do not overbake the cake or the texture will be dry.

Sponge cake

Troubleshooting: Sponge cake

	PROBLEMS	CAUSES
APPEARANCE	Cracked crust	Eggs overwhisked Mixture too stiff
	Hard, brown crust	Oven temperature too high Baking time too long
	Sticky crust	Too much sugar Baking time too short
	Crust smooth and shiny on the sides	Tin was greased
	Shrinkage	Too little or too much acid added Baking temperature too low Baking time too short Tin was greased Cooled too rapidly
	White flecks on the crust	Sugar not dissolved Air bubbles drying out on the surface
	Low volume	Oven temperature too high Egg whites whisked too little or too much Too much sugar Overmixed after adding the cake flour
TEXTURE	Coarse	Sugar too coarse No acid added Eggs and sugar mixture not whisked enough Cake flour not folded in carefullly Batter mixed too little or too much Oven temperature too high
	Dry	Egg whites whisked until too dry Too much cake flour Too little sugar Oven temperature too low Baking time too long
	Dense and heavy	Egg whites whisked too little or too much Cake flour not folded in carefully Batter overmixed
	A dense layer at the bottom	Eggs not fresh Batter left to stand before baking Ingredients not properly mixed
	Sticky or hard	Too much cake flour No acid added Baked too long Batter mixed too much
	Uneven texture	Ingredients not mixed properly Oven temperature too low

Chocolate sponge cake

This sponge cake, made with only egg whites, is as light as a soufflé, says Marika Jooste of Kuilsrivier, who sent in this recipe years ago.

80 ml (⅓ c) cocoa
60 ml (¼ c) boiling water
10 ml (2 t) vanilla essence
500 ml (2 c) egg whites (about 12 eggs), at room temperature
10 ml (2 t) cream of tartar
430 ml caster sugar
250 ml (1 c) cake flour
1 ml (¼ t) salt
cocoa and caster sugar

Preheat the oven to 180 °C. Line the bottom of a ring tin with greased baking paper, sprinkle it with caster sugar and knock out the excess sugar. Do not grease the sides of the tin.

Mix together the cocoa and boiling water to form a smooth paste and add the vanilla essence.

Whisk the egg whites until frothy and add the cream of tartar.

Whisk until stiff peaks form and add the caster sugar by the spoonful, whisking continuously while adding the sugar. Whisk until the mixture is thick and shiny. Add about 250 ml (1 c) of the meringue to the cocoa mixture and, using a metal spoon, fold in gently.

Sift the cake flour and salt over the remaining meringue and fold in gently. Fold the cocoa mixture into this mixture.

Turn the batter into the tin and gently tap the bottom of the tin on the work surface to remove large air bubbles.

Bake for 40 minutes or until done or the cake is springy to the touch.

Invert the tin on the work surface and leave the cake to cool in the tin. Carefully run a knife along the inside of the tin and turn out the cake. Dust with a little cocoa and caster sugar to decorate.

MAKES 1 LARGE CAKE.

Carmen says

How to fold in the flour: Use a figure-eight motion and spatula or metal spoon for best results. Sweep the spatula or spoon up against the nearest side, draw it through the centre of the mixture at an angle, lift the spatula or spoon towards the surface and high up into the air and draw it through the mixture to complete the figure-eight. Rotate the mixing bowl a quarter turn while folding. Repeat a few times until all the flour is folded in.

Butter cake

The cream method is the most common, flop-proof method used to make a butter cake. This is a wonderful standard recipe that you can adapt in several ways.

CAKE
120 g butter or margarine, at room temperature
200 ml sugar
5 ml (1 t) vanilla essence
2 extra-large eggs
500 ml (2 c) cake flour
10 ml (2 t) baking powder
1 ml (¼ t) salt
125 ml (½ c) milk

FILLING AND ICING
butter icing (see p. 204)

Preheat the oven to 190 °C and grease two 20 cm sandwich cake tins.

CAKE Beat the butter or margarine until creamy. Gradually add the sugar, beating until light and creamy. Add the vanilla essence.
Whisk the eggs well and gradually beat them into the butter mixture, beating until smooth.
Sift together the dry ingredients and carefully add them to the butter mixture, alternating with the milk.
Mix carefully and well.
Turn the batter into the prepared tins and bake for 20–25 minutes. Leave the cakes to cool in the tins before turning them out onto a wire rack to cool completely.

FILLING AND ICING Prepare the butter icing as described and sandwich the cake layers together with a little of the icing. Decorate the cake with the remaining icing.

MAKES 1 LARGE SANDWICH CAKE.

VARIATIONS
Marble cake: Divide the batter into two equal parts. Mix 25 ml (5 t) cocoa, 5 ml (1 t) sugar and 25 ml (5 t) boiling water and stir the mixture into the one half of the batter. Spoon alternating mounds of the two batters into a greased 18 cm square cake tin and run a skewer through the batters to mix them slightly. Bake, ice and decorate with chocolate curls.
Orange cake: Substitute orange juice for a quarter of the milk and grated lemon zest for the vanilla essence.
Nut cake: Stir 50 g (125 ml) chopped walnuts or any other nuts into the batter.
Spice cake: Sift 5 ml (1 t) ground cinnamon, 5 ml (1 t) ground ginger and 1 ml (¼ t) ground cloves or 15 ml (1 T) mixed spice with the dried ingredients. Omit the vanilla essence.
Coconut cake: Add 60 ml (¼ c) desiccated coconut to the milk and leave to soak a little. Add to the batter.

Carmen says
■ The success of a butter cake depends largely on how thoroughly the butter and sugar are creamed together. Beat until you no longer feel the sugar crystals when you rub the mixture between your thumb and forefinger.
■ A butter cake usually rises in the centre to form a dome. For a level cake, make a slight hollow in the middle of the batter or bake a feather or chiffon cake instead.
■ Occasionally the butter mixture splits once the eggs have been added. This is easily remedied by adding a little flour to the mixture.

Marble cake

Troubleshooting: Butter cake

	PROBLEMS	CAUSES
APPEARANCE	Cracked crust	Batter too stiff Oven temperature too high at the start of the baking time Tin too deep
	Cake forms a dome	Ingredients overmixed Batter too stiff Oven temperature too high Tin too deep
	Cake rises over tin	Too much butter Tin too shallow or small for amount of batter
	Cake sinks in the centre	Batter too thin Too much sugar, shortening, leavening agent or liquid Oven temperature too low Batter not mixed well Oven door opened too soon or cake moved during baking process Baking time too short
	Uneven shape	Oven heat distributed unevenly Oven shelf is uneven Tin uneven
	Speckled crust	Sugar too coarse Sugar not fully dissolved Air bubbles drying out on the surface because too much air has been incorporated
	Pale colour	Batter overmixed
	Sugary crust	Too much sugar or leavening agent Ingredients not properly mixed
	Crust brown and shiny with coarse surface	Too much sugar Batter not mixed enough
	Moist, sticky crust	Too much sugar or butter Batter too slack Baking time too short
	Sides have sticky marks and loose crumbs	Not cooled long enough in tin before turning out
	Dry and sticky	Too much egg, flour or leavening agent Too little shortening, sugar or liquid Batter overmixed Baking time too long
	Low volume	Butter and sugar not creamed enough Too much butter or leavening agent Batter not mixed enough Oven temperature too low Very shiny cake tins used
TEXTURE	Coarse texture with large holes and thick sides	Bread flour used instead of cake flour Butter and sugar not creamed enough Too much cake flour, sugar or leavening agent Oven thermostat faulty Ingredients not mixed properly or overmixed
	Tunnels and large holes	Batter overmixed Leavening agent not evenly distributed in batter Oven temperature too high

Dry texture	Too little shortening, liquid and sugar Too much baking powder or cake flour Ingredients overmixed Cocoa added without reducing cake flour or adding extra liquid Egg whites overwhisked Baking time too long	
Dense, heavy texture	Too much shortening or sugar Too little leavening agent Too little or too much liquid Overmixed Baking time too short Oven thermostat faulty Too much batter in tin Tin overgreased	
Too light and crumbly	Too much leavening agent Oven temperature too low	
Moist and sticky	Too much sugar, liquid and leavening agent Not mixed enough	

Madeira cake

A Madeira cake is a very rich butter cake. The method is the same as for a butter cake except that the eggs are not whisked before being added. This traditional English cake has a lovely citrus flavour. For an almond-flavoured cake add almond essence instead of the lemon zest.

CAKE
250 g butter
250 g caster sugar
5 extra-large eggs
grated zest of ½ lemon or
    3 ml almond essence
250 g (520 ml) cake flour
1 ml (¼ t) salt
15 ml (1 T) milk

ICING
icing sugar
lemon juice
glacé orange slices (see p. 210)

Preheat the oven to 160 °C. Grease a deep round cake tin (18 cm in diameter and 8 cm deep) and line it with greased baking paper.

CAKE Beat the butter until soft and creamy. Gradually add the sugar, beating until the mixture is light and fluffy. If using a mixer set it at medium speed.
Add the eggs one by one, beating well after each addition. Add the zest or essence. The sugar must be completely dissolved before the flour is added.
Sift the flour and salt together and gradually add a third of the mixture at a time to the butter mixture. Add just enough milk to make a fairly stiff batter.
Turn the batter into the prepared tin, spreading it evenly, and bake for about 1 hour or until a skewer comes out clean when inserted into the centre of the cake. Turn out and leave to cool.

ICING Mix just enough icing sugar with lemon juice to make a drop mixture and drizzle it over the cake. Decorate with glacé orange slices.

MAKES 1 LARGE SINGLE-LAYER CAKE.

Troubleshooting: Madeira cake

	PROBLEMS	CAUSES
APPEARANCE	White specks on the crust	Sugar not properly dissolved Too much air incorporated, causing white flecks on the surface when air bubbles dry out
	Crust cracked or domed	Too much batter in the tin, causing the crust to form before the batter has risen in the centre. It rises later, causing the crust to crack Batter too stiff Oven temperature too high
	No cracks in crust or slightly sunken	Batter too slack
TEXTURE	Coarse	Sugar not dissolved or too coarse Ingredients not mixed enough Batter too slack Oven temperature not well regulated
	Spongy	Proportions of ingredients incorrect for a Madeira cake
	Sticky crust	Sugar not properly dissolved Too much sugar

Gingerbread

Gingerbread

Quick flour mixtures such as those for gingerbread and brandy snaps are prepared according to the melting method. The shortening, sugar and liquid are melted together and the dry ingredients are stirred in followed by the eggs. Quick and easy.

CAKE
500 ml (2 c) cake flour
10 ml (2 t) ground ginger
5 ml (1 t) mixed spice
5 ml (1 t) ground cinnamon
5 ml (1 t) bicarbonate of soda
2 ml (½ t) salt
120 g butter
125 ml (½ c) golden syrup
125 ml (½ c) sugar
125 ml (½ c) boiling water
1 extra-large egg, whisked

DECORATION
whole ginger preserve, diced

Preheat the oven to 180 °C. Grease a small loaf tin and line it with greased baking paper.

CAKE Sift the flour, spices, bicarbonate of soda and salt together.
Mix the butter, syrup, sugar and boiling water together, stirring until the sugar has dissolved.
Blend the two mixtures and stir in the whisked egg. Turn the batter into the prepared tin, scatter the diced ginger on top and bake for 45–50 minutes or until done.
Leave the loaf to cool in the tin for 5 minutes before turning it out onto a wire rack to cool completely.

MAKES 1 SMALL LOAF.

Carmen says
- Do not leave the batter to stand in the tin before putting it in the oven. The batter is very thin so the solids will sink to the bottom, resulting in a loaf with a moist, dense bottom layer and poor volume.
- This gingerbread tastes at its best two days after baking.
- The crust of a gingerbread is always domed and slightly cracked.

Troubleshooting: Gingerbread

	PROBLEMS	CAUSES
APPEARANCE	Large crack	Loaf tin not the correct size Too much leavening agent Too little liquid Oven temperature too high at the beginning
TEXTURE	Dry	Too little syrup Batter too stiff
	Hollow under the crust	Batter not mixed enough
TASTE	Disappointing taste	Ginger old Poor spice mix ratio Soapy taste caused by too much bicarbonate of soda

Granny Carmen's feather cake

The recipe for this cake, which my mom used to call a hot-milk cake, comes from my Granny Carmen. It was the standard recipe my mom used to teach us the art of baking.

A combination of the melting and sponge-cake methods is used for a feather cake. Unlike a butter cake where the sugar and shortening are creamed together, the butter for a feather cake is melted in the liquid so less shortening is needed.

CAKE
160 ml (⅔ c) milk
60 ml (¼ c) butter
4 extra-large eggs
375 ml (1½ c) caster sugar
5 ml (1 t) vanilla essence
500 ml (2 c) cake flour
2 ml (½ t) salt
10 ml (2 t) baking powder

FILLING AND ICING
butter icing (see p. 204)
crystallised orange peel (see p. 210)

Preheat the oven to 200 °C. Grease the bottoms of two 22 cm sandwich cake tins or line 24 muffin tin hollows with paper cups.

CAKE Heat the milk and butter until the milk comes to the boil. Remove from the heat and stir until the butter has melted. Set aside.
Whisk the eggs until light and fluffy. Gradually add the sugar, beating until it has dissolved. Add the essence.
Sift the flour, salt and baking powder together and fold the mixture into the egg mixture. Add the lukewarm milk mixture and beat well.
Turn the batter into the prepared tins or paper cups and bake for 20–25 minutes. Leave the cakes to cool in the tins before turning them out onto a wire rack to cool completely.

FILLING AND ICING Prepare a butter icing, sandwich the cake layers together with a little of the icing and spread the remaining icing on top. Decorate with crystallised orange peel.

MAKES 1 MEDIUM-SIZED SANDWICH CAKE.

VARIATION
To make a light chocolate cake add 20–45 ml (4–9 t) cocoa and reduce the cake flour accordingly.

Carmen says
- Sift the dry ingredients together three times.
- Always add the liquid at the end, beating the mixture well.
- Turn the batter into the tins and put them in the oven immediately; do not let the batter stand in the tins.
- The batter is thinner than that of a butter cake and spreads evenly in the tins.
- The oven temperature is higher than for other cakes. Leave the cakes to cool in the tins before turning them out.
- If you loosen the sides of the cakes and turn them out while still hot the air bubbles will break and form doughy layers.

Granny Carmen's feather cake

Three-tier chiffon cake

Three-tier chiffon cake

A chiffon cake is like an instant cake (similar to an oil cake), where all the ingredients are mixed together, except that stiffly beaten egg whites are added last. This is a combination of instant and sponge-cake methods.

CAKE
750 ml (3 c) cake flour
470 ml sugar
22 ml (4½ t) baking powder
4 ml salt
190 ml oil
7 extra-large eggs, separated
270 ml cold water
15 ml (1 T) lemon juice
7 ml (1½ t) grated lemon zest
3 ml (generous ½ t) cream of tartar

ICING
caramel condensed milk
icing sugar

Preheat the oven to 180 °C. Line the bases of three 22 cm sandwich cake tins with ungreased baking paper. Do not grease the tins.

CAKE Sift the flour, sugar, baking powder and salt together. Make a well in the centre of the ingredients.
Add the oil, whole egg yolks, cold water and lemon juice and zest in this order and beat with a spoon or beater until the mixture is smooth.
Add the cream of tartar to the egg whites and whisk until stiff but not dry. Gently fold the stiffly beaten egg whites into the batter.
Turn the batter into the prepared tins and bake for 25–30 minutes. Leave to stand for 5 minutes, run a knife along the inside of the tins and turn out the cakes on a wire rack to cool completely.

ICING Sandwich the cakes together with caramel condensed milk. Mix icing sugar with enough water to make a runny paste and drizzle the icing over the cake.

MAKES 1 TRIPLE-LAYERED CAKE.

VARIATIONS

Walnut chiffon cake: Add 100 g finely chopped walnuts to the batter just before folding in the egg whites. Decorate the cake with caramel cream icing (see p. 205) and walnut halves.

Chocolate chiffon cake: Substitute 80 ml (⅓ c) cocoa for 80 ml (⅓ c) flour.

Carmen says
- Fold in the egg whites carefully to ensure the incorporated air does not escape.
- A chiffon cake has a delicate, fine, airy texture but is not as spongy as a sponge cake. It rises to a great height and is much higher than a feather cake.
- Chiffon or feather cake batter is ideal for oven-pan cakes or cupcakes.

Large cakes

Light, risen to perfection and with a fine texture — that's what a large cake should look like. Bakers' skill was often measured by the height of their cakes but fortunately this requirement no longer applies and you can pick and choose from sandwich cakes, Swiss rolls, ring cakes and loaf cakes. If you have to bake for large numbers bake a cake in an oven pan.

Cheesecake, chocolate cake and fruitcake always deserve a special mention, while cakes packed with fresh ingredients and wholesome health cakes are high on the agenda too. If you need to rustle up a cake in a jiffy, you can use the microwave oven.

SANDWICH CAKES

Cake layers sandwiched together with filling: for me the enjoyment of a sandwich cake lies in the many ways a delicious filling or icing can transform a plain cake into delectable confection.

Mariëtte Crafford's buttermilk sandwich cake

"In our house this cake is for festive occasions but also comfort food and sometimes our daily bread," wrote well-known food writer Mariëtte Crafford when sharing her favourite food with YOU. "For us it's confirmation of an important event and everyday goodwill. We usually have it just because we love it. For special occasions it can be decorated with fresh fruit and rose geranium and lemon verbena leaves or simply dusted with icing sugar. If baking it for a bazaar or birthday smother it with a thick layer of vanilla icing. It's a real standby and child's play to bake."

CAKE
125 g softened butter
310 ml (1¼ c) caster sugar
3 extra-large eggs
250 ml (1 c) buttermilk or Bulgarian
   yoghurt, at room temperature
   (or equal quantities of buttermilk
   and crème fraîche)
5 ml (1 t) vanilla essence or seeds
   of ½ vanilla pod
450 ml (1¾ c) self-raising flour

FILLING AND ICING
cream cheese icing (see p. 204)
60–125 ml (¼–½ c) orange curd
   (see p. 206)
fresh organic roses
200 g dark chocolate, melted

Preheat the oven to 180 °C. Grease a 23 cm springform tin with butter, margarine or nonstick spray. Dust the tin with cake flour or line the bottom with greased baking paper.

CAKE Beat the butter and caster sugar together until thick and pale yellow. **Add** the eggs one at a time, beating well after each addition. Add the buttermilk or yoghurt and vanilla essence or seeds and beat until smooth. **Sift** the self-raising flour on top and fold in gently. **Spoon** the batter into the prepared tin and bake for 40–50 minutes or until a testing skewer comes out clean when inserted into the centre of the cake. Leave the cake to cool in the tin for a few minutes before turning it out onto a wire rack to cool completely. Halve the cake.

FILLING AND ICING Prepare the cream cheese icing as described, add the orange curd and mix well. Spread the icing over the cake layers and stack them on top of each other. Dip the roses in the melted chocolate and leave them to harden on a wire rack. Decorate the cake with fresh roses.

MAKES 1 MEDIUM-SIZED SANDWICH CAKE.

VARIATION
Add 50 ml granadilla pulp to the Bulgarian yoghurt and reduce the yoghurt accordingly. Decoration: Mix 375 ml (1½ c) icing sugar with about 60 ml (¼ c) granadilla pulp and drizzle the runny icing over the cake instead of using the cream cheese icing.

Mom Rinie's hot-milk feather cake

Landbouweekblad's food editor and former YOU test kitchen team member Arina du Plessis learnt to bake using this recipe. She says it's the only cake recipe that's used in the Du Plessis household. The variations and fillings are the result of many years of experimenting.

CAKE

500 ml (2 c) cake flour
3 ml (generous ½ t) salt
125 ml (½ c) water
125 ml (½ c) milk
100 ml oil
4 extra-large eggs
500 ml (2 c) sugar
10 ml (2 t) baking powder

NOUGAT FILLING

15 ml (1 T) gelatine
125 ml (½ c) water
250 ml (1 c) butter, at room
    temperature
30 ml (2 T) caster sugar
1 can (375 g) condensed milk
5 ml (1 t) vanilla essence
1 ml (¼ t) almond essence
1 ml (¼ t) salt
5 ml (1 t) cream of tartar
5 ml (1 t) lemon juice
125 ml (½ c) finely chopped
    red glacé cherries
125 ml (½ c) finely chopped walnuts
sherry or muscadel

ICING

125 ml (½ c) cream, chilled
30 ml (2 T) caster sugar
2 ml (½ t) vanilla essence
30 ml (2 T) thick yoghurt
fresh berries (optional)

Preheat the oven to 180 °C. Grease two 23 cm cake tins with butter, margarine or nonstick spray. Line the tins with greased baking paper.

CAKE Sift the cake flour and salt together and set aside.
Bring the water, milk and oil to the boil. Remove from the heat and leave to cool.
Whisk the eggs until thick and pale yellow. Add the sugar by the spoonful while beating continuously until thick and light.
Sift the flour over the egg mixture and fold in. Sift over the baking powder, add the milk mixture and mix.
Turn the batter into the prepared tins, spreading it evenly.
Bake for 20–25 minutes or until a testing skewer comes out clean when inserted into the centre of the cakes. Leave the cakes to cool in the tins for a few minutes before turning them out onto a wire rack to cool completely.

NOUGAT FILLING In a glass bowl, sprinkle the gelatine over the cold water and leave it to sponge. Heat the sponged gelatine over a saucepan with hot water until it has just melted. Leave it to cool for a few minutes.
Cream the butter and sugar together and add the gelatine drop by drop while beating continuously.
Add the condensed milk, vanilla and almond essences, salt, cream of tartar and lemon juice, beating until blended. Chill until slightly set.
Fold in the glacé cherries and nuts and leave to set further.
Halve each cake layer and sprinkle each half with sherry or muscadel. Evenly spread a little of the filling on the bottom cake layer and cover with the next cake layer, pressing it down gently. Repeat until all the cake layers have been used. Do not cover the top of the last layer with filling.

ICING Whip the cream, caster sugar and vanilla essence together until stiff. Carefully fold in the yoghurt. Spoon the icing on top of the cake and decorate with fresh berries.

MAKES 1 LARGE SANDWICH CAKE.

VARIATIONS

Chocolate cake with coffee filling: Prepare the recipe as described but use 400 ml cake flour and 100 ml cocoa instead of 500 ml (2 c) cake flour.
Coffee filling: Cream together 200 ml butter (at room temperature) and 250 ml (1 c) icing sugar. Add 7 ml (1½ t) coffee powder dissolved in 10 ml (2 t) boiling water, whisking until blended. Stir in 5 ml (1 t) vanilla essence. Sprinkle a little brandy over the four cake layers and sandwich them together with a thin layer of coffee filling. The moistened cake layers will absorb the filling. Decorate the cake with whipped cream.

Granny Marjorie's Victoria sandwich

Award-winning food editor of **Taste**, Abigail Donnelly, has loved cooking since she used to help her granny, Marjorie Millard, in the kitchen. This cake was a favourite.

CAKE
500 ml (2 c) butter, at room temperature
400 ml caster sugar
6 extra-large eggs, lightly whisked
600 ml self-raising flour
pinch salt
15–25 ml (3–5 t) milk (optional)

FILLING AND ICING
smooth apricot jam
icing sugar for dusting on top
fresh roses or crystallised
   pansies (see p. 213) to decorate the cake

Preheat the oven to 180 °C. Grease two 23 cm cake tins with butter, margarine or nonstick spray and line them with greased baking paper.

CAKE Beat the butter and caster sugar together until thick and pale yellow.
Add the eggs a little at a time, beating continuously.
Sift the flour and salt together and sift a third of the mixture over the batter.
Fold in with a metal spoon and repeat with the remaining flour. Add a little of the milk if the batter is too stiff.
Divide the batter between the cake tins, spreading it evenly. Bake for 45–60 minutes or until golden and a testing skewer comes out clean when inserted into the centre of the cakes. Leave the cakes to cool in the tins for a few minutes before turning them out onto a wire rack to cool completely.
Halve each cake layer horizontally.

FILLING AND ICING Spread a thin layer of smooth apricot jam over one cake layer, put the other layer on top and dust the cake with icing sugar. Decorate with fresh roses or crystallised pansies.

MAKES 2 MEDIUM-SIZED SANDWICH CAKES.

Chocolate 'n spice feather cake

This chocolate hot-milk cake is given extra flavour with spices and is sandwiched together with a date filling. We were sent the recipe by Mrs E Moller of Kuruman.

CAKE
250 ml (1 c) milk
30 ml (2 T) sugar
30 ml (2 T) butter
30 ml (2 T) cocoa
250 ml (1 c) cake flour
10 ml (2 t) baking powder
5 ml (1 t) ground cinnamon
5 ml (1 t) grated nutmeg
pinch cloves
pinch salt
250 ml (1 c) sugar
2 extra-large eggs

FILLING AND ICING
15 ml (1 T) sugar
15 ml (1 T) cocoa
250 ml (1 c) water
125 g butter
250 g dates, pitted and finely chopped
chopped nuts for sprinkling on top

Preheat the oven to 190 °C. Grease two 20 cm cake tins with butter, margarine or nonstick spray and line them with greased baking paper.

CAKE Bring the milk, 30 ml (2 T) sugar, butter and cocoa to the boil. Remove from the heat and leave to cool.
Sift the dry ingredients together, except the sugar.
Beat the sugar and eggs together until thick and light.
Fold the dry ingredients into the egg mixture and add the cooled milk mixture. Mix gently.
Turn the batter into the prepared tins and bake for 30–45 minutes. Leave the cakes to cool in the tins for a few minutes before turning them out onto a wire rack.

FILLING AND ICING Mix the sugar, cocoa and water. Add the butter and dates. Bring to the boil and, stirring occasionally, simmer the mixture until thick. Cool slightly and sandwich the cake layers together with the filling. Spread a little of the filling on top of the cake and scatter with chopped nuts.

MAKES 1 MEDIUM-SIZED SANDWICH CAKE.

Three-tier orange custard sandwich cake

Cecile Strydom of Middelburg sent us this recipe in 1992. She says she searched high and low for a light cake with a soft, creamy filling. When the women from the Women's Agricultural Association raved about this chiffon cake she knew her search was over.

CAKE
400 ml cake flour
50 ml cornflour
15 ml (1 T) baking powder
3 ml (generous ½ t) salt
5 extra-large eggs, at room
 temperature, separated
350 ml sugar
100 ml fresh orange juice
finely grated zest of 1 large orange
125 ml (½ c) oil
100 ml boiling water
2 ml (½ t) cream of tartar

FILLING AND ICING
50 ml cake flour
50 ml cornflour
25 ml (5 t) custard powder
1 ml (¼ t) salt
200 ml sugar
500 ml (2 c) fresh orange juice
finely grated zest of 1 large orange
2 extra-large eggs
250 ml (1 c) fresh cream

Preheat the oven to 190 °C. Line three 20 cm cake tins with greased baking paper.

CAKE Sift the dry ingredients together twice. Set aside.
Whisk the egg yolks until thick and pale yellow. Add the sugar by the spoonful, beating well after each addition. Beat until very light and creamy. Beat in the orange juice and zest. Mix the oil and boiling water and gradually beat the mixture into the egg mixture.
Sift the dry ingredients over the egg mixture and fold them in with a metal spoon.
Whisk the egg whites in a clean, dry bowl until soft peaks form. Fold in the cream of tartar.
Fold the egg whites into the batter and divide it among the three prepared cake tins.
Make a slight hollow in the middle of the batter.
Place the tins in the oven, immediately reduce the temperature to 180 °C and bake for about 35 minutes or until a testing skewer comes out clean when inserted into the centre of the cakes. Remove the cakes from the oven and leave them to cool in the tins for 2 minutes. Turn them out onto a tea towel on a wire rack. Cover with a thin tea towel and leave to cool.

FILLING AND ICING Sift the dry ingredients together and add the sugar. Bring 100 ml of the orange juice and zest to the boil in a small saucepan and reduce rapidly for about 3 minutes. Remove the saucepan from the heat and strain the reduction through a sieve to remove the zest. Add the reduction to the remaining orange juice and add enough water to make up 500 ml. Whisk the eggs until frothy. Add the dry ingredients, beating until the mixture resembles whipped cream.
Bring the orange juice mixture to the boil and add half to the egg mixture, beating well. Add everything to the remaining orange juice mixture in the saucepan. Stirring continuously, simmer over low heat until the mixture thickens and is cooked. Spoon the custard mixture into a mixing bowl and cover the surface with clingfilm to prevent a skin forming. Leave to cool completely.
Whip the cream until stiff. Beat the custard into the cream by the spoonful until everything has been incorporated. Chill until firm. Sandwich the cake layers together with some of the filling and decorate the cake with the remaining filling. Put the cake in an airtight container and leave for at least 4 hours or overnight to allow the flavour to develop.

MAKES 1 LARGE THREE-TIER SANDWICH CAKE.

Ginger sandwich cake

The chopped ginger preserve gives this cake a wonderfully spicy flavour. The cake will last in an airtight container for up to a week. Decorate it just before serving.

CAKE
200 g butter
250 ml (1 c) soft brown sugar
45 ml (3 T) golden syrup
150 ml milk
2 large eggs, whisked
4 pieces ginger preserve, chopped
625 ml (2½ c) self-raising flour
15 ml (1 T) ground ginger
pinch salt

FILLING AND ICING
560 ml (2¼ c) icing sugar, sifted
140 g butter
60 ml (¼ c) ginger syrup from the
**   ginger preserve**
10 ml (2 t) lemon juice

Preheat the oven to 160 °C. Grease a 23 cm cake tin and line it with greased baking paper.

CAKE Heat the butter, brown sugar and golden syrup in a saucepan until melted. Stir and leave to cool slightly. Add the milk, gradually beat in the eggs, then add the chopped ginger preserve.

Sift the flour, ground ginger and salt together and gradually stir the mixture into the butter mixture.

Turn the batter into the prepared tin.

Bake for 30–35 minutes or until a testing skewer comes out clean when inserted into the centre of the cake and the cake has shrunk slightly from the sides of the tin. Leave the cake to cool in the tin before turning it out onto a wire rack. Halve the cake. (The cake can be frozen at this stage.)

FILLING AND ICING Beat the icing sugar, butter and 30 ml (2 T) of the ginger syrup and lemon juice together until thick. Prick the cake layers and pour over the remaining ginger syrup. Sandwich the cake layers together with the filling, ice the top and decorate with extra chopped ginger preserve.

MAKES 1 MEDIUM-SIZED CAKE.

Carmen says
Serve the ginger cake with ginger strawberries (see p. 211).

SWISS ROLLS

A Swiss roll always impresses as you need to master the knack of rolling it up without cracking it. The secret lies in not baking it too long and to work rapidly when it comes out of the oven. Usually a Swiss roll is spread with only a thin layer of apricot jam but the variations include one where ground almonds are added to the batter. If only a meringue mixture is used the roll is called a roulade. It's simply delicious spread with a thin layer of lemon curd or chocolate.

Lemon Swiss roll

Janet Shelford of Marshalltown loves making this feather-light Swiss roll with a lemon filling.

SWISS ROLL
150 ml cake flour
15 ml (1 T) cornflour
7 ml (1½ t) baking powder
4 extra-large eggs, separated
220 ml caster sugar
finely grated zest of 1 lemon
15 ml (1 T) lemon juice

CITRUS CURD CREAM
250 ml (1 c) cream, chilled
   and stiffly whipped
125 ml (½ c) orange or
   lemon curd (see p. 206)

Preheat the oven to 190 °C and lightly grease a 33 x 25 cm Swiss roll tin with butter, margarine or nonstick spray. Line the tray with baking paper (see below). Grease again and sprinkle with sugar and a little flour.

SWISS ROLL Sift the flour, cornflour and baking powder together and set aside.
Whisk the egg whites until soft peaks form and gradually whisk in 60 ml (4 T) caster sugar. Whisk until the mixture is thick and glossy.
Whisk the egg yolks, lemon zest and remaining sugar together until thick and pale yellow. Whisk in the lemon juice. Using a metal spoon, fold the egg white mixture into the egg yolk mixture, followed by the flour.
Turn the batter into the prepared tin, spreading it evenly. Bake for 15 minutes or until golden.
Sprinkle a large sheet of wax paper or a damp tea towel with caster sugar. Turn out the Swiss roll onto the wax paper or tea towel. Remove the paper clips and slowly and carefully peel away the paper. Roll up the sponge with the sheet of wax paper or tea towel and leave it to cool.

CITRUS CURD CREAM Fold the stiffly whipped cream into the curd. Carefully unroll the cooled sponge, spread it with the cream mixture and roll it up again.

MAKES 1 SWISS ROLL OF ABOUT 10–12 SLICES.

tip
The Swiss roll can be baked a day in advance.

Carmen says
How to line a Swiss roll tin: Tear a sheet of wax or baking paper about 7 cm bigger all around than the tin. Invert the tin, put the paper on the back of the tin and fold in the sides along the edges of the tin. Cut an incision to each corner of the tin. Turn the tin the right way up, put the sheet of paper inside and secure it with paper clips where it overlaps the corners.

Lemon Swiss roll

Meringue Swiss roll (Roulade)

Marizahn van Breda of Stellenbosch makes a soft meringue mixture which contains no flour. She sprinkles the mixture with almond flakes and fills the roulade with lemon curd.

ROULADE
6 extra-large egg whites
1 ml (¼ t) salt
3 ml (generous ½ t) lemon juice
350 ml caster sugar
5 ml (1 t) vanilla essence
15 ml (1 T) boiling water
15 ml (1 T) cornflour
50 g flaked almonds

FILLING
icing sugar
citrus curd cream (see p. 38)

Preheat the oven to 140 °C. Put the oven shelf one position below the middle. Line a 25 x 35 cm baking tray with baking paper (see p. 38), grease the tray and dust with cornflour.

ROULADE Whisk the egg whites and salt together until slightly frothy. Add the lemon juice and whisk until stiff peaks begin to form. Gradually add the caster sugar, beating continuously until the mixture is stiff and glossy. Whisk in the essence and boiling water.
Sift the cornflour over the mixture and fold it in with a metal spoon.
Spoon the mixture onto the baking paper and, using a spatula, spread it evenly. Scatter over the almond flakes.
Bake for 20–25 minutes or until the meringue is pale brown and spongy and easy to roll up. (Do not overbake or the roulade will become stiff and impossible to roll up.)
Turn out onto a clean tea towel that has been sprinkled with icing sugar. Roll up and leave to cool.
Prepare the citrus curd cream as described.
Unroll the roulade, spread with the filling and reroll it. Slice and serve immediately.

MAKES 1 MEDIUM-SIZED ROULADE.

Chocolate and almond Swiss roll

This recipe works beautifully. The ground almonds in the mixture make it slightly heavier than a conventional sponge mixture. The sponge is filled with cream cheese and cherries.

SWISS ROLL
5 extra-large eggs, separated
200 ml caster sugar
60 ml (¼ c) cake flour
125 ml (½ c) cocoa
60 ml (¼ c) ground almonds
60 ml (¼ c) milk

FILLING
45 ml (3 T) softened butter
45 ml (3 T) caster sugar
250 g cream cheese
100 g ground almonds
5 maraschino cherries, finely chopped

Preheat the oven to 200 °C. Lightly grease a 35 x 20 cm Swiss roll tin, line it with greased baking paper (see p. 38) and sprinkle it with caster sugar and flour.

SWISS ROLL Whisk the egg yolks and caster sugar together until thick and pale yellow.
Sift the cake flour and cocoa together and stir in the almonds. Fold the flour mixture into the egg yolk mixture, alternating with the milk.
Whisk the egg whites until stiff and fold them into the batter.
Turn the batter into the prepared tin, spreading it evenly. Bake for 10–12 minutes or until done. Turn out onto a damp tea towel sprinkled with caster sugar. Roll up firmly with the tea towel and leave to cool.

FILLING Cream the butter and sugar together. Beat in the cream cheese and add the almonds and cherries, mixing well. Chill until needed. Unroll the sponge and evenly spread the filling over the cake. Roll up firmly and cut into neat, thin slices.

MAKES 1 MEDIUM-SIZED SWISS ROLL.

Chocolate Swiss roll

This decadent Swiss roll is filled with chocolate spread and whipped cream. If the filling is too rich, substitute strawberry jam for the chocolate spread.

SWISS ROLL
4 extra-large eggs
100 ml caster sugar
180 ml (¾ c) cake flour
30 ml (2 T) cocoa, sifted
caster sugar for rolling

FILLING
90 ml (6 T) chocolate spread (see tip)
200 ml cream, chilled
icing sugar for dusting

Preheat the oven to 190 °C. Grease a Swiss roll tin, line it with greased baking paper (see p. 38) and dust it with cocoa.

SWISS ROLL Whisk the eggs and sugar together until thick and pale yellow. (The mixture must fall off the beater in a thick ribbon.)
Sift the cake flour and cocoa over the egg yolk mixture and, using a metal spoon, fold in gently.
Turn the mixture into the prepared tin, gently spreading it evenly. Bake for 8–10 minutes or until puffed and the sponge is springy to the touch.
Meanwhile moisten a tea towel and wring it out so it is slightly damp. Spread it out on the work surface, cover it with a sheet of wax paper and sprinkle with caster sugar. Turn out the cake onto the sheet of wax paper and carefully peel away the baking paper from the bottom of the sponge. Roll up the sponge, starting from the long end, and leave it to cool. Unroll the sponge when completely cooled and spread it with a thin layer of the chocolate spread. Beat the cream until stiff and spread over the chocolate layer. Carefully reroll the sponge and dust with icing sugar.

MAKES 1 MEDIUM-SIZED SWISS ROLL.

Carmen says
There are many chocolate spreads to choose from but you can also make your own. Melt 200 g dark chocolate, broken into pieces, with 150 ml cream. Stir until the mixture is smooth and leave it to cool before spreading it over the Swiss roll.

RING CAKES

I've always associated ring cakes with special occasions. With their unique shape and decorative pattern they hardly need any icing. My first introduction to ring cakes was as a child when my mom used to make a fruit and buttermilk cake. It was saturated with a citrus syrup that ensured it lasted well and, of course, also improved the flavour over time.

In 2007 Daleen van der Merwe, who was assistant food editor at YOU at the time and is now cookery book editor at Human & Rousseau, collected several ring cake recipes, from plain ring cakes with nuts to carrot cakes, including delicious icings, and ring cakes rose even further in my esteem.

Mom Jo's fruit ring cake

My mom was given this recipe by a neighbour. In the seventies, during the "border war", farmers' wives in the Citrusdal region used to make food parcels for the soldiers. They baked plenty of these cakes and put a can of boiled condensed milk in the centre of each and surrounded it with dried fruit.

SYRUP
250 ml (1 c) sugar
180 ml (¾ c) orange juice
10 ml (2 t) finely grated orange zest

CAKE
250 g butter
250 ml (1 c) sugar
2 extra-large eggs
500 ml (2 c) cake flour
2 ml (½ t) salt
150–180 ml (generous ½–¾ c)
   buttermilk
5 ml (1 t) bicarbonate of soda
125 ml (½ c) roughly chopped
   walnuts or pecan nuts
30 ml (2 T) mixed peel
250 ml (1 c) finely chopped dates
30 ml (2 T) cake flour

Carmen says
This cake freezes well and will keep for up to a month in an airtight container.

SYRUP Prepare the syrup well in advance of making the cake so it will be ice cold when spooned over the hot cake. Slowly heat the syrup ingredients until the sugar has melted. Bring the mixture to the boil and simmer for 1 minute. Remove the saucepan from the heat and leave the syrup to cool. Chill until ice cold.

Preheat the oven to 180 °C and grease a 27 cm loose-bottom ring tin with butter, margarine or nonstick spray.

CAKE Cream the butter and sugar together until the mixture is pale and fluffy. Add the eggs one at a time, beating well after each addition.

Sift the cake flour and salt together. Add 250 ml (1 c) of the flour mixture and half the buttermilk to the butter mixture and fold in until just blended.

Dissolve the bicarbonate of soda in the remaining buttermilk and add to the butter mixture, alternating with the remaining flour mixture.

Mix the nuts, peel and dates with the 30 ml (2 T) cake flour and mix lightly into the batter.

Turn the batter into the prepared tin, spreading it evenly. Bake for 45–55 minutes or until a testing skewer comes out clean when inserted into the centre of the cake. Spoon the chilled syrup over the hot cake. Prick the cake with a testing skewer so the syrup can be easily absorbed. Return the cake to the oven and bake it for another 20 minutes or until the syrup is no longer visible. Remove the cake from the oven and leave it to cool in the tin before turning it out carefully.

MAKES 1 MEDIUM-SIZED CAKE.

Fig 'n spice ring cake

This cake is made with dried figs and moistened with a spicy syrup. The recipe was sent in by Mrs ME Steenkamp of Ceres.

CAKE
80 ml (⅓ c) softened butter
310 ml (1¼ c) sugar
250 ml (1 c) milk
5 ml (1 t) grated lemon zest
750 ml (3 c) cake flour
20 ml (4 t) baking powder
2 ml (½ t) salt
4 egg whites
5 ml (1 t) ground cinnamon
5 ml (1 t) grated nutmeg
375 ml (1½ c) finely chopped dried figs
30 ml (2 T) cake flour
15 ml (1 T) honey

SPICY SYRUP
250 ml (1 c) sugar
250 ml (1 c) water
2 star anise
2 cinnamon sticks
4 thick strips lemon peel

Preheat the oven to 190 °C. Grease a 30 cm ring tin and dust it with flour.

CAKE Cream the butter and sugar together until the mixture is pale and fluffy. Beat in the milk and lemon zest.
Sift the dry ingredients together and fold into the butter mixture. Whisk the egg whites until stiff and fold into the batter. Spoon two-thirds of the batter into a bowl and add the spices. Dust the figs with flour and add them to the remaining third of the batter. Add the honey.
Turn the spice batter into the tin, alternating with the fig batter. Bake for 20 minutes.
Reduce the oven temperature to 180 °C and bake the cake for another 40 minutes or until a testing skewer comes out clean when inserted into the centre of the cake.

SPICY SYRUP Slowly bring the syrup ingredients to the boil in a saucepan. Boil rapidly for about 5 minutes or until slightly syrupy. Remove from the heat. Pour the syrup over the cake as soon as it comes out of the oven. Leave the cake to cool in the tin before carefully turning it out.

MAKES 1 LARGE CAKE.

Granadilla ring cake

Anneli van Zyl of Pretoria sent us this recipe in 1990. Her husband loves granadilla cake and after searching high and low she found this recipe.

CAKE
250 g butter
430 ml (1¾ c) caster sugar
4 extra-large eggs
5 ml (1 t) vanilla essence
560 ml (2¼ c) cake flour
10 ml (2 t) baking powder
180 ml (¾ c) cornflour
250 ml (1 c) evaporated milk
1 can (110 g) granadilla pulp
pinch salt

ICING
250 ml (1 c) sifted icing sugar
granadilla pulp

Preheat the oven to 180 °C. Grease a 25 cm ring tin with butter, margarine or nonstick spray.

CAKE Cream the butter and caster sugar together until the mixture is light and fluffy. Add the eggs one at a time, beating well after each addition. Add the vanilla essence and mix.
Sift the dry ingredients together and add to the egg mixture, alternating with the evaporated milk.
Add the granadilla pulp and salt and mix.
Turn the batter into the prepared tin and bake for 25–35 minutes or until a testing skewer comes out clean when inserted into the centre of the cake. Leave the cake to cool in the tin for a few minutes before turning it out onto a wire rack.

ICING Mix the icing sugar with just enough granadilla pulp to make a thick, runny icing. Drizzle it over the cake.

MAKES 1 LARGE RING CAKE.

Carmen says
A ring cake is usually moist and heavy and should preferably be baked in a ring tin. The hole in the centre ensures better heat distribution so the cake bakes more evenly. If baked in an ordinary tin the cake tends to sink in the centre.

Citrus and poppy seed ring cake

This cake, drenched in a sweet 'n sour citrus syrup, is decorated with citrus zest cooked in the syrup until soft.

CAKE
125 g butter
250 ml (1 c) caster sugar
4 extra-large eggs, whisked
560 ml (2¼ c) cake flour
12 ml (2½ t) baking powder
180 ml (¾ c) milk
60 ml (¼ c) poppy seeds
grated zest of 1 orange
grated zest of 1 lemon
10 ml (2 t) vanilla essence

SYRUP AND DECORATION
125 ml (½ c) lemon juice
250 ml (1 c) orange juice
500 ml (2 c) sugar
zest of 2 oranges, cut into thin strips
zest of 2 lemons, cut into thin strips
whipped cream to serve (optional)

Preheat the oven to 180 °C. Grease a 22 cm ring tin and dust with a little cake flour. Knock out the excess flour.

CAKE Cream the butter and sugar together until the mixture is pale and fluffy. Gradually add the eggs, beating well after each addition.
Sift the flour and baking powder together and fold the mixture into the egg mixture, alternating with the milk. Add the poppy seeds, orange and lemon zests and vanilla essence and fold in.
Turn the batter into the prepared tin and bake for 45–50 minutes or until a testing skewer comes out clean when inserted into the centre of the cake.

SYRUP Heat the lemon and orange juices and sugar over low heat, stirring until the sugar has dissolved. Add the zests and bring the mixture to the boil. Simmer for 5 minutes or until the zest is soft. Remove the zest with a slotted spoon and set aside.
Prick the cake with a skewer as soon as it comes out of the oven and pour over the hot syrup. Arrange the zest strips on the cake and leave the cake to cool completely. Remove the cake from the tin and serve it with whipped cream if desired.

MAKES 1 LARGE RING CAKE.

Fig and pecan nut ring cake

I love a heavy cake like this one, made with plenty of dried fruit and nuts. All it needs is a little drop icing, but for special occasions you can decorate it with caramelised nuts.

CAKE
200 g butter
375 ml (1½ c) sugar
15 ml (1 T) finely grated lemon zest
3 extra-large eggs
15 dried Smyrna figs,
  roughly chopped
250 ml (1 c) roughly chopped
  pecan nuts
430 ml self-raising
  flour, sifted
250 ml (1 c) milk

ICING
creamy lemon drop icing (p. 203)
  and caramelised nuts (see p. 209)

Preheat the oven to 180 °C. Grease a 24 cm ring tin and dust with cake flour.

CAKE Beat the butter, sugar and lemon zest together until the mixture is pale yellow and fluffy. Add the eggs one at a time, beating well after each addition.
Stir in the figs and pecan nuts and, using a large metal spoon, fold the self-raising flour into the batter, alternating with the milk. The batter must be smooth.
Turn the batter into the prepared tin and bake for 50–60 minutes or until a testing skewer comes out clean when inserted into the centre of the cake. Leave the cake to cool in the tin for 20 minutes before turning it out onto a wire rack to cool completely.

ICING Prepare the icing and caramelised nuts as described and drizzle the icing over the cake so it runs down the sides. Scatter the nuts on top.

MAKES 1 LARGE RING CAKE.

Macadamia and polenta ring cake

I love the coarse texture of polenta cakes. The icing we chose to go with this cake is called 7-minute icing because that's how long it takes to whisk it over hot water until it's firm enough to use.

CAKE
125 ml (½ c) macadamia
   or hazelnuts
300 ml icing sugar, sifted
125 g butter, at room temperature
2 extra-large eggs, whisked
250 ml (1 c) cake flour
5 ml (1 t) baking powder
1 ml (¼ t) bicarbonate of soda
pinch salt
100 ml buttermilk
45 ml (3 T) honey
90 ml (6 T) polenta
   or coarse maize meal

ICING
7-minute icing (see p. 205)
fresh berries to serve

Preheat the oven to 190 °C. Grease a 20 cm loose-bottomed ring tin and dust it with a little cake flour. Knock out the excess flour.

.

CAKE Toast the nuts in the preheated oven for about 5 minutes. Roughly chop them and stir in a spoonful of flour to coat them.

Beat the icing sugar and butter together until light and creamy. Add the whisked eggs by the spoonful, beating continuously.

Sift the flour, baking powder, bicarbonate of soda and salt together and fold the mixture into the egg mixture, alternating with the buttermilk.

Fold in the nuts, honey and polenta.

Turn the batter into the prepared tin and bake for 35–40 minutes or until done. Leave the cake to cool in the tin for 15 minutes.

Turn out onto a wire rack to cool completely.

ICING Prepare the icing as described and drizzle it over the cake. Decorate with fresh berries just before serving.

MAKES 1 LARGE RING CAKE.

Carmen says
Sprinkle a spoonful of flour over the nuts or fruit to prevent them sinking to the bottom of the tin while baking.

LOAF CAKES

Loaves such as banana, date and ginger loaves are fuss-free and can be baked in small loaf tins or even food tins in the case of Boston loaf. They can also be baked in small round cake tins if desired. The fruit and nuts give the loaves their special flavour. A small crack in the surface is no reflection on your baking skills — it's completely acceptable. Most loaves need little if any icing — some drop icing should suffice. Some loaves are served with butter.

Lemon loaf

We first published this recipe in 2001 with a single remark: "Irresistibly delicious!"

CAKE
750 ml (3 c) cake flour
3 ml (generous ½ t) baking powder
3 ml (generous ½ t) salt
230 g butter, at room temperature
750 ml (3 c) sugar
6 extra-large eggs
60 ml (¼ c) lemon juice
30 ml (2 T) finely grated lemon zest
250 ml (1 c) sour cream

ICING
creamy lemon drop icing (see p. 203)

Preheat the oven to 180 °C. Grease two 20 x 10 cm loaf tins or two 20 cm cake tins with butter, margarine or nonstick spray. Dust them with cornflour and knock out the excess cornflour.

Sift the flour, baking powder and salt together and set aside.

Cream the butter and sugar together until the mixture is pale and fluffy. Add the eggs one at a time, beating well after each addition. Beat in the lemon juice and zest.

Fold in the dry ingredients. Stir in the sour cream and turn the batter into the prepared tins, spreading it evenly.

Bake for about 1 hour or until a testing skewer comes out clean when inserted into the centre of the loaves. Leave the loaves to cool in the tins.

Carefully run a knife along the inside of the tins and turn out the loaves onto wire racks. Leave them to cool completely before decorating with lemon drop icing.

MAKES 2 MEDIUM-SIZED LOAVES.

Carmen says
- The loaves taste at their best if left to stand for a day or two to ripen.
- Leave the loaves to cool in the tins for a few minutes; the steam ensures they come out easily. Do not leave them in the tins for too long, however, as they'll sweat and the sides will become stodgy.

Dark ginger loaf

This dark ginger loaf is richer than a standard gingerbread, writes Lionel Slabbert of Benoni. The molasses gives the loaf its dark colour, while the ginger preserve and walnuts add to its rich flavour.

125 g margarine
160 ml (⅔ c) caster sugar
2 extra-large eggs, whisked
10 ml (2 t) golden syrup
15 ml (1 T) molasses
390 ml cake flour
3 ml (generous ½ t) ground ginger
3 ml (generous ½ t) baking powder
125 g ginger preserve in syrup,
    roughly chopped
80 ml (⅓ c) chopped walnuts

Preheat the oven to 180 °C. Grease a small loaf tin or 20 cm cake tin with a little butter, margarine or nonstick spray and line the bottom with greased baking paper.
Cream the margarine and sugar together. Beat in the eggs, syrup and molasses.
Sift the flour, ginger and baking powder together and stir the mixture into the margarine mixture. Fold in the ginger pieces and turn the batter into the prepared tin.
Scatter the chopped nuts on top and bake for 60–70 minutes or until a testing skewer comes out clean when inserted into the centre of the loaf.
Turn out the loaf and leave it to cool on a wire rack.
Serve with ginger strawberries (see p. 211) if desired.

MAKES 1 SMALL LOAF.

Madeira loaf with nuts and cherries

The butter in this rich cake will keep it deliciously moist for a week or two.

250 g butter, at room temperature
300 ml (250 g) caster sugar
6 extra-large eggs
3 ml (generous ½ t) almond essence
525 ml (250 g) cake flour
10 ml (2 t) baking powder
2 ml (½ t) salt
50 ml milk
125 g pecan nuts, halved lengthways
125 g red glacé cherries, rinsed
    and drained

Preheat the oven to 160 °C and line a 25–27 cm loaf tin with greased baking paper.
Cream the butter and sugar together until the mixture is pale and fluffy. Add the eggs one at a time, beating well after each addition. Beat the mixture until the sugar has dissolved completely. Add the essence.
Sift the flour, baking powder and salt together and gradually stir the mixture into the egg mixture, alternating with the milk. Add the pecan nuts and whole cherries and mix well.
Turn the batter into the prepared tin and bake for 1 hour or until a testing skewer comes out clean when inserted into the centre of the loaf. Leave the loaf to cool in the tin for a few minutes before turning it out onto a wire rack to cool completely.

MAKES 1 LARGE LOAF.

Carmen says
Wrap loaves in clingfilm and store them in an airtight container. They'll keep for two weeks.

Pineapple loaf

This yummy loaf, made with granadilla yoghurt, tastes even better if left to stand for a day, writes Neville Arendse of Heidedal in Bloemfontein.

CAKE
500 ml (2 c) cake flour
5 ml (1 t) baking powder
5 ml (1 t) grated nutmeg
1 ml (¼ t) salt
100 g butter
250 ml (1 c) light brown sugar
1 can (410 g) crushed pineapple, drained
1 extra-large egg
5 ml (1 t) bicarbonate of soda
250 ml (1 c) granadilla yoghurt

ICING (OPTIONAL)
icing sugar
milk
granadilla pulp

Preheat the oven to 180 °C. Grease a 26 x 10 cm loaf tin with butter, margarine or nonstick spray and line the bottom with greased baking paper.

CAKE Sift the cake flour, baking powder, nutmeg and salt together and set aside.
Cream the butter and brown sugar together until the mixture is light and fluffy.
Add the pineapple and mix well.
Whisk the egg, bicarbonate of soda and yoghurt together. Add to the pineapple mixture and mix lightly.
Add the mixture to the dry ingredients.
Turn the batter into the prepared tin and bake for 45–50 minutes or until a testing skewer comes out clean when inserted into the centre of the loaf.

ICING Serve plain or decorate with a drop icing made with a little icing sugar, milk and granadilla pulp.

MAKES 1 LARGE LOAF.

Apple loaf

Grated apple and nuts add extra fibre to this buttermilk loaf. The recipe was sent in by Ellen Ritter of George.

500 ml (2 c) cake flour
1 ml (¼ t) salt
5 ml (1 t) bicarbonate of soda
125 ml (½ c) butter or margarine
250 ml (1 c) sugar
2 extra-large eggs
60 ml (¼ c) buttermilk
60 ml (¼ c) finely chopped pecan nuts
250 ml (1 c) finely grated apple
5 ml (1 t) vanilla essence

Preheat the oven to 180 °C and grease a 20 x 10 cm loaf tin with butter, margarine or nonstick spray.
Sift the cake flour, salt and bicarbonate of soda together. Set aside.
Cream the butter or margarine and sugar together until the mixture is light and fluffy. Add the eggs one at a time, beating well after each addition.
Stir the dry ingredients into the butter mixture, alternating with the buttermilk.
Add the pecan nuts, grated apple and vanilla essence.
Mix gently, turn the batter into the prepared tin and bake for about 1 hour or until golden and a testing skewer comes out clean when inserted into the centre of the loaf. Leave the loaf to cool in the tin for a few minutes before turning it out onto a wire rack.

MAKES 1 MEDIUM-SIZED LOAF.

Peanut Boston loaf

This full-flavoured loaf lasts well and tastes even better the next day, writes Mrs EJ Eager-Schultz of Sasolburg.

500 ml (2 c) cake flour
pinch salt
5 ml (1 t) baking powder
250 ml (1 c) brown sugar
5 ml (1 t) mixed spice
250 ml (1 c) fruitcake mix
250 ml (1 c) dates, pitted and
   finely chopped
15 ml (1 T) peanut butter
5 ml (1 t) bicarbonate of soda
250 ml (1 c) boiling water
peanuts for sprinkling over (optional)

Preheat the oven to 180 °C. Grease a 24 x 12 cm loaf tin with butter, margarine or nonstick spray and line the bottom with greased baking paper.

Sift the flour, salt and baking powder together and add the brown sugar and mixed spice.

Add the fruit, dates and peanut butter. Dissolve the bicarbonate of soda in the boiling water and add to the fruit mixture, mixing well.

Turn the batter into the prepared tin, scatter peanuts on top if using and bake for about 1¼ hours or until done. Leave the loaf to cool in the tin for a few minutes before turning it out onto a wire rack to cool completely. Serve with butter.

MAKES 1 MEDIUM-SIZED LOAF.

Buttermilk fruit loaf

Marié Keulder of Florida Hills in Gauteng often bakes this loaf. We used a round tin but a 22 x 10 cm loaf tin works equally well.

500 ml (2 c) cake flour
pinch salt
125 g softened butter or margarine
250 ml (1 c) sugar
5 ml (1 t) bicarbonate of soda
10 ml (2 t) mixed spice
5 ml (1 t) ground cinnamon
3 ml (generous ½ t) grated nutmeg
125 ml (½ c) currants
125 ml (½ c) mixed peel,
   finely chopped
15 ml (1 T) golden syrup
300 ml buttermilk

Preheat the oven to 180 °C. Grease a 20 x 10 cm jam tin with butter, margarine or nonstick spray and line the bottom with greased baking paper.

Sift the cake flour and salt together and rub in the butter or margarine with your fingertips.

Add the sugar, bicarbonate of soda, spices, currants and mixed peel and mix well.

Mix the syrup and buttermilk and add, stirring until everything is just mixed. Turn the batter into the prepared tin.

Bake for 1–1½ hours or until done and a testing skewer comes out clean when inserted into the centre of the loaf. Remove the loaf from the oven and leave it to cool in the tin for a few minutes before turning it out. Leave to cool completely and serve as is or with butter.

MAKES 1 MEDIUM-SIZED LOAF.

Nut and banana loaf

This banana loaf is moistened with a syrup made of milk and sugar. We were sent the recipe by Bets van der Linde of Pretoria North.

CAKE
125 g butter or margarine
375 ml (1½ c) sugar
2 extra-large eggs, whisked
375 ml (1½ c) cake flour
5 ml (1 t) bicarbonate of soda
3 ml (generous ½ t) salt
250 ml (1 c) mashed ripe banana
125 ml (½ c) finely chopped
   mixed nuts
125 ml (½ c) seedless raisins

SYRUP
125 ml (½ c) soft brown sugar
250 ml (1 c) milk
5 ml (1 t) vanilla essence

Preheat the oven to 180 °C. Grease a 20 x 10 cm loaf tin with butter, margarine or nonstick spray and line it with greased baking paper.

CAKE Cream the butter or margarine together and sugar until the mixture is light and fluffy. Add the eggs one at a time, beating well after each addition. Sift over the dry ingredients and add the banana, nuts and raisins. Mix gently until the ingredients are just blended. Turn the batter into the prepared tin, spreading it evenly. Bake for 35–45 minutes or until a testing skewer comes out clean when inserted into the centre of the loaf.

SYRUP Slowly heat the sugar and milk together until the sugar has melted. Bring the mixture to the boil and simmer for about 3 minutes. Add the vanilla essence. Pour the hot syrup over the loaf as soon as it comes out of the oven. Leave the loaf to cool in the tin for a few minutes before turning it out. Work carefully as the loaf is very moist.

MAKES 1 MEDIUM-SIZED LOAF.

Carmen says
Line deep muffin tin hollows with paper cups and bake cupcakes. Decorate them with caramel icing (p. 53).

OVEN-PAN CAKES

Cake sales, bazaars, birthdays — these are but a few occasions when you need a plentiful supply of cake. My trusty oven-pan cake recipes came to the rescue many a time when the kids suddenly remembered just before bedtime that they needed to take something to eat to school the next day. The last thing you need at that time of the night is creaming butter and sugar together and separating and whisking eggs. All you want is a recipe where you can just mix everything together and decorate the cake with caramel condensed milk, melted chocolate or a light dusting of icing sugar.

Versatile one-bowl cake

All the ingredients for this cake are mixed in only one bowl before the batter is turned into an oven pan and baked. That's it. Daleen van der Merwe developed several variations for this versatile cake. You can make up to eight different cakes using this basic recipe.

BASIC CAKE RECIPE
400 ml caster sugar
375 g softened butter or margarine
7 extra-large eggs
750 ml (3 c) self-raising flour, sifted
18 ml (3½ t) baking powder, sifted
2 ml (½ t) salt
60 ml (¼ c) milk
10 ml (2 t) vanilla essence

Carmen says
The butter or margarine must be soft but not melted.

Preheat the oven to 180 °C. Line an oven pan or roasting tin with baking paper and grease it with butter, margarine or nonstick spray.
Put all the cake ingredients in a large mixing bowl and beat well until the batter is smooth. Turn the batter into the prepared pan, spreading it evenly with a spatula or the back of a spoon.
Bake for 25–30 minutes or until a testing skewer comes out clean when inserted into the centre of the cake. Turn out the cake onto a wire rack and leave it to cool completely. Decorate with a butter icing (see p. 204) or as desired.

MAKES ABOUT 24 SQUARES.

VARIATIONS
Use the basic recipe to make these eight delectable variations, each with its own icing.

Almond cake
Add 150 ml chopped almonds to the cake batter and substitute 2 ml (½ t) almond essence for the vanilla essence.

WHIPPED CREAM ICING
Whip 400 ml cream until stiff peaks form. Stir in 1 ml (¼ t) almond essence. Spread the cream over the cake and sprinkle it with toasted almond flakes.

To toast almonds
Heat 15 ml (1 T) butter in a pan and add 110 g flaked almonds. Stir over medium heat or until the almonds are evenly browned. Work rapidly as almonds burn easily. Turn out onto paper towels.

Granadilla cake

Stir 1 can (115 g) granadilla pulp into the cake batter and mix well.

GRANADILLA ICING

Mix 500 g mascarpone or cream cheese with 100 ml caster sugar and 1 can (115 g) granadilla pulp. Beat well. Spread the icing evenly over the cake once it has cooled.

Orange and poppy seed cake

Substitute 20 ml (4 t) grated orange zest for the vanilla essence and add 100 ml poppy seeds to the cake batter.

ORANGE GLACÉ ICING

Sift 600 ml icing sugar into a heat-resistant mixing bowl. Add 30 ml (2 T) orange juice. Put the bowl over a saucepan with a little boiling water and stir for 1 minute. Add 15 ml (1 T) thin orange zest strips and rapidly pour the icing over the cake, spreading it evenly with the back of a spoon that has been dipped in hot water. Scatter extra orange zest strips and poppy seeds over the cake.

Coffee and walnut cake

Sift 30 ml (2 T) instant coffee powder with the flour and add 250 ml (1 c) chopped walnuts.

SYRUPY COFFEE ICING

Stir 250 ml (1 c) sugar and 375 ml (1½ c) water over low heat until the sugar has dissolved. Bring to the boil and simmer for 5 minutes. Remove from the heat and stir in 75 ml (5 T) coffee cream liqueur or 25 ml (5 t) instant coffee powder. Arrange whole walnuts on top of the cake, spacing them evenly, and pour the syrup over the nuts and cake.

Marble cake

Divide the cake batter into two equal parts. Mix 40 ml cocoa with a little boiling water and stir it into one half of the batter. Spoon alternate mounds of the batter into the prepared pan.

CARAMEL ICING

Spread 2 cans (360 g each) caramel condensed milk over the cake and sprinkle with chocolate vermicelli.

Chocolate cake

Mix 60 ml (¼ c) cocoa with 30 ml (2 T) water. Heat the milk, add the cocoa mixture and stir it into the cake batter.

GANACHE ICING

Slowly bring 600 ml cream to the boil in a saucepan. Remove from the heat and add 200 g grated dark chocolate, stirring until the mixture is smooth. Chill until firm. Beat until the mixture begins to thicken and is slightly paler in colour. Spread over the cake and decorate with chocolate shavings.

Apple and spice cake

Sift 5 ml (1 t) ground cinnamon, 5 ml (1 t) mixed spice, 2 ml (½ t) ground cloves and 2 ml (½ t) ground ginger with the flour. Arrange 1 can (385 g) apple slices in the bottom of the prepared pan and carefully spoon the batter on top of the apples.

CRUMB TOPPING

Scatter the topping over the cake halfway through the baking time. Return the cake to the oven and bake until done.

Mix 125 ml (½ c) light brown sugar and 125 ml (½ c) cake flour and rub in 150 g butter with your fingertips until the mixture resembles breadcrumbs. Add 100 g roughly chopped macadamia nuts to the sugar mixture. Scatter the crumb mixture over the cake halfway through the baking time.

Coconut cake

Soak 150 ml desiccated coconut in the milk for 1 hour and stir it into the batter.

COCONUT ICING

Mix 750 ml (3 c) desiccated coconut, 375 ml (1½ c) sugar, 180 ml (¾ c) milk, 180 ml (¾ c) water and 5 egg yolks in a saucepan. Stirring continuously, heat over medium heat until the egg yolks are done. Leave the mixture to cool and spoon it over the cake.

Lemon meringue cake

This cake has a lemon meringue topping. The recipe was sent in by Joey Cilliers of Hermanus.

CAKE
500 ml (2 c) cake flour
250 ml (1 c) sugar
pinch salt
10 ml (2 t) baking powder
125 g softened margarine
250 ml (1 c) milk
grated zest of 1 lemon
2 extra-large eggs, whisked

TOPPING
1 can (395 g) condensed milk
2 extra-large eggs, separated
125 ml (½ c) lemon juice
pinch cream of tartar
80 ml (⅓ c) sugar
100 ml flaked almonds

Preheat the oven to 180 °C. Grease a 20 x 30 cm oven pan or roasting tin with butter, margarine or nonstick spray.

CAKE Sift the flour, sugar, salt and baking powder together.
Add the remaining cake ingredients and beat with an electric beater until the mixture forms a smooth batter.
Turn the batter into the prepared pan and bake for 30–35 minutes or until a testing skewer comes out clean when inserted into the centre of the cake.

TOPPING Whisk the condensed milk, egg yolks and lemon juice together and spread the mixture over the hot cake.
Bake for another 5–10 minutes or until firm.
Whisk together the egg whites and cream of tartar until soft peaks begin to form. Gradually add the sugar while beating continuously.
Spoon the meringue on top of the cake, scatter over the almond flakes and bake until the meringue is pale brown. Leave to cool and cut into squares.

MAKES 24–32 SQUARES.

Blueberry lemon cake

CAKE
200 g butter, at room temperature
180 ml (¾ c) caster sugar
350 ml self-raising flour
3 large eggs
finely grated zest of 1 lemon
25 ml (5 t) milk
125 g frozen blueberries

TOPPING
90 g sugar cubes, roughly crumbled
juice of 1 lemon

Preheat the oven to 180 °C. Line a 22 x 28 cm oven pan or roasting tin with baking paper and grease it with butter, margarine or nonstick spray.

CAKE Put the butter, caster sugar, flour, eggs, lemon zest and milk in a mixing bowl and beat with an electric beater until well blended and smooth.
Turn the batter into the prepared pan. Scatter the blueberries on top of the batter and sprinkle over the sugar cubes.
Bake in the middle of the oven for 50–70 minutes or until firm and a testing skewer comes out clean when inserted into the centre of the cake. Remove the cake from the oven and sprinkle over the lemon juice. Leave the cake to cool in the tin for 10–15 minutes before turning it out onto a wire rack and cutting into squares.

MAKES ABOUT 24 SQUARES.

Lemon meringue cake

Semolina and coconut cake

The semolina and coconut in this buttermilk cake make it deliciously different. Sadhna Kalichuran of Shallcross in KwaZulu-Natal sent us the recipe in 2002.

CAKE
250 ml (1 c) butter or margarine
375 ml (1½ c) caster sugar
400 ml cream
500 ml (2 c) buttermilk
500 ml (2 c) semolina
500 ml (2 c) desiccated coconut
375 ml (1½ c) cake flour
20 ml (4 t) baking powder
125 ml (½ c) milk

ICING (optional)
drop icing (see p. 203)

Preheat the oven to 180 °C and grease a 25 x 40 cm oven pan or roasting tin with butter, margarine or nonstick spray.

CAKE Cream the butter or margarine and caster sugar together until the mixture is light and fluffy. Slowly add the cream and buttermilk, beating until well blended.
Combine the semolina, coconut, cake flour and baking powder. Add the buttermilk mixture and mix gently. Add the milk and mix until smooth.
Turn the batter into the prepared pan and bake for 50–60 minutes or until done and a testing skewer comes out clean when inserted into the centre of the cake. Leave to cool in the tin for about 20 minutes.

ICING Decorate the cake with a drop icing made with lemon juice and icing sugar or milk and icing sugar. Leave the icing to harden slightly before cutting the cake into squares.

MAKES 1 LARGE CAKE OR ABOUT 24 SQUARES.

Egg-free oven-pan chocolate cake

This was my standby recipe for school functions. Today our 17-year-old daughter Hanje uses the recipe to bake cupcakes. She decorates the cupcakes with chocolate ganache and colourful chocolate beads. Perfect for dessert or birthdays.

CAKE
750 ml (3 c) cake flour
350–500 ml sugar
90 ml (6 T) cocoa
10 ml (2 t) bicarbonate of soda, sifted
160 ml (⅔ c) oil
30 ml (2 T) vinegar
10 ml (2 t) vanilla essence
500 ml (2 c) cold water

ICING
1 can (385 g) caramel condensed milk
  or yoghurt ganache (see p. 208)
edible beads

Preheat the oven to 180 °C. Grease an oven pan or roasting tin with nonstick spray.

CAKE Sift the dry ingredients together and make a well in the centre.
Whisk the oil, vinegar, vanilla essence and water together and pour the mixture into the well. Beat until well blended.
Turn the batter into the prepared pan, tapping it gently to remove any large air bubbles. Bake for 30–40 minutes or until a testing skewer comes out clean when inserted into the centre of the cake. Cover the cake with aluminium foil if it darkens too quickly.

ICING Spread the cake with caramel condensed milk or prepare a ganache as described and decorate the cake with beads.

MAKES 1 LARGE CAKE

VARIATION
Mocha cake: Add 40 ml instant coffee powder to the cake mixture.

CHOCOLATE CAKES

I confess: I simply love chocolate cake. While writing I can taste the seductive creaminess of these cakes from our test kitchen. My favourite chocolate cake is not a voluminous prize-winner because the higher the cake rises the lighter and fluffier it is. I like my chocolate cakes dense, dark and moist, which means some of these cakes will be fairly flat when they come out of the oven.

CAKES MADE WITH REAL CHOCOLATE
Chocolate mud cake

Mud cakes are fairly flat, moist and sticky with a dense texture. They're made with plenty of chocolate and butter and only a little flour, which makes them very rich. This deliciously decadent cake needs no icing; a dusting of cocoa and icing sugar will suffice.

CAKE
350 g dark chocolate,
broken into squares
190 ml (generous ¾ c) caster sugar
185 g butter, diced
5 extra-large eggs, separated
80 ml (⅓ c) cake flour

ICING
cocoa, sifted
icing sugar, sifted

How to melt chocolate
Chocolate can be melted in a double boiler or in a glass bowl in the microwave oven on 70 per cent power or over a saucepan with boiling water (put a glass bowl over the saucepan with boiling water but take care that the bottom of the bowl does not touch the water). Break the chocolate into squares and put them in the glass bowl. Stir occasionally.

If using a microwave oven, stir the chocolate squares every few seconds because they will keep their shape though melted already and will burn if heated for too long.

Preheat the oven to 180 °C. Grease a 23 cm springform tin with butter, margarine or nonstick spray and line the bottom with greased baking paper.

CAKE Put the chocolate, sugar and butter in a double boiler or in a glass bowl over a saucepan with a little boiling water and stir until the chocolate has melted and the mixture is smooth. Leave the mixture to cool for a few minutes. Add the egg yolks one at a time, beating well after each addition. Sift over the flour and fold in gently.

Whisk the egg whites until stiff peaks begin to form and fold them into the chocolate mixture.

Turn the batter into the prepared tin and bake for 45 minutes or until a testing skewer comes out clean when inserted into the centre of the cake. Leave the cake to cool in the tin for a few minutes before turning it out onto a cake platter.

ICING Dust the cake with alternating stripes of cocoa and icing sugar just before serving.

MAKES 1 MEDIUM-SIZED CAKE.

VARIATION
Cut the cake into 12 squares and put each square into a paper cup. Decorate them with roses, nuts and glacé fruit.

Chocolate meringue cake

This is a gluten-free cake with a dense base made with real chocolate and crisp hazelnut and meringue topping.

CAKE
160 ml (⅔ c) butter
180 ml (¾ c) light brown sugar
6 extra-large eggs, separated
350 g dark chocolate, broken into
    squares and melted
15 ml (1 T) vanilla essence
pinch salt

MERINGUE
250 ml (1 c) hazelnuts, toasted, skins
    removed and roughly chopped
15 ml (1 T) cornflour
4 egg whites
250 ml (1 c) caster sugar
1 ml (¼ t) cream of tartar

Preheat the oven to 180 °C. Grease a 22 cm springform tin with butter, margarine or nonstick spray and line the bottom with greased baking paper.

CAKE Cream the butter and brown sugar together until the mixture is light and fluffy. Add the egg yolks one at a time, beating well after each addition.
Add the melted chocolate in a thin stream, beating continuously. Add the vanilla essence.
Whisk the egg whites in a clean bowl until soft peaks form. Add the salt.
Mix one-third of the egg whites with the chocolate mixture and gently fold in the rest until just blended.
Turn the batter into the prepared tin and bake for 35 minutes.

MERINGUE Mix the hazelnuts and cornflour and set aside. Whisk the egg whites until frothy, add the caster sugar a little at a time and beat until stiff peaks form. Sprinkle over the cream of tartar and beat in. Gently fold in the hazelnut mixture.

Remove the cake from the oven, gently spread the meringue mixture on top and return the cake to the oven. Bake for another 25–30 minutes or until the meringue is pale brown and crisp.

MAKES 1 MEDIUM-SIZED CAKE.

Carmen says
- To remove the skins from hazelnuts, put the hot toasted hazelnuts in a tea towel and rub them until all the skins have been removed.
- The art of making a perfect meringue is to ensure the caster sugar is well blended with the egg whites, which is why it is added a little at a time. Beat well after each addition. Rub the meringue mixture between your thumb and forefinger: it must be completely smooth and you shouldn't be able to feel any sugar granules.

Almond chocolate cake

Another winning recipe. The cake, which is made with chocolate and ground almonds, is fairly flat. Sandwich the layers together with chocolate ganache and cover the top of the cake with the remaining ganache for a cake that looks as good as it tastes.

CAKE
180 g butter
200 ml caster sugar
4 extra-large eggs, separated
1 slab (100 g) dark chocolate, broken into squares
1 packet (100 g) ground almonds
80 ml (⅓ c) self-raising flour
60 ml (¼ c) cornflour
pinch salt

ICING
chocolate ganache (see p. 208)

Preheat the oven to 160 °C. Grease two 20 cm loose-bottomed tins and line them with greased baking paper.

CAKE Cream the butter and caster sugar together. Add the egg yolks one at a time, beating well after each addition.
Melt the chocolate in a glass bowl over boiling water or in the microwave oven at 70 per cent power, stirring every few seconds. Add the melted chocolate to the butter mixture and mix well. Add the almonds and mix well.
Sift the self-raising flour, cornflour and salt over the chocolate mixture and fold in.
Whisk the egg whites until stiff and, using a metal spoon, fold them into the chocolate mixture. Turn the mixture into the prepared tins.
Bake for 40–45 minutes or until done. Cool the cakes in the tins for a few minutes before turning them out onto a wire rack to cool completely.

ICING Prepare the ganache as described and sandwich the cake layers together with the mixture. Use the remaining ganache to cover the top of the cake.

MAKES 1 MEDIUM-SIZED CAKE.

Carmen says
Make small individual cakes by baking the mixture in large muffin cups. Decorate the cakes with the ganache. Perfect for serving as a dessert.

Chocolate and whisky fudge cake

This deliciously moist cake is sheer heaven.

180 g butter
190 ml (generous ¾ c) caster sugar
3 extra-large eggs, separated
60 ml (¼ c) whisky
15 ml (1 T) vanilla essence
200 g dark chocolate, melted
250 ml (1 c) self-raising flour, sifted
chocolate curls to decorate (see p. 209)

Preheat the oven to 180 °C. Grease a 23 cm springform tin with butter, margarine or nonstick spray and line the bottom with greased baking paper.
Cream the butter and 125 ml (½ c) of the sugar together until the mixture is light and fluffy. Add the egg yolks, whisky and vanilla essence and beat until well blended. Add the cooled chocolate and beat gently.
Fold the sifted flour into the mixture.
Whisk the egg whites until soft peaks begin to form. Gradually add the remaining sugar, beating continuously.
Stir a quarter of the egg white mixture into the chocolate mixture and, using a metal spoon, carefully fold in the rest.
Turn the batter into the prepared tin. Cover it with aluminium foil and bake for 30 minutes. Remove the aluminium foil and bake for another 60 minutes or until the cake is done and springy to the touch. Run a knife along the inside of the tin to loosen the cake and leave it to cool in the tin. Remove the cake from the tin and decorate it with chocolate curls.

MAKES 1 MEDIUM-SIZED CAKE.

Carmen says
The cake will sink in the centre while cooling.

Chocolate torte

This is an impressive-looking cake with four layers sandwiched together with a ganache filling.

CAKE

155 g dark chocolate,
  broken into squares
250 ml (1 c) soft brown sugar
125 ml (½ c) cream
2 egg yolks
200 g butter, softened
250 ml (1 c) white sugar
5 ml (1 t) vanilla essence
2 extra-large eggs, lightly whisked
250 ml (1 c) cake flour
250 ml (1 c) self-raising flour
180 ml (¾ c) milk
3 egg whites

ICING

chocolate ganache (see p. 208)
chocolate curls, glazed cherries
  and chocolate truffles to
  decorate (optional)

Preheat the oven to 180 °C. Grease two 23 cm cake tins with butter, margarine or nonstick spray and line the bottoms with greased baking paper.

CAKE Heat the chocolate, brown sugar, cream and egg yolks in a double boiler or in a glass bowl over boiling water. Stir continuously until the mixture is smooth. Remove the mixture from the heat and leave it to cool slightly.

Cream the butter, white sugar and vanilla essence together until the mixture is light and fluffy. Gradually add the whisked eggs, beating continuously.

Sift the flour and self-raising flour over the butter mixture.

Add the chocolate mixture and milk and mix until well blended.

Beat the egg whites until stiff and fold it into the chocolate mixture.

Turn the batter into the prepared cake tins and bake for 40 minutes or until done. Leave the cakes to cool in the tins for 5 minutes before turning them out onto a wire rack.

ICING Prepare the chocolate ganache as described. Halve each cake layer horizontally and sandwich them together with the ganache. Cover the top and sides of the cake with the remaining ganache. Decorate the cake with the chocolate curls, cherries and truffles.

MAKES 1 LARGE WELL-RISEN CAKE.

Test your terms

Torte: In Europe torte or torta refers to a rich multi-tier cake, while in America a chocolate torte is a rich, moist, sticky chocolate cake that contains little flour.

Ganache: This is the French word for a smooth mixture made with chopped chocolate and cream, usually in equal quantities, that is used to decorate cakes and make truffles. The mixture is runny while hot but thickens to a spreadable consistency when beaten while cooling.

Chocolate praline upside-down cake

It's hard to believe how little effort it takes to make this impressive cake. While it's baking, a sticky praline (caramelised nut) layer forms below the decadent chocolate layers. The cake layers are sandwiched together with sweetened cream. The batter is quick and easy to prepare: simply mix everything together.

PRALINE LAYER

250 ml (1 c) soft brown sugar, firmly packed

125 g butter

60 ml (¼ c) cream

180 ml (¾ c) roughly chopped pecan nuts

CAKE LAYERS

560 ml (2¼ c) cake flour

310 ml (1¼ c) white sugar

180 ml (¾ c) sour cream

60 ml (4 T) margarine or butter

250 ml (1 c) water

6 ml (1¼ t) bicarbonate of soda

5 ml (1 t) salt

5 ml (1 t) vanilla essence

3 ml (generous ½ t) baking powder

2 extra-large eggs

125 g dark chocolate, melted and slightly cooled

FILLING

250 ml (1 c) cream

30 ml (2 T) icing sugar

2 ml (½ t) vanilla essence

pecan nuts to decorate

Preheat the oven to 180 °C. Grease three deep round 20 cm cake tins with butter, margarine or nonstick spray and line them with greased baking paper.

PRALINE LAYER Heat the brown sugar, butter and cream together over moderate heat in a saucepan. Stir occasionally until the butter has melted; the sugar crystals will not be completely dissolved. Divide the syrup among the three prepared tins, spreading it evenly. Scatter over the chopped nuts and set aside.

CAKE LAYERS Using an electric beater set on low, whisk all the cake ingredients together for 30 seconds. Set the speed at moderately high and continue beating for 3 minutes.

Pour the batter over the nuts in the tins, spreading it evenly.

Bake for 22–25 minutes or until a testing skewer comes out clean when inserted into the centre of the cakes. Leave the cakes to cool in the tins for 5 minutes before turning them out onto a wire rack to cool completely.

FILLING Whip the cream, icing sugar and vanilla essence in a cold bowl until the cream is stiff. Put a cake layer on a cake platter, praline-side facing up. Spread over half the cream. Repeat the layers and decorate the top of the cake with pecan nuts.

MAKES 1 LARGE CAKE.

Fancy polka-dot chocolate cake

With its smart polka-dot band this cake is perfect for a special occasion. It's also ideal as a wedding cake because it has a firm texture, doesn't crumble much and is easy to stack.

CAKE
375 ml (1½ c) sugar
125 g butter
15 ml (1 T) hot water
2 extra-large eggs
125 ml (½ c) cocoa
125 ml (½ c) hot water
500 ml (2 c) cake flour
5 ml (1 t) bicarbonate of soda
2 ml (½ t) cream of tartar
pinch salt
125 ml (½ c) sour milk
10 ml (2 t) vanilla essence

BUTTER ICING
125 g butter or margarine, softened
480 ml icing sugar, sifted
50 ml cocoa, sifted
pinch salt
milk

CHOCOLATE BAND
50 g white chocolate
200 g dark chocolate
chocolate curls and red roses
   to decorate (see p. 209)

Preheat the oven to 180 °C. Grease two 20 cm round cake tins with butter, margarine or nonstick spray and line the bottoms with greased baking paper.

CAKE Cream the sugar, butter and 15 ml (1 T) hot water together. Add the eggs one at a time, beating well after each addition.
Dissolve the cocoa in the 125 ml (½ c) water and add the mixture to the sugar mixture.
Sift the flour, bicarbonate of soda, cream of tartar and salt together. Add the sifted dry ingredients to the cocoa mixture, alternating with the sour milk and essence. Mix well.
Turn the batter into the prepared tins and bake for 45 minutes or until done. Leave the cakes to cool in the tins for 5 minutes before turning them out onto wire racks to cool completely.

ICING Beat the butter, icing sugar, cocoa, salt and just enough milk together to make a creamy icing with a spreadable consistency. Sandwich the two cake layers together with the icing and ice the top and sides of the cake.

CHOCOLATE BAND Cut out a band from a sheet of acetate or transparencies that have been taped together. The band must be slightly longer than the circumference of the cake and slighter wider than the height of the cake.
Melt the white chocolate in a double boiler or glass bowl over boiling water or in the microwave oven at 70 per cent power.
Spoon the mixture into a piping bag with a small smooth nozzle and pipe white dots on the acetate sheet and leave them to harden (picture 1). Melt the dark chocolate and spread it evenly over the band. Work carefully so the white dots do not come unstuck (picture 2). Leave to harden slightly.
Once the chocolate is no longer runny but is still slightly pliable, fold the band, chocolate-side facing the cake, around the cake so the ends overlap slightly (picture 3). Gently press the band onto the cake and leave the chocolate to harden completely before carefully removing the acetate band.
Decorate the top of the cake with chocolate curls and red roses.

MAKES 1 LARGE CAKE

Chocolate mousse cake

Most people love chocolate mousse cake. The mousse for this cake is made with white chocolate, while ground almonds are mixed into the batter for the cake layers. The recipe was sent in by Sheehaam Shabodien of Garlandale.

CAKE LAYERS
10 large eggs
325 ml (1⅓ c) caster sugar
160 ml (⅔ c) oil
300 ml self-raising flour
125 ml (½ c) cocoa
160 ml (⅔ c) ground almonds

MOUSSE
350 g white cooking chocolate,
　　broken into squares
45 ml (3 T) honey
100 ml water
20 ml (4 t) gelatine
75 ml (5 T) water
3 large eggs, separated
250 ml (1 c) cream

DECORATION
selection of fresh summer berries

Preheat the oven to 190 °C. Grease two 23 cm springform tins with butter, margarine or nonstick spray. Dust the tins with cake flour.

CAKE Beat the eggs and caster sugar together until thick and pale yellow. Beat in the oil.
Sift the flour and cocoa together and fold into the egg mixture, alternating with the almonds.
Turn the batter into the prepared tins and bake for 25 minutes or until the cakes are firm to the touch. Leave them to cool in the tins for a few minutes before turning them out and leaving them to cool on a wire rack. Halve each cake horizontally.

MOUSSE Heat the chocolate, honey and 100 ml water in a glass bowl over a saucepan with boiling water or in the microwave oven on 70 per cent power. Stir until the chocolate has melted. Leave to cool. Sprinkle the gelatine over the 75 ml cold water and leave it to sponge. Heat the sponged gelatine in the microwave oven until melted, taking care it doesn't come to the boil.
Whisk the egg yolks until pale yellow and creamy. Slowly beat the melted gelatine into the egg yolks. Beat the egg mixture into the cooled chocolate mixture.
Whip the cream until stiff. In a clean bowl and using clean beaters, whisk the egg whites until stiff peaks form. Fold the cream into the chocolate mixture, then fold in the egg whites. Leave the mixture to cool until it resembles lightly whipped cream.

TO ASSEMBLE THE CAKE Spray a clean springform tin with nonstick spray. Return one cake layer to the tin and spoon a quarter of the mousse on top, spreading it evenly. Repeat the layers, reserving a little mousse for the top of the cake. Put the cake in the fridge until nearly set (chill the remaining mousse in a separate bowl). Transfer the cake to a platter. Spoon the remaining mousse into a piping bag and decorate the top of the cake. Scatter fresh berries on top of the cake and keep it in the fridge.

MAKES 1 LARGE CAKE.

Carmen says
- When melting chocolate do not expose it to hot water or steam as it will burn, separate and form a thick, solid mass which will not melt. Milk and white chocolate will form lumps. If adding water to the mixture at the start (as in the above recipe), stir it continuously to prevent the chocolate from solidifying.

- If the chocolate does solidify add a little oil, butter or cream, 5 ml (1 t) at a time, stirring until the mixture becomes smooth.

Orange and chocolate marble cake

Orange and chocolate are a divine combination. In this marble cake the lighter part is flavoured with aromatic orange while real chocolate is added to the other part. The cake is decorated with a delicious chocolate ganache and strips of orange zest.

CAKE
250 g butter
250 ml (1 c) caster sugar
4 extra-large eggs
450 ml (250 g) self-raising flour
30 ml (2 T) juice and finely grated zest of 1 orange
30 ml (2 T) cocoa
100 g dark chocolate, grated

ICING
chocolate ganache (see p. 208)
crystallised orange peel (see p. 210)

Preheat the oven to 180 °C. Grease a deep 20 cm cake tin with butter, margarine or nonstick spray.

CAKE Cream the butter and caster sugar together until the mixture is light and fluffy. Add the eggs one at a time, beating well after each addition. (Add a little of the flour if the mixture looks as if it's about to split.)
Sift the self-raising flour over the egg mixture and fold it in.
Divide the mixture in half. Add the orange juice and zest to the one half. Sift the cocoa and add it to the other half of the mixture. Add the grated chocolate and mix well.
Spoon alternating mounds of the two mixtures into the cake tin and stir gently with a testing skewer.
Bake for 1 hour or until a testing skewer comes out clean when inserted into the centre of the cake. Cool the cake in the tin for 5 minutes before turning it out onto a wire rack to cool completely.

ICING Prepare the ganache as described, pour it over the cake and tap the wire rack gently on the work surface to get a smooth surface. Prepare the orange zest strips as described and pile them on top of the cake.

MAKES 1 MEDIUM-SIZED CAKE.

Kinds of chocolate
Chocolate consists of cocoa solids and cocoa butter. The more cocoa solids it contains the better the quality and the more intense the flavour.

Research has shown that dark chocolate with at least 65 per cent cocoa solids is rich in antioxidants. The darker the chocolate the more cocoa solids it contains.

There is a difference between baking and milk chocolate. Rather use baking chocolate for cooking because it's easier to melt and doesn't burn as easily as milk chocolate.

WHITE AND CARAMEL CHOCOLATE
It contains no cocoa solids or cocoa syrup, only cocoa butter. It can be exposed to only low temperatures and must be heated carefully and for a short period.

BITTER CHOCOLATE
This quality chocolate is imported and is much more expensive than chocolate made in South Africa. Use it when you want to be sure of an exceptional quality and taste. For decoration purposes it must first be softened, which is a complicated process, so rather use baking chocolate.

BAKING CHOCOLATE
Baking chocolate contains only six to ten per cent cocoa solids. Dark baking chocolate melts and handles easily, making it ideal for decorations such as curls, lace and leaves. It is generally used in dishes.

MILK CHOCOLATE
Milk chocolate contains milk powder, sugar, milk and vegetable fat and little cocoa solids. It's suitable for cold dishes such as mousse and is seldom used in baking. It's also used to make sweets. Milk chocolate contains hardly any antioxidants.

CHOCOLATE DISCS
Chocolate discs (Magic Melt) are made from sugar, plant oil, cocoa and flavourings. Because the discs are all the same size they melt simultaneously and quickly so there is no need to chop or grate the chocolate first. It's ideal for making decorations such as curls and lace.

BUDGET CHOCOLATE CAKES

Moist chocolate cake

This chocolate cake is made with a generous scoop of blackcurrant jam.

CAKE
125 g butter, at room temperature
125 ml (½ c) caster sugar
80 ml (⅓ c) icing sugar, sifted
2 extra-large eggs, lightly whisked
5 ml (1 t) vanilla essence
60 ml (¼ c) blackcurrant jam
310 ml (1¼ c) self-raising flour
125 ml (½ c) cocoa
5 ml (1 t) bicarbonate of soda
250 ml (1 c) milk

ICING
70 g dark chocolate
25 g butter
60 ml (¼ c) icing sugar, sifted
60 ml (¼ c) cream

Preheat the oven to 180 °C. Grease a 20 cm square tin with butter, margarine or nonstick spray and line it with greased baking paper.

CAKE Cream the butter, caster sugar and icing sugar together until pale yellow and fluffy. Gradually add the eggs, beating well. Add the vanilla essence and jam and stir until just blended.
Sift the self-raising flour, cocoa and bicarbonate of soda together and fold into the creamed mixture, alternating with the milk.
Turn the batter into the prepared tin, spreading it evenly.
Bake for 45 minutes or until a testing skewer comes out clean when inserted into the centre of the cake. Leave the cake to cool in the tin for 15 minutes before turning it out onto a wire rack.

ICING Heat all the ingredients over low heat, stirring until smooth. Remove the saucepan from the heat and leave the icing to cool slightly before spreading over the cake.

MAKES 1 MEDIUM-SIZED CAKE.

Coca-Cola cake

The recipe for this cake with its feather-light texture was sent in by Lauren Ashworth of Wynberg.

CAKE
500 ml (2 c) self-raising flour
45 ml (3 T) cocoa
2 ml (½ t) bicarbonate of soda
310 ml (1¼ c) caster sugar, sifted
200 g butter
250 ml (1 c) Coca-Cola
100 ml milk
2 extra-large eggs, lightly whisked
5 ml (1 t) vanilla essence

ICING
150 g butter
50 ml Coca-Cola
45 ml (3 T) cocoa, sifted
750 ml (3 c) icing sugar

Preheat the oven to 180 °C and grease two 20 cm cake tins with butter, margarine or nonstick spray.

CAKE Sift the self-raising flour, cocoa, bicarbonate of soda and caster sugar together in a mixing bowl.
Slowly heat the butter and Coca-Cola until the butter has melted. Beat the milk, eggs and vanilla essence together. Slowly add the butter mixture to the dry ingredients, alternating with the egg mixture. Stir until smooth and turn the batter into the prepared tins.
Bake for 40 minutes or until done and a testing skewer comes out clean when inserted into the centre of the cakes. Leave the cakes to cool in the tins for 10 minutes before turning them out onto a wire rack to cool completely.

ICING Slowly heat the butter, Coca-Cola and cocoa until the butter has melted. Add the mixture to the icing sugar and stir or beat until well blended. Sandwich the cake layers together with the icing, saving some to ice the top of the cake.

MAKES 1 MEDIUM-SIZED CAKE.

Chocolate and buttermilk cake

This deliciously moist buttermilk cake is quick and easy to make.
The recipe was sent in by Mrs Ruth Dodds of George.

CAKE
125 ml (½ c) oil
250 ml (1 c) water
125 ml (½ c) margarine
45 ml (3 T) cocoa
500 ml (2 c) cake flour
500 ml (2 c) sugar
125 ml (½ c) buttermilk
5 ml (1 t) vanilla essence
2 extra-large eggs, whisked
5 ml (1 t) bicarbonate of soda,
    blended with a little milk

ICING
100 g margarine
15 ml (1 T) cocoa
125 ml (½ c) icing sugar
30 ml (2 T) buttermilk
2 ml (½ t) vanilla essence

Preheat the oven to 180 °C. Grease a 24 cm loose-bottomed cake tin with a tight-fitting base with butter, margarine or nonstick spray.

CAKE Bring the oil, water, margarine and cocoa to the boil over medium heat. Leave the mixture to cool slightly.
Sift the cake flour and add it to the oil mixture along with the sugar.
Whisk the buttermilk, vanilla essence, eggs and bicarbonate of soda together and add to the oil mixture, mixing well.
Turn the batter into the prepared tin, put it on a baking sheet and bake for about 30 minutes or until done.

ICING Bring all the icing ingredients, except the vanilla essence, to the boil over medium heat. Simmer gently for about 1 minute. Remove from the heat, stir in the vanilla essence and leave to cool for 5 minutes. Pour the hot sauce over the hot cake. If the sauce is too thick heat it in the microwave oven for a few seconds. Leave the cake to cool in the tin before removing. Or decorate the cake with white chocolate strips and rose petal strips.

MAKES 1 MEDIUM-SIZED CAKE.

SPECIAL CAKES

These cakes, like fruitcakes, are not your everyday standbys. Instead they are reserved for special occasions.

Frangipane

Daleen van der Merwe was given the family recipe for this delicious fruitcake baked in a puff pastry crust by her grandmother and we've never come across it again. (Frangipane is the French term for baking with an almond filling or flavour.)

1 packet (400 g) puff pastry
160 ml (⅔ c) sugar
125 g butter
3 extra-large eggs
260 ml (generous 1 c) cake flour
10 ml (2 t) baking powder
60 ml (¼ c) milk
200 ml raisins
200 ml currants
200 ml glacé cherries
½ packet (125 g) dates, chopped
125 ml (½ c) flaked almonds
30 ml (2 T) smooth apricot jam
icing sugar

Preheat the oven to 150 °C.

Roll out the puff pastry on a floured surface and line a 23–25 cm pie dish with the pastry. Trim the edges and prick the bottom with a fork. Chill until needed.

Cream the sugar and butter together and add the eggs one at a time while beating continuously.

Sift the flour and baking powder together and fold the mixture into the egg mixture, alternating with the milk. Carefully stir in the raisins, currants, cherries, dates and almonds and turn the batter into the unbaked puff pastry shell.

Bake for 1½–2 hours or until a testing skewer comes out clean when inserted into the centre of the cake. Heat the apricot jam and spread it over the filling. Dust with icing sugar and serve cold.

MAKES 1 LARGE CAKE.

Panforte

This delectable Italian confection is flat, dense and packed with nuts. Keep it for special occasions only and serve it thinly sliced with coffee.

rice paper
2 packets (100 g each) flaked almonds
½ packet (50 g) walnuts
1 packet (100 g) pecan nuts
100 g dates, finely chopped
175 g mixed peel
90 ml (6 T) cake flour
60 ml (4 T) cocoa
5 ml (1 t) ground cinnamon
1 ml (¼ t) grated nutmeg
200 ml sugar
180 ml (¾ c) honey
icing sugar

Preheat the oven to 180 °C. Grease a 23 cm cake tin with butter, margarine or nonstick spray and line it with greased baking paper. Line the bottom and sides with rice paper.

Toast the nuts lightly in a dry pan. Chop roughly and mix them with the dates and peel.

Sift the cake flour, cocoa and spices. Add the mixture to the nuts and mix well.

Heat the sugar and honey together, stirring until the sugar has melted. Bring to the boil and boil rapidly for 2 minutes without stirring. Add the syrup to the nut mixture and mix well. Spoon the mixture into the prepared tin, pressing down firmly.

Bake for 30–40 minutes until firm. Turn out onto a wire rack to cool. Peel away the baking paper but not the rice paper. Dust with a generous layer of icing sugar and wrap in clingfilm. Store in an airtight container.

MAKES 1 MEDIUM-SIZED CAKE.

Stollen

Stollen is a German fruit loaf made with yeast and filled with marzipan. It is traditionally made for Christmas and symbolises the body of Christ. The longer you keep it the more the flavour improves.

100 ml currants
100 ml seedless raisins
200 ml mixed peel
60 ml (¼ c) rum
75 ml (5 T) sugar
780 ml (3 generous c) cake flour
10 ml (2 t) active dry yeast
5 ml (1 t) vanilla essence
pinch salt
grated zest of 1 lemon
150 g butter
2 extra-large eggs, whisked
200 ml ground almonds
125 ml (½ c) lukewarm milk, or as needed
100 g marzipan
90 g butter, melted, for brushing over
150 ml icing sugar

Soak the currants, raisins and peel in the rum overnight. In a mixing bowl mix the sugar, flour, yeast, essence, salt and lemon zest.

Melt the butter and add the eggs and almonds. Mix the egg mixture with the flour mixture. Gradually add the lukewarm milk. Knead for about 10 minutes or until the dough is smooth. Cover and leave for 2 hours to rise.

Knead the marinated fruit mixture into the dough and leave it to rise for another 2 hours.

Preheat the oven to 180 °C and line a baking sheet with greased baking paper.

Knock down the dough and shape it into an oval. Roll the marzipan into a sausage shape the same length as the dough and put it in the centre of the dough oval.

Fold the dough over the marzipan and put it on the prepared baking sheet, seam-side facing down. Leave the dough to rise for about 15 minutes.

Bake for 1 hour or until done. Brush with the melted butter until absorbed. Dust with the icing sugar. The thick white layer of icing sugar is characteristic of stollen. Serve sliced with coffee.

MAKES 1 LARGE STOLLEN.

Easter cake

This is a South African version of simnel cake which is served on Easter Sunday. Traditionally it has a marzipan topping with 11 marzipan balls symbolising the 11 loyal disciples.

625 ml (2½ c) cake flour
12 ml (2½ t) baking powder
10 ml (2 t) ground cinnamon
270 g unsalted butter
250 ml (1 c) caster sugar
5 extra-large eggs
grated zest of 1 orange
juice of 2 oranges
300 ml ground almonds
250 ml (1 c) currants
250 ml (1 c) sultanas
80 ml (⅓ c) seedless raisins
500 g marzipan

Preheat the oven to 170 °C. Grease a 23 cm springform tin with butter and line the inside with five layers of baking paper, cut so they protrude 2.5 cm above the rim of the tin.

Sift the flour, baking powder and cinnamon together twice.

Cream the butter and caster sugar together until the mixture is light and fluffy. Add the eggs one at a time, beating well after each addition.

Using your hands, mix in the sifted flour mixture, orange zest and juice, almonds and dried fruit. Turn half the batter into the prepared tin, spreading it evenly. Roll half the marzipan into a 22 cm circle and put it on top of the batter in the tin.

Spoon the remaining batter on top of the marzipan and bake for 2 hours or until a testing skewer comes out clean when inserted into the centre of the cake. Leave the cake to cool in the tin. Remove the cake from the tin and transfer it to a cake platter.

Roll the remaining marzipan into a 22 cm circle and put it on top of the cake. Crimp the edge of the marzipan circle between your thumb and forefinger.

Decorate the cake as desired.

MAKES 1 LARGE CAKE.

Polenta cake

This beautiful cake, served with poached fruit, is not too rich as it contains very little sugar and shortening.

CAKE
375 ml (1½ c) cake flour
10 ml (2 t) baking powder
2 ml (½ t) salt
180 ml (¾ c) polenta or yellow maize meal
4 extra-large eggs
180 ml (¾ c) sugar
grated zest of 1½ lemons
10 ml (2 t) chopped rosemary
100 ml melted butter

SYRUP
80 ml (⅓ c) sugar
125 ml (½ c) water
20 ml (4 t) chopped rosemary
zest and juice of 1 lemon

Preheat the oven to 180 °C. Grease a 23 cm cake tin with margarine, butter or nonstick spray. Dust with flour.

CAKE Mix the flour, baking powder, salt and polenta together.
Cream the eggs and sugar together until the mixture is light and fluffy. Add the lemon zest and rosemary towards the end of the creaming process. Fold in about one-third of the dry ingredients, followed by half the melted butter. Repeat until everything has been folded in.
Turn the batter into the cake tin and bake for 35–40 minutes and until the cake has shrunk slightly from the inside of the tin.

SYRUP Prepare the syrup while the cake is in the oven. Dissolve the sugar in the water and add the rosemary and lemon zest. Bring to the boil and simmer for 15 minutes. Strain the syrup through a sieve and set it aside. Add the lemon juice just before using.

Leave the cake to cool in the tin for 10 minutes. Evenly pour the syrup over the cake while it's still in the tin. Leave the cake to cool in the tin before removing it. Serve at room temperature as is or with whipped cream or poached fruit or blueberry sauce (see p. 213).

MAKES 1 LARGE CAKE.

Panpepato

This traditional Italian chocolate loaf is packed with dried fruit and nuts. It's traditionally served with Parmesan cheese shavings and sweet fortified wine.

125 ml (½ c) sultanas
60 ml (¼ c) dry marsala or brandy
2 packets (100 g each) walnuts, toasted and chopped
5 ml (1 t) ground cinnamon
5 ml (1 t) finely ground black pepper
100 g dates, chopped
100 g mixed peel, chopped
180 ml (¾ c) cake flour
22 ml (4½ t) cocoa
125 ml (½ c) caster sugar
15 ml (1 T) honey
30 ml (2 T) softened butter
80 ml (⅓ c) milk

Preheat the oven to 150 °C. Grease a 16 x 7 x 6 cm loaf tin.
Soak the sultanas in the marsala or brandy. Add the walnuts, spices, dates and mixed peel.
Sift over the flour and cocoa.
Melt the sugar, honey and butter together. Add to the cake mixture along with the milk and mix well.
Turn the batter into the prepared tin, spreading it evenly.
Bake for 45–60 minutes. Leave the cake to cool in the tin for a few minutes before turning it out onto a wire rack to cool completely. Cut into thin slices and serve with Parmesan cheese shavings and sherry or port.

MAKES 1 LOAF.

Baked cheesecake

CHEESECAKES

Cheesecake has been around for generations. It was even served to the ancient Greek athletes during the first Olympic Games held in 776 BC.

I always opt for a basic baked cheesecake, preferably with a slight lemon tang. But now that we've tried and tested a ricotta cheesecake with fewer kilojoules and a savoury cheesecake I'll definitely be more adventurous.

If you've shied away from baking a cheesecake because it always ends up with a deep crack on top, relax. Our tips will ensure your cheesecake is beautifully smooth and, even if it cracks, don't worry; it will still taste heavenly.

Baked cheesecake

I was treated to this delicious cheesecake by Beate Joubert of the Joubert-Tradauw boutique cellar near Barrydale. The recipe, which calls for eight eggs for the filling, makes a large cake that is especially good served with a little grape jam.

CRUST
125 g butter or margarine
60 ml (¼ c) sugar
1 extra-large egg
500 ml (2 c) cake flour
7 ml (1½ t) baking powder

FILLING
1 kg (4 c or 4 x 250 g)
cream cheese
375 ml (1½ c) sugar
250 ml (1 c) cream
10 ml (2 t) vanilla essence
grated zest of 1 lemon
juice of 1½ lemons
8 extra-large eggs

Preheat the oven to 200 °C. Grease a 25 cm springform tin with butter, margarine or nonstick spray.

CRUST Cream the butter and sugar together until the mixture is light and fluffy.
Beat in the egg until well blended.
Sift the flour and baking powder together and stir it into the creamed mixture to make a fairly stiff dough. Press the dough onto the bottom and against the inside of the tin, taking care that the crust is not too thick.

FILLING Whisk the filling ingredients together until just blended (do not overbeat) and pour the mixture into the crust.
Bake for 45 minutes. The filling will not be completely set. Leave the cheesecake to cool in the oven with the door slightly ajar. Chill until firm. Cut into slices and serve with a little merlot jam.

MAKES 1 LARGE CHEESECAKE.

TO MAKE A LOW-FAT CHEESECAKE:
- Cheesecake is ideal for diabetics because, unlike other cakes that consist of mainly carbohydrates (flour and sugar), it consists mainly of protein (cheese and eggs). Carbohydrates are the culprits that play havoc with blood-sugar levels, while protein does not have a glycemic index. Cheesecake is, however, inclined to be very rich because it's usually made with cream cheese and cream. For a less rich version use a combination of smooth cottage cheese (with hardly any fat) and creamed cottage cheese (which contains less than 10 per cent fat) instead of the cream cheese and omit the cream. The cake will be somewhat drier and I suggest you reduce the baking time slightly.
- Use less sugar. (When baking cheesecake the effect of the sugar on the texture is not as important as in other cakes.)
- Use phyllo pastry for the crust; it's fat free. Use four layers and spray each with nonstick spray.

Coconut and sour cream cheesecake

The toasted coconut and coconut milk give this cheesecake its outstanding flavour.

CRUST
250 g Tennis biscuits, crushed
120 g butter, melted

FILLING
1 tub (250 g) cream cheese
  or smooth cottage cheese
300 ml sour cream
60 ml (¼ c) coconut liqueur
3 extra-large eggs
250 ml (1 c) coconut milk
125 ml (½ c) desiccated coconut, toasted
60 ml (4 T) cornflour
125 ml (½ c) caster sugar

Preheat the oven to 180 °C.

CRUST Mix the crushed biscuits and melted butter and press the mixture onto the bottom and along the sides of a 22 cm springform tin. Chill for 30 minutes.

FILLING Using an electric beater, whisk the filling ingredients together until creamy.
Pour the filling into the crust and bake for 1¼ hours or until the filling has just set.
Switch off the oven and leave the cheesecake to cool in the oven with the door slightly ajar.
Chill the cheesecake for at least 3 hours.

MAKES 1 LARGE CAKE.

THE DIFFERENCE BETWEEN CREAM CHEESE AND CREAMED COTTAGE CHEESE
Both are fresh cheeses but cream cheese, such as Philadelphia cream cheese, contains at least 33 per cent fat while creamed cottage cheese is cottage cheese to which 4–8 per cent cream has been added.

Apple cheesecake

YOU's editorial staffers loved this cheesecake with its apple layer at the bottom of the filling and crumb topping.

CRUST
200 g ginger cookies, crushed
60 ml (¼ c) butter, melted

FILLING
3 apples, peeled and cored
60 ml (¼ c) sugar
30 ml (2 T) butter
30 ml (2 T) cream
1 tub (230 g or 250 g) cream cheese
125 ml (½ c) sugar
2 extra-large eggs
250 ml (1 c) sour cream
juice and grated zest of 1 lemon

TOPPING
125 ml (½ c) cake flour
60 ml (¼ c) soft brown sugar
1 ml (¼ t) ground ginger
60 ml (¼ c) butter

Preheat the oven to 180 °C and line a 20 cm springform tin with baking paper. Grease with butter, margarine or nonstick spray.

CRUST Mix the crushed cookies and melted butter and press the mixture onto the bottom and along the inside of the prepared tin.

FILLING Cut the apples into 8 mm thick slices. Heat the apple slices, sugar and butter in a large pan over medium heat and sauté the fruit for 3–5 minutes or until soft. Add the cream and simmer for 5 minutes. Set aside. Whisk the cream cheese and sugar until smooth. Beat in the eggs one at a time until just blended. Beat in the sour cream and lemon juice and zest. Arrange the apples slices on the crust and pour over the cheese mixture.

TOPPING Mix the topping ingredients until crumbly and sprinkle the mixture over the filling. Bake for 45 minutes or until just set. Leave the cheesecake to cool in the oven and chill for at least 4 hours before serving.

MAKES 1 LARGE CHEESECAKE.

THE FOUR MOST COMMON REASONS FOR CRACKS IN A CHEESECAKE:
1. Too much air in the mixture; 2. Cooled down too rapidly; 3. Underdone; 4. Overdone.

1. If the mixture is beaten for too long or too fast, extra air is incorporated into the batter. During the baking process the air expands, causing the cheesecake to rise. The air bubbles burst as there are few or no added ingredients that offer structural support and the cake collapses. To avoid this beat the mixture slowly, especially after the eggs have been added. Once the tin has been filled you can also pick it up and drop it gently on the worktop before putting it in the oven. This will force the air bubbles to the surface. You can also run a knife in an S movement through the mixture once it has been poured into the tin.
2. A cheesecake shrinks slightly as it cools. If cooled too rapidly it can burst. Leave the cheesecake to cool in the oven for at least 20 minutes – switch off the oven and leave the door slightly ajar. Leave the cheesecake to cool to room temperature before putting it in the fridge.
3. If the centre of the cheesecake is not baked through it can burst while cooling. The filling should still be slightly wobbly in the centre and the sides must be firm. A thermometer is perfect for testing the doneness – the temperature must be between 75 °C and 80 °C.
4. If the cheesecake is overdone, too much moisture will evaporate, leaving the cake dried out and with a cracked surface. To test if a cheesecake is done, tap the tin lightly while it's still in the oven. The edge must be firm and the centre still slightly wobbly. The cake will set during the cooling process. Baking the cheesecake in a water bath will prevent it drying out too much.

Another tip is to run a knife around the inside of the tin 10 minutes after the cheesecake has come out of the oven. This will also reduce the risk of cracks when the cheesecake shrinks from the inside of the cake tin. If it sticks the cheesecake will crack. Also line the sides of the tin with baking paper.

Lemon meringue cheesecake

This quick and easy cake is like a lemon meringue pie and cheesecake all in one. Delicious!

CRUST
250 g Tennis biscuits, crushed
110 g butter, melted

FILLING
1 tub (230 g or 250 g) cream cheese
1 can (398 g) condensed milk
2 extra-large eggs, separated
60 ml (¼ c) lemon juice
15 ml (1 T) grated lemon zest
125 ml (½ c) caster sugar

Preheat the oven to 200 °C. Line the bottom of a 20 cm springform tin with baking paper and grease it with butter, margarine or nonstick spray.

CRUST Mix the crushed biscuits and melted butter and press one-third of the mixture onto the bottom of the tin and the rest about three-quarters of the way up the inside of the tin.

FILLING Beat the cream cheese until smooth. Beat in the condensed milk, egg yolks and lemon juice and zest and pour the mixture into the crust.
Whisk the egg whites until soft peaks form and gradually beat in the caster sugar until the mixture is stiff, smooth and shiny. Spoon the meringue mixture on top of the filling and bake for 10–15 minutes or until the meringue is pale brown.
Leave the cheesecake to cool completely in the tin before removing it.

MAKES 1 LARGE CHEESECAKE.

Carmen says
To easily loosen the crust, steam the bottom of the tin for a few seconds over a boiling kettle.

Double chocolate cheesecake

Dark chocolate is added to the cream cheese for this deliciously rich cheesecake, while white chocolate squares are scattered over the filling just before the cake goes into the oven.

CRUST

1 packet (200 g) chocolate digestive biscuits
250 ml (1 c) cake flour
125 ml (½ c) caster sugar
125 g butter
1 extra-large egg

FILLING

160 ml (⅔ c) thick cream
200 g dark chocolate, broken into pieces
2 tubs (230 g each) cream cheese
2 extra-large eggs
60 ml (¼ c) caster sugar
10 ml (2 t) vanilla essence
100 g white chocolate, broken into pieces

Preheat the oven to 180 °C. Grease a 22 x 28 cm tin with butter, margarine or nonstick spray.

CRUST Put all the ingredients except the butter and egg in a food processor and blitz until the mixture resembles breadcrumbs. Add the butter and blitz until mixed. Add the egg and blitz until a soft ball forms. Spread the mixture over the bottom of the tin.

FILLING Bring the cream to the boil and remove from the heat. Add the dark chocolate, stirring until melted. Leave the mixture to cool slightly but do not let it set.
Whisk the cream cheese, eggs, caster sugar and vanilla essence together. Whisk the cooled chocolate mixture into the cream cheese mixture. Mix well and spoon the filling into the prepared crust. Scatter the white chocolate pieces on top.
Bake for 1 hour in the centre of the oven, reduce the temperature to 140 °C and bake for another 30–40 minutes or until firm in the centre. Switch off the oven and leave the cheesecake to cool in the oven with the door slightly ajar.

MAKES 1 MEDIUM-SIZED CHEESECAKE.

Baked mocha cheesecake

This cheesecake is delicately flavoured with aromatic coffee.

CRUST

75 g butter
50 ml soft brown sugar
200 g caramel cookies (such as Nuttikrust), crushed

FILLING

2 tubs (250 g each) cream cheese
160 ml (⅔ c) soft brown sugar
125 ml (½ c) cake flour
2 ml (½ t) vanilla essence
3 extra-large eggs
30 ml (2 T) cream
10 ml (2 t) instant coffee granules, dissolved in 10 ml (2 t) boiling water

TOPPING

250 ml (1 c) dark chocolate discs
80 ml (⅓ c) cream
30 ml (2 T) strong coffee

Preheat the oven to 160 °C. Grease a 21 cm springform tin with butter, margarine or nonstick spray.

CRUST Mix the ingredients for the crust and press the mixture onto the bottom of the prepared tin.

FILLING Whisk the filling ingredients together until well blended and smooth and pour the mixture into the crust. Bake for about 1 hour or until the filling has just set. Leave to cool in the oven.

TOPPING Heat the chocolate discs, cream and coffee together, stirring until the chocolate has melted. Drizzle over the cheesecake in a zigzag pattern.

MAKES 1 MEDIUM-SIZED CAKE.

Fruity cheesecake with phyllo pastry crust

This typically Mediterranean cheesecake, made with almonds, sultanas, dates and ricotta cheese, has a lovely dense texture. It's not too sweet and not as rich as other cheesecakes.

CRUST
8 sheets phyllo pastry
60 g butter, melted

FILLING
60 ml (¼ c) cake flour
30 ml (2 T) ground almonds
75 ml (5 T) caster sugar
250 ml (1 c) milk
3 extra-large eggs, lightly whisked
250 g ricotta cheese
60 ml (¼ c) sultanas
60 ml (¼ c) finely chopped dates
a few drops almond essence
2 ml (½ t) vanilla essence
5 ml (1 t) lemon juice
2 ml (½ t) grated orange zest
  (optional)
icing sugar for dusting

Preheat the oven to 180 °C. Grease a 20–22 cm round pie dish with butter, margarine or nonstick spray.

CRUST Cut the phyllo pastry sheets into 30 cm squares and brush each with the melted butter. Line the pie dish with one of the pastry sheets and arrange the next five sheets in the pie dish so the corners fan out over the edge of the dish.

FILLING Mix the cake flour, almonds and caster sugar in a saucepan. Add the milk and bring to the boil over medium heat, stirring until the mixture thickens. Pour it into a mixing bowl and put the bowl in cold water to rapidly cool the mixture.
Whisk in the eggs and ricotta cheese until the mixture is smooth and lump free. Stir in the sultanas, dates, essences, lemon juice and orange zest and pour the mixture into the phyllo pastry crust. Cut the remaining two phyllo pastry sheets so they are slightly bigger than the pie dish and brush them with butter. Lay them on top of the filling.
Fold the overlapping pastry sheets over the filling and brush the top layer with melted butter. Bake for 35–40 minutes or until the filling has set and the crust is golden and crisp. Cool slightly, then dust with icing sugar. Serve lukewarm or cold.

MAKES 1 LARGE CHEESECAKE.

Orange and fig cheesecake

This cheesecake is former YOU assistant food editor Daleen van der Merwe's favourite.

CRUST
125 ml (½ c) ground Brazil nuts
125 g Tennis biscuits, crushed
80 g butter, melted

FILLING
250 ml (1 c) orange juice
250 g dried figs, finely chopped
1 cinnamon stick
pinch ground cloves
1 tub (250 g) cream cheese or
  smooth cottage cheese, at room
  temperature
12 ml (2½ t) grated orange zest
180 ml (¾ c) caster sugar
5 ml (1 t) vanilla essence
250 g mascarpone cheese
2 extra-large eggs, separated

Preheat the oven to 160 °C. Grease a 22 cm springform tin with butter, margarine or nonstick spray.

CRUST Mix the nuts, crushed biscuits and butter and press the mixture onto the bottom of the prepared tin. Chill until cold and firm.

FILLING Heat the orange juice, figs, cinnamon stick and cloves together and simmer for 10 minutes or until nearly all the liquid has evaporated. Leave to cool and remove the cinnamon stick. Evenly spread the fig mixture over the crust.
Using an electric beater, whisk the cream cheese, orange zest and caster sugar together until blended. Add the essence, mascarpone cheese and egg yolks and whisk until blended.
Whisk the egg whites until soft peaks form and fold them into the cheese mixture.
Pour the filling over the fig layer and bake for 1¼ hours or until the filling is just firm. Switch off the oven and leave the cheesecake to cool in the oven with the door slightly ajar. Chill the cheesecake for at least 3 hours.

MAKES 1 LARGE CHEESECAKE.

Savoury cheesecake

This mouthwatering savoury cheesecake
is a delicious alternative to a quiche.

CRUST
200 g savoury biscuits, crushed
60 ml (¼ c) melted butter

FILLING
250 g Philadelphia cream cheese
2 tubs (230 g or 250 g each) cream cheese
3 extra-large eggs
2 egg yolks
250 ml (1 c) sour cream
15 ml (1 T) lemon juice
**200 g smoked salmon or smoked
    snoek, flaked**
100 g piquant peppers, sliced into strips
15 ml (1 T) chopped chives
2 ml (½ t) finely grated lemon zest

Preheat the oven to 180 °C. Line a 22 cm springform tin
with baking paper and grease it with butter, margarine or
nonstick spray.

CRUST Mix the crushed biscuits and melted butter and
press the mixture onto the bottom of the prepared tin.
Bake for 10–12 minutes and remove from the oven. Reduce
the oven temperature to 150 °C.

FILLING Using an electric beater, whisk the cream
cheeses together until smooth.
Add the eggs, egg yolks, sour cream and lemon juice
and beat slowly until smooth. Stir in the salmon or snoek,
piquant peppers, chives and lemon zest.
Pour the mixture into the baked shell and bake for
40–50 minutes or until set. Leave to cool, preferably in
the oven. Cover and chill overnight.

MAKES 1 LARGE CHEESECAKE.

Individual blue-cheese cakes

Serve this delicious blue-cheese cake
with clementine marmalade instead of the
usual cheese and biscuits. It's perfect if
you're looking for dishes that are low in
fat and contain no sugar.

CRUST
1 packet (200 g) cream crackers, crushed
4 extra-large egg whites, whisked

FILLING
2 tubs (250 g each) creamed cottage cheese
100 g blue cheese, crumbled
4 extra-large egg yolks, whisked with 125 ml (½ c) milk
1 ml (¼ t) cayenne pepper
few basil leaves, chopped
salt and black pepper to taste

Preheat the oven to 180 °C. Grease six 8 cm loose-
bottomed pie tins with butter, margarine or nonstick spray.

CRUST Mix the crust ingredients together and set aside.

FILLING Stir the filling ingredients together and divide the
mixture among the prepared tins. Scatter over a thick layer
of the crust mixture. Bake the cakes for about 40 minutes
or until firm and leave them to cool in the oven. Serve with
spicy clementine marmalade (see p. 212).

MAKES 6 INDIVIDUAL CAKES.

Chocolate carrot cake

CAKES WITH FRUIT AND VEGETABLES

It's easy to get kids to eat fruit and vegetables with these wonderful cakes. They're packed with veggies such as carrots, beetroot and pumpkin and fruit such as apples, pears, blueberries, bananas and apricots, making them not only nutritious but deliciously filling and moist. The cakes are even better served with a cottage cheese, yoghurt, buttermilk or nutty caramel topping.

These cakes are a healthier alternative to a butter cake but don't be fooled: the cakes contain their fair share of butter and sugar.

Chocolate carrot cake

This cake is made with pecan nuts, coconut, sultanas and real chocolate, writes Alta de Scande of Swakopmund in Namibia.

CAKE
375 ml (1½ c) self-raising flour
60 ml (¼ c) cocoa
5 ml (1 t) ground cinnamon
1 ml (¼ t) grated nutmeg
pinch salt
125 ml (½ c) chopped pecan nuts
125 ml (½ c) sultanas
80 ml (⅓ c) desiccated coconut
3 extra-large eggs
180 ml (¾ c) soft brown sugar
125 ml (½ c) oil
125 g dark chocolate, melted
750 ml (3 c) finely grated carrots

ICING
1 tub (250 g) creamed cottage cheese
125 g dark chocolate, melted
500 ml (2 c) sifted icing sugar
pecan nuts, roughly chopped

Preheat the oven to 180 °C and grease a 23 cm ring cake tin with butter, margarine or nonstick spray.

CAKE Sift the self-raising flour, cocoa and spices together. Stir in the pecan nuts, sultanas and coconut.

Whisk the eggs, sugar and oil together until the sugar has dissolved. Stir the melted chocolate into the egg mixture, mixing until smooth. Fold the chocolate mixture into the flour mixture, alternating with the carrots.

Turn the mixture into the prepared tin and bake for about 1 hour or until a testing skewer comes out clean when inserted into the centre of the cake. Leave the cake to cool in the tin for 10 minutes before turning it out onto a wire rack to cool completely.

ICING Beat the cottage cheese and melted chocolate together until smooth. Stir in the icing sugar and pour the mixture over the cake so it runs down the sides. Sprinkle over chopped nuts.

MAKES 1 LARGE RING CAKE.

VARIATIONS
- Substitute the same quantity sweet potatoes for the carrots.
- Substitute beetroot for 250 ml (1 c) of the carrots.
- To make the cake even more special, use caramel cream icing (see p. 205) instead of the cream cheese icing.

Spicy apple cake

The recipe for this winner was sent in by Elna Mattheus of Faerie Glen in Pretoria. We decorated the cake with baby apples.

CAKE

400 g (2–3 large) apples, peeled, cored and cut into pieces
30 ml (2 T) water
juice of 1 lemon
400 ml cake flour
10 ml (2 t) baking powder
1 ml (¼ t) salt
7 ml (1½ t) mixed spice
125 g butter, at room temperature
160 ml (⅔ c) light brown sugar
1 extra-large egg
5 ml (1 t) vanilla essence

ICING

250 ml (1 c) cream, chilled
160 ml (⅔ c) caster sugar
125 g (½ tub) creamed cottage cheese
60 ml (¼ c) thick Greek yoghurt
1 can (425 g) baby apples, stems intact
125 ml (½ c) white sugar
brown sugar for sprinkling on top

Preheat the oven to 180 °C and grease a 20 cm loose-bottomed tin with butter, margarine or nonstick spray.

CAKE Put the apples, water and lemon juice in a saucepan and bring everything to the boil. Simmer gently for about 10 minutes or until the mixture forms a purée. Beat gently with a wooden spoon and, stirring continuously, heat for 2 minutes more or until the mixture is no longer watery. Remove from the heat and leave to cool. Sift the dry ingredients together and set aside.

Cream the butter and sugar together until the mixture is light and fluffy. Lightly whisk the egg and vanilla essence together and stir the mixture into the apple sauce. Fold the apple mixture into the butter mixture, alternating with the flour mixture. Mix gently but thoroughly. Turn the batter into the prepared tin, spreading it evenly.

Bake for 40–45 minutes or until a testing skewer comes out clean when inserted into the centre of the cake. Leave the cake to cool in the tin before turning it out onto a wire rack. Once the cake has cooled completely, halve it horizontally.

ICING Whip the cream and caster sugar until stiff. Mix the creamed cottage cheese and yoghurt until well blended and carefully fold it into the whipped cream. Drain the apples but reserve 125 ml (½ c) of the syrup. Slowly heat the sugar and apple syrup until the sugar has dissolved. Bring the mixture to the boil and simmer until the syrup turns a light caramel colour. Remove from the heat and dip the apples in the syrup. Leave them to dry on wax paper. Sandwich the two cake layers together with half the icing and spoon the rest on top. Sprinkle the cake with light brown sugar just before serving and decorate with the caramelised apples.

MAKES 1 TWO-TIER CAKE.

Apricot and chocolate chip cake

She won first prize in a Safari Dried Fruit competition with this cake, writes Ursula Schuster of Port Elizabeth. She leaves the cake to stand overnight so it can ripen.

CAKE
250 ml (1 c) finely chopped dried apricots
250 ml (1 c) apricot juice
125 g butter
160 ml (⅔ c) light brown sugar
2 extra-large eggs
375 ml (1½ c) self-raising flour
5 ml (1 t) baking powder
375 ml (1½ c) desiccated coconut
125 ml (½ c) chocolate chips or roughly
    chopped dark chocolate

ICING
1 slab (100 g) dark chocolate, roughly chopped
100 ml cream or plain yoghurt

Preheat the oven to 180 °C. Grease a 22 cm cake tin with margarine, butter or nonstick spray and line it with greased baking paper.

CAKE Soak the apricots in the apricot juice for at least 1 hour. Cream the butter and sugar together until the mixture is light and fluffy. Add the eggs one at a time, whisking well after each addition.
Sift the self-raising flour and baking powder together.
Stir the coconut and half the sifted flour into the butter mixture. Stir in the remaining flour, soaked apricots and chocolate chips or pieces. Turn the batter into the prepared tin, spreading it evenly.
Bake for 1¼ hours or until a testing skewer comes out clean when inserted into the centre of the cake. Leave the cake to cool in the tin for 5 minutes before turning it out onto a wire rack to cool completely.

ICING Melt the chocolate and stir in the cream or yoghurt. Cool the mixture slightly before pouring it over the cooled cake.

MAKES 1 MEDIUM-SIZED CAKE.

Blueberry and sour cream cake

Blueberries work well in baking because their firm skins retain their juiciness and burst when you bite into them.

CAKE
175 g butter, softened
200 ml caster sugar
3 extra-large eggs
400 ml self-raising flour
5 ml (1 t) baking powder
10 ml (2 t) vanilla essence
60 ml (¼ c) sour cream
375 g blueberries

ICING
200 g Philadelphia cream cheese
75 ml (5 T) sour cream
200 ml icing sugar

Preheat the oven to 180 °C. Grease a 22 cm loose-bottomed cake tin with butter, margarine or nonstick spray and line it with greased baking paper.

CAKE Cream the butter and sugar together until the mixture is light and fluffy. Add the eggs one at a time, beating well after each addition.
Sift the self-raising flour and baking powder over the creamed mixture and fold in. Whisk in the vanilla essence and sour cream and carefully stir in half the berries. Turn the mixture into the prepared cake tin, spreading it evenly.
Bake for 50 minutes or until a testing skewer comes out clean when inserted into the centre of the cake. Leave the cake to cool in the tin for about 10 minutes before turning it out onto a wire rack. Peel away the baking paper and leave the cake to cool completely.

ICING Whisk the cream cheese, sour cream and icing sugar together until the mixture is smooth and creamy. Spread the cheese mixture over the cooled cake and scatter the remaining blueberries over the cake. The cake will keep well in the fridge for a few days.

MAKES 1 MEDIUM-SIZED CAKE.

Carmen says
Serve this cake at room temperature.

Pear cake with ginger and cream cheese icing

A full-flavoured cake with a coarse texture similar to that of carrot cake. The ginger icing makes it extra special.

ICING
200 g cream cheese
30 ml (2 T) finely chopped
    ginger preserve
30 ml (2 T) ginger preserve syrup
60 ml (¼ c) softened butter
125 ml (½ c) icing sugar, sifted
ground cinnamon
dried fruit slices (see p. 213)

CAKE
500 ml (2 c) cake flour
200 ml sugar
10 ml (2 t) baking powder
3 ml (generous ½ t) salt
10 ml (2 t) ground cinnamon
3 ml (generous ½ t)
    grated nutmeg
45 ml (3 T) finely grated
    lemon zest
180 ml (¾ c) oil
100 ml honey
2 extra-large eggs
80 ml (⅓ c) milk
7 ml (1½ t) vanilla essence
750 ml (3 c) grated fresh pears
125 ml (½ c) toasted and finely
    chopped walnuts

Preheat the oven to 180 °C. Grease two 20 cm cake tins with butter, margarine or nonstick spray and dust them with flour.

ICING Whisk the cream cheese, ginger pieces and syrup together and set aside. Cream the butter and icing sugar together and mix with the cream cheese mixture. Chill.

CAKE Mix the dry ingredients, spices and lemon zest in a mixing bowl. Make a well in the centre.
Whisk the oil, honey, eggs, milk and vanilla essence together and add the mixture to the dry ingredients, stirring until just blended.
Fold the grated pears and nuts into the batter and turn the mixture into the prepared tins.
Bake for 40–45 minutes or until a testing skewer comes out clean when inserted into the centre of the cakes.
Leave the cakes to cool in the tins for a few minutes before turning them out onto a wire rack to cool completely.
Sandwich the cakes together with some of the icing and spread the rest on top of the cake. Dust the cake with a little ground cinnamon and decorate with dried fruit slices.

MAKES 1 MEDIUM-SIZED TWO-TIER CAKE.

VARIATION
Use apples instead of pears.

Apricot cake with buttermilk icing

Nicky Young of Bellville always sends in cake recipes that are real winners.

250 ml (1 c) chopped dried apricots
500 ml (2 c) water
350 ml caster sugar
450 ml cake flour
pinch salt
3 ml (generous ½ t) bicarbonate
    of soda
7 ml (1½ t) baking powder
125 g butter, softened
2 egg yolks
60 ml (¼ c) water
5 ml (1 t) orange essence
3 ml (generous ½ t) vanilla essence

BUTTERMILK ICING
60 ml (¼ c) caster sugar
30 ml (2 T) cornflour
3 egg yolks, whisked
500 ml (2 c) buttermilk
5 ml (1 t) orange essence
2 ml (½ t) vanilla essence
chopped dried apricots to
    decorate (optional)

Preheat the oven to 180 °C. Grease a 20 cm cake tin with butter, margarine or nonstick spray.

CAKE Bring the apricots, 500 ml (2 c) water and 100 ml of the caster sugar to the boil and simmer for 15–20 minutes. Purée.

Sift the dry ingredients together and set aside.

Cream the butter and remaining caster sugar together until the mixture is light and fluffy. Beat in the egg yolks. Fold the dry ingredients into the butter mixture, alternating with the apricot purée and 60 ml (¼ c) water. Add the essences.

Turn the batter into the tin, spreading it evenly. Bake for 45 minutes or until a testing skewer comes out clean when inserted into the centre of the cake.

Leave the cake to cool in the tin before turning it out.

BUTTERMILK ICING Combine the caster sugar and cornflour in a saucepan and add the egg yolks. Add the buttermilk and mix. Put the saucepan on the stove and, stirring continuously, slowly heat the mixture until it thickens and coats the back of a wooden spoon. Add the essences and leave the mixture to cool. Halve the cake horizontally and sandwich the two cake halves together with the icing. Decorate the cake with the remaining icing. Sprinkle with chopped apricots if desired.

MAKES 1 LARGE CAKE.

Banana cake with caramelised walnut topping

The flavour of this cake, with its walnut topping that's caramelised under the oven grill, improves the longer the cake is left to stand.

175 g butter, softened
310 ml (1¼ c) soft brown sugar
4 extra-large eggs
3 large ripe bananas, mashed
150 g walnuts, roughly chopped
625 ml (2½ c) self-raising flour
5 ml (1 t) baking powder
pinch salt
1 ml (¼ t) grated nutmeg
300 ml thick Greek yoghurt

TOPPING
75 g butter
200 ml soft brown sugar
30 ml (2 T) thick cream
½ packet (50 g) walnuts,
    chopped

Preheat the oven to 180 °C. Grease a 25 cm loose-bottomed tin with butter, margarine or nonstick spray and line it with greased baking paper.

CAKE Cream the butter and sugar together until the mixture is light and fluffy.

Add the eggs one at a time, beating well after each addition. Stir in the mashed bananas and walnuts.

Sift the flour, baking powder, salt and nutmeg together and gently fold the flour mixture into the banana mixture. Fold in the yoghurt.

Turn the batter into the prepared tin and bake for about 1 hour or until risen and golden. Remove the cake from the oven and preheat the oven grill.

TOPPING Slowly heat the butter, sugar and cream in a saucepan on top of the stove until the sugar has melted. Bring the mixture to the boil and stir in the nuts. Spoon the mixture over the cake and put it under the oven grill until the mixture starts to bubble. Leave the cake to cool in the tin.

MAKES 1 MEDIUM-SIZED CAKE.

Banana and coconut cake

This cake is a hit with everyone, writes Desiré Hayward of Steytlerville. The cake layers are sandwiched together with caramel condensed milk and the cake is decorated with butter icing and walnuts.

CAKE
225 g butter
280 ml sugar
4 extra-large eggs, separated
3 large, ripe bananas, mashed
½ packet (50 g) walnuts, roughly chopped
625 ml (2½ c) cake flour
15 ml (1 T) baking powder
1 ml (¼ t) salt
160 ml (⅔ c) desiccated coconut
60 ml (¼ c) caster sugar

ICING
butter icing (see p. 204)
1 can (375 g) caramel condensed milk
1 packet (100 g) walnut halves

Preheat the oven to 180 °C. Line two greased 22 cm cake tins with baking paper and grease the paper with butter, margarine or nonstick spray.

CAKE Cream the butter and sugar together until the mixture is light and fluffy. Add the egg yolks, mashed banana and nuts and mix.
Sift the flour, baking powder and salt together and fold into the banana mixture, alternating with the coconut.
Whisk the egg whites until stiff peaks begin to form.
Add the caster sugar and whisk for 30 seconds. Fold the meringue mixture into the flour mixture and turn the batter into the prepared tins.
Bake for about 40 minutes or until golden and a testing skewer comes out clean when inserted into the centre of the cakes. Turn the cakes out onto a wire rack. When cooled, halve the cakes horizontally.

ICING Prepare the butter icing as described. Spread the bottom cake layer with half the condensed milk, cover with a cake layer and spread it with half the icing. Repeat the layers and decorate the cake with the nuts.

MAKES 1 LARGE FOUR-TIER CAKE.

Pear upside-down cake

The batter for this cake, with its topping of caramelised pear slices, contains finely grated pears and ginger preserve, which give the cake a wonderful spicy flavour.

CARAMEL LAYER
80 ml (⅓ c) butter
180 ml (¾ c) soft brown sugar
4 firm pears, sliced

CAKE
330 ml (1⅓ c) cake flour
160 ml (⅔ c) white sugar
45 ml (3 T) chopped ginger preserve
5 ml (1 t) bicarbonate of soda
2 ml (½ t) ground ginger
2 ml (½ t) salt
3 extra-large eggs
125 ml (½ c) oil
5 ml (1 t) vanilla essence
5 ml (1 t) finely grated orange zest
250 ml (1 c) peeled and finely grated firm pears
    (about 2 pears)

Preheat the oven to 180 °C and grease a 25 cm cake tin with butter, margarine or nonstick spray.

CARAMEL LAYER Melt the butter in the cake tin over low heat. Remove from the heat and sprinkle the brown sugar in the bottom of the tin. Arrange the pear slices in a pretty pattern in the bottom of the tin.

CAKE Mix the cake flour, sugar, ginger preserve, bicarbonate of soda, ground ginger and salt.
Whisk the eggs, oil, vanilla essence and orange zest together in a large bowl.
Stir in the grated pears, mixing well. Add the flour mixture to the egg mixture and mix well. Carefully spoon the batter over the pears in the cake tin.
Bake for 40–45 minutes or until a testing skewer comes out clean when inserted into the centre of the cake.
Leave the cake to cool in the tin for about 20 minutes. Run a knife along the inside of the tin and invert the cake onto a platter. Serve lukewarm with extra caramelised pears and ice cream.

MAKES 1 MEDIUM-SIZED CAKE.

Pineapple upside-down cake

The buttermilk batter for this cake has a delicate orange flavour.

CARAMEL LAYER
200 ml caster sugar
1 can (440 g) pineapple rings, drained

CAKE
250 ml (1 c) self-raising flour
145 ml caster sugar
2 extra-large eggs
grated zest of 1 orange
200 ml buttermilk
60 ml (¼ c) melted butter

Preheat the oven to 200 °C and grease a 20 cm cake tin (round or fluted) with butter, margarine or nonstick spray.

CARAMEL LAYER Heat the caster sugar in a nonstick pan over medium heat for about 5 minutes or until it turns a caramel colour. Do not stir but take care that it doesn't burn. Put the pineapple rings in the bubbling caramel and leave them to simmer for a few minutes or until they begin to brown. Rapidly spoon the mixture into the prepared cake tin and arrange the pineapple rings in a pretty pattern in the bottom of the tin.

CAKE Sift the self-raising flour and caster sugar together in a mixing bowl.
Whisk the eggs, orange zest, buttermilk and melted butter and gently fold the mixture into the flour mixture.
Turn the batter into the prepared tin.
Put the cake tin on a baking sheet and bake it for 20–25 minutes or until done and golden on top. Leave the cake to cool in the tin for a few minutes. Put a serving platter over the tin and carefully invert the cake onto the platter. Serve warm with cream or ice cream.

MAKES 1 MEDIUM-SIZED CAKE.

Carmen says
To invert an upside-down cake, run a knife along the inside of the tin to loosen the cake. Put a plate on the tin and quickly invert the tin. Leave the tin to rest on the platter for a few minutes. The filling will sink into the fruit layer.

Pineapple and macadamia upside-down mini-cakes

These individual cakes, each with its own pineapple ring, are baked in muffin tins or ramekins. Quick and easy to prepare, as the pineapple rings are caramelised while baking.

CARAMEL LAYER
45 ml (3 T) butter, melted
80 ml (⅓ c) soft brown sugar, firmly packed
15 ml (1 T) rum
125 ml (½ c) chopped macadamia nuts, toasted
6 fresh or canned pineapple rings

CAKE
300 ml cake flour
250 ml (1 c) white sugar
10 ml (2 t) baking powder
1 ml (¼ t) salt
160 ml (⅔ c) milk
60 g butter, at room temperature
1 extra-large egg
5 ml (1 t) vanilla essence
cream to serve

Preheat the oven to 180 °C.

CARAMEL LAYER Pour the butter into six ramekins or muffin tin hollows of a large muffin tin. Sprinkle the brown sugar, rum and nuts over the butter. Put a pineapple ring on top of the nuts in each ramekin or hollow and set aside.

CAKE Sift the flour, sugar, baking powder and salt together in a large mixing bowl.
Add the milk, butter, egg and vanilla essence and, using an electric beater set on low, whisk the mixture for 30 seconds. Increase the speed to moderate and whisk the mixture for another 2 minutes, regularly scraping the inside of the bowl. Turn the batter into the ramekins or muffin tin hollows.
Bake for 25–30 minutes or until a testing skewer comes out clean when inserted into the centre of the cakes. Leave the cakes to cool in the ramekins or muffin tin for 2 minutes. Carefully run a sharp knife along the inside of the ramekins or muffin tin hollows and invert the cakes onto an even surface. Serve warm or at room temperature with whipped cream.

MAKES 6 SMALL CAKES.

Banana and walnut upside-down cake

The caramelised nuts impart a delicious crunchy texture to this cake.

CARAMEL LAYER
250 ml (1 c) soft brown sugar,
    firmly packed
60 ml (¼ c) butter
45 ml (3 T) golden syrup
60 ml (¼ c) roughly chopped walnuts
3 large bananas, cut into 6 mm thick
    diagonal slices

CAKE
250 ml (1 c) cake flour
10 ml (2 t) baking powder
2 ml (½ t) ground cinnamon
1 ml (¼ t) salt
180 ml (¾ c) white sugar
90 ml (6 T) butter, at room
    temperature
1 extra-large egg
2 ml (½ t) vanilla essence
90 ml (6 T) milk

Preheat the oven to 160 °C and grease a deep 20 cm cake tin with butter, margarine or nonstick spray.

CARAMEL LAYER Heat the sugar, butter and syrup over low heat, stirring until the butter has melted. Pour the syrup into the prepared cake tin, spreading it evenly. Sprinkle the nuts over the syrup in an even layer. Arrange the banana slices on top of the nuts in concentric, slightly overlapping circles.

CAKE Sift the flour, baking powder, cinnamon and salt together.
Cream the sugar and butter together until the mixture is pale and fluffy. Add the egg and vanilla essence and whisk until creamy.
Beat the flour mixture into the butter mixture in three batches, alternating each batch with the milk. Carefully spoon the batter over the bananas, spreading it evenly.
Bake for 50–55 minutes or until a testing skewer comes out clean when inserted into the centre of the cake. Leave the cake to cool in the tin for 15 minutes. Run a sharp knife along the inside of the tin to loosen the cake and invert it onto a cake platter. Leave the tin on the cake for 3 minutes before removing it carefully. Serve warm or at room temperature.

MAKES 1 LARGE CAKE.

Pineapple upside-down cake

LUXURIOUS FRUITCAKES

It's not every day that you bake a fruitcake at the drop of a hat. They are reserved for special occasions such as Christmas, weddings and christenings. The ingredients are expensive but fruitcakes last long and their flavour improves over time. Serve sparingly and thinly sliced.

My mother-in-law, Suzie, who's now deep in her eighties still spoils the family with her special fruitcake but refuses point blank to part with the recipe!

Over the years YOU readers have shared their best fruitcake recipes with us. Here's a selection of them; I still can't decide which is my favourite.

English fruitcake

English fruitcake

Don't have the right size cake tin called for in a recipe? Luckily we found this wonderful recipe from British celebrity chef Delia Smith; it gives the ingredients for four round and square tin sizes. Square tins with the same side measurements as the diameter of a round tin hold about 25 per cent more ingredients. The baking temperature is the same but the baking time longer.

INGREDIENTS	15 cm round or 13 cm square cake	20 cm round or 18 cm square cake	23 cm round or 20 cm square cake	28 cm round or 25 cm square cake
currants	360 ml	720 ml	920 ml	5 x 250 ml (5 c)
sultanas	120 ml	280 ml	360 ml	560 ml (2¼ c)
raisins	120 ml	280 ml	360 ml	560 ml (2¼ c)
glacé cherries, rinsed and finely chopped	50 ml	60 ml (¼ c)	80 ml (⅓ c)	140 ml
mixed citrus peel, finely chopped	60 ml (¼ c)	75 ml (5 T)	90 ml (6 T)	160 ml (⅔ c)
brandy	45 ml (3 T)	45 ml (3 T)	60 ml (¼ c)	90 ml (6 T)
cake flour	200 ml	430 ml	530 ml	860 ml
salt	2 ml (½ t)	2 ml (½ t)	2 ml (½ t)	2 ml (½ t)
grated nutmeg	1 ml (¼ t)	1 ml (¼ t)	2 ml (½ t)	2 ml (½ t)
mixed spice	1 ml (¼ t)	2 ml (½ t)	4 ml (¾ t)	5 ml (1 t)
soft brown sugar	125 ml (½ c)	250 ml (1 c)	300 ml	500 ml (2 c)
butter	110 g	225 g	275 g	450 g
eggs, whisked	2 extra-large	4 extra-large	5 extra-large	8 extra-large
molasses	7 ml (1½ t)	12 ml (2½ t)	15 ml (1 T)	25 ml (5 t)
almonds, chopped	70 ml	85 ml	100 ml	190 ml
grated lemon zest	of ½ lemon	of 1 lemon	of 1 large lemon	of 2 large lemons
grated orange zest	of ½ orange	of 1 orange	of 1 orange	of 2 large oranges
APPROX. BAKING TIME	3½ HOURS	4½–4¾ HOURS	4¾ HOURS	5½ HOURS

Put the dried fruit and peel in a mixing bowl, add the brandy, cover and leave to soak overnight.

Grease the tin and line as described on p. 92.

Preheat the oven to 140 °C.

Sift the flour, salt and spices together in a large mixing bowl.

Cream the sugar and butter together until light and fluffy. Add the eggs, 15 ml (1 T) at a time, beating well after each addition.

Gently fold in the flour mixture and stir in the fruit mixture, molasses, almonds and lemon and orange zest.

Turn the batter into the prepared tin, spreading it evenly with the back of a spoon. If leaving the cake plain, arrange whole blanched almonds on top of the batter.

Bake according to the length of time given in the table. Turn out the cake onto a wire rack and leave it to cool completely. Wrap the cake in clingfilm until needed. Sprinkle over a little brandy at five-day intervals if desired.

Decorate the cake as desired just before serving.

MAKES 1 LARGE CAKE.

HOW TO LINE A TIN FOR FRUITCAKE

A fruitcake has a long baking time so the cake tin must be lined to ensure that the cake doesn't dry out.

The conventional method: Grease the tin with butter, margarine or nonstick spray. Cut a strip of baking paper 5 cm wider than the depth of the tin and long enough to fit around the inside of the tin so the edges overlap. Fold in one long edge 3 cm, unfold again and cut notches up to the fold mark at regular intervals. Put the strip on the inside of the tin with the notches facing the bottom of the tin. Cut out a circle from baking paper the same size as the bottom of the tin. Put it in the tin and grease it. Using string, secure a few layers of newspaper around the outside of the tin.

My short-cut method: After many years of experimenting I've found it's easiest to bake a fruitcake in a cardboard box. Line the tin with a sheet of heavy-duty aluminium foil and line the bottom once more with a sheet of baking paper. Cover the outside of a cardboard box large enough to hold the tin with two layers of brown paper and a sheet of aluminium foil. Put the tin with the fruitcake batter inside the box and bake it at the required temperature. If the top of the cake turns too dark too quickly, cover it with a sheet of aluminium foil.

> **Carmen says**
> - Level the batter in the tin and sprinkle over a little brandy or water to prevent the cake drying out while baking.
> - A fruitcake will keep for at least three months. Ensure the cake is wrapped airtight before storing it.

Troubleshooting: Fruitcakes

	PROBLEMS	CAUSES
APPEARANCE	Cake sinks in the centre	Batter too thin – too much liquid and/or eggs Too much sugar, shortening or leavening agent Oven temperature too low or too many layers of protective paper Baking time too short
	Fruit on top too dark or burnt	Fruit not covered with batter before putting the cake in the oven
	Holes in crust	Protective lid or sheet of aluminium foil too tight-fitting, causing condensation and drops of water to fall on top of cake. Rather use a brown-paper lid.
TEXTURE	Moist and dense like a steamed pudding	Fruit too moist Cake steamed without baking it again Oven temperature too low
TASTE	Taste of fruit not evenly distributed	Poor-quality fruit Cake not matured long enough

Deliciously moist mini-fruitcakes

This outstanding fruitcake recipe was sent in by Ronnie Trieloff of Viljoenskroon. Wrapped in cellophane, the cakes make lovely gifts. Ronnie bakes the cakes in empty tuna cans and annually makes hundreds of them for corporate gifts. The cake can also be baked in a 20 cm cake tin, in which case reduce the oven temperature to 140 °C and bake the cake for 3-4 hours.

FRUITCAKES

125 g margarine, melted

125 g dates, finely sliced

250 ml (1 c) sugar

5 ml (1 t) bicarbonate of soda

750 ml (3 c) fruitcake mix

190 ml boiling water

125 ml (½ c) brandy

125 ml (½ c) glacé cherries

1 jar (175 g) ginger preserve,
   drained and quartered

1 jar (310 g) watermelon preserve,
   drained and cut into smaller pieces

5 ml (1 t) rum essence

2 extra-large eggs, whisked

500 ml (2 c) cake flour

2 ml (½ t) mixed spice

2 ml (½ t) ground cinnamon

2 ml (½ t) ground ginger

5 ml (1 t) baking powder

125 ml (½ c) roughly chopped
   mixed nuts

TO FINISH

80 ml (⅓ c) sherry

80 ml (⅓ c) brandy

80 ml (⅓ c) fortified wine

meringue icing (see p. 205) (optional)

FRUITCAKES Put the margarine, dates, sugar, bicarbonate of soda, fruitcake mix, boiling water and 60 ml (¼ c) of the brandy in a saucepan. Bring the mixture to the boil, reduce the heat and simmer for 20 minutes. Remove the saucepan from the heat and leave the mixture to stand overnight.

Soak the cherries and ginger and watermelon preserve in the rum essence and remaining brandy overnight.

Preheat the oven to 160 °C. Grease 9 empty tuna cans or the hollows of giant muffin tins with butter, margarine or nonstick spray.

Mix the fruitcake and soaked cherry mixtures well and add the eggs, flour, spices, baking powder and nuts. Mix well and turn the batter into the prepared tins, filling them to the top.

Bake for 1 hour or until a testing skewer comes out clean when inserted into the centre of the cakes.

TO FINISH Mix the sherry, brandy and fortified wine and slowly pour the mixture over the cakes as soon as they come out of the oven. Leave the cakes to cool in the tins before turning them out. Wrap the cakes in clingfilm until needed. Decorate with meringue icing if desired.

MAKES 9 MINI-FRUITCAKES.

VARIATION

Substitute 200 ml each currants, raisins, sultanas and lemon peel for the fruitcake mix.

Carmen says

Remember to moisten fruitcakes with a tot of brandy or sherry once a week so it can ripen. Wrap the cake in clingfilm so it doesn't dry out.

Dark fruitcake

We baked these fruitcakes in biscuit tins with tight-fitting lids so they can be neatly packed. The cakes are made with, among others, red jam and buttermilk and are moistened with brandy.

250 g butter, softened
375 ml (1½ c) sugar
3 extra-large eggs, separated
5 ml (1 t) bicarbonate of soda
125 ml (½ c) buttermilk
750 ml (3 c) cake flour
7 ml (1½ t) ground cinnamon
2 ml (½ t) grated nutmeg
2 ml (½ t) ground cloves
125 ml (½ c) red mixed-fruit jam
250 ml (1 c) chopped pecan nuts
250 ml (1 c) chopped red glacé cherries
250 ml (1 c) seedless raisins
250 ml (1 c) chopped dates
250 ml (1 c) brandy

Preheat the oven to 150 °C. Grease 12 cm and 18 cm cake tins with butter, margarine or nonstick spray. Line the tins with a double layer of baking paper and grease again. Dust the paper with cake flour.
Cream the butter and sugar together until the mixture is light and fluffy. Beat in the egg yolks.
Dissolve the bicarbonate of soda in the buttermilk and beat the mixture into the butter mixture.
Sift 625 ml (2½ c) of the flour and spices together and beat the mixture into the butter mixture, alternating with the jam.
Whisk the egg whites until stiff and fold them into the batter. Mix the remaining flour with the nuts and fruit and fold the mixture into the batter.
Turn the batter into the prepared tins, cover the cakes with aluminium foil and put each in a cardboard box.
Bake for 1¼ hours (small tin) and 2¾ hours (large tin) or until a testing skewer comes out clean when inserted into the centre of the cakes. Sprinkle the brandy over the cakes as soon as they come out of the oven. Leave the cakes to cool in the tins and cover them with the lids. Alternatively, turn out the cakes, wrap them in aluminium foil and store them in an airtight container.

MAKES 1 LARGE AND 1 SMALL CAKE.

Golden fruitcake

Doreen Patterson of Bromhof sent us the recipe for this delicious cake.

CAKE
125 ml (½ c) chopped glacé pineapple
250 ml (1 c) halved glacé cherries
125 ml (½ c) chopped dried apricots
250 ml (1 c) sultanas
45 ml (3 T) brandy
250 ml (1 c) butter
250 ml (1 c) caster sugar
juice and grated zest of 1 lemon
4 extra-large eggs
330 ml (1⅓ c) self-raising flour
100 ml ground almonds
180 ml (¾ c) roughly chopped blanched
    almonds or pecan nuts
100 ml whole blanched almonds or pecan nuts
30 ml (2 T) brandy

DECORATION
glacé fruit
blueberries

Preheat the oven to 140 °C and prepare a 26 cm cake tin as described on p. 92.

CAKE Mix the pineapple, cherries, apricots and sultanas and pour over the 45 ml (3 T) brandy.
Cream the butter and sugar together until light and fluffy.
Add the lemon juice and zest and mix well. Add the eggs one at a time, beating well after each addition.
Sift the self-raising flour over the creamed mixture and sprinkle the ground almonds on top. Fold in gently. Add the brandy-soaked fruit and chopped nuts and mix.
Turn the batter into the prepared tin, arrange the whole nuts on top and bake the cake for about 3 hours or until a testing skewer comes out clean when inserted into the centre of the cake. Leave the cake to cool in the tin. Sprinkle the cake with the extra brandy, wrap it in aluminium foil and store it in an airtight container. Decorate the cake just before serving with glacé fruit and blueberries.

MAKES 1 LARGE CAKE.

Golden fruitcake

Last-minute fruitcake

If the festive season is around the corner and you still haven't baked a cake, this recipe will come to your rescue. Cook the fruit the day before and leave it to cool overnight. The cake needs only one week to mature.

125 g butter
500 g fruitcake mix
125 g dates, chopped
250 ml (1 c) soft brown sugar
2 ml (½ t) mixed spice
5 ml (1 t) ground cinnamon
5 ml (1 t) bicarbonate of soda
200 ml water
125 ml (½ c) whole glacé cherries
125 ml (½ c) whole nuts
50 ml brandy
500 ml (2 c) cake flour
pinch salt
2 extra-large eggs
5 ml (1 t) baking powder
extra brandy

Melt the butter and add the fruitcake mix, dates, sugar and spices. Mix the bicarbonate of soda with the water and add the mixture to the fruit mixture. Bring the mixture to the boil and simmer it for 15 minutes. Leave to cool overnight.

Preheat the oven to 150 °C and prepare a 20 cm cake tin (see p. 92). Add the cherries, nuts and brandy to the fruit mixture.

Sift the flour and salt together and fold the mixture into the fruit mixture. Add the eggs and baking powder and mix.

Turn the batter into the prepared cake tin and bake for about 2½ hours or until a testing skewer comes out clean when inserted into the centre of the cake. Leave the cake to cool in the tin. Sprinkle over a little brandy, wrap the cake in aluminium foil and store it in an airtight container.

MAKES 1 MEDIUM-SIZED CAKE.

Economical fruitcake

The fruit for this cake, which is mostly affordable raisins, sultanas, currants and dates, is cooked together.

250 ml (1 c) raisins
250 ml (1 c) sultanas
250 ml (1 c) currants
1 packet (250 g) dates, finely sliced
250 ml (1 c) mixed peel
250 ml (1 c) sugar
130 g butter or margarine
250 ml (1 c) water
5 ml (1 t) bicarbonate of soda
500 ml (2 c) cake flour
3 ml (generous ½ t) baking powder
2 ml (½ t) allspice
2 ml (½ t) ground ginger
2 ml (½ t) salt
2 extra-large eggs, whisked
blanched almonds to decorate (optional)
25 ml (5 t) brandy

Prepare a deep 18 cm cake tin or 9–10 small loaf tins as described on p. 92.

Bring the raisins, sultanas, currants, dates, mixed peel, sugar, butter and water to the boil and cook for 5 minutes, stirring occasionally. Add the bicarbonate of soda to the hot fruit mixture. Remove the saucepan from the heat and leave the mixture to cool completely.

Preheat the oven to 140–150 °C.

Sift the flour, baking powder, allspice, ginger and salt together. Add the flour mixture to the fruit mixture, alternating with the whisked eggs. Mix well. Turn the batter into the prepared tins, spreading it evenly. Arrange the blanched almonds on top if desired.

Bake for 3 hours or 1 hour if using small loaf tins. Leave the cake to cool in the tin and sprinkle over the brandy. Turn out the cake, wrap it in aluminium foil and store it in an airtight container.

MAKES 1 SMALL CAKE OR 9 SMALL LOAVES.

Last-minute fruitcake

Mom Jo's 11 o'clock tea cake

CAKES FOR MORNING TEA AND AFTERNOON COFFEE

My mom loves her tea. Every morning at eleven tea is served on the stoep using pretty teacups and a teapot kept warm in a tea cosy for a second cup. For special occasions or on Saturdays cake, like a honey syrup cake still lukewarm from the oven, is served with tea.

Coffee is served after meals or in the late afternoon, often with a slice of freshly baked cake. These cakes have a coarser texture than teatime cakes, though are still delicate and prettily dressed with a streusel topping. Coffee cake is not necessarily cake that's made with coffee; it can also be cake that's served with coffee. These cakes are traditionally made with yeast.

Mom Jo's 11 o'clock tea cake

This cake was a huge favourite in the Van Zyl family. The original recipe came from Kata van Zyl who lived on the old family farm, Middelpos, near Citrusdal. The recipe was passed on to other family members, including my mom, who used to bake the cake in a glass dish and serve it lukewarm.

CAKE
2 extra-large eggs
60 ml (¼ c) sugar
30 ml (2 T) butter
60 ml (¼ c) milk
180 ml (¾ c) cake flour
5 ml (1 t) baking powder
pinch salt
3 ml (generous ½ t) vanilla essence
2 ml (½ t) almond essence

SYRUP
45 ml (3 T) golden syrup or honey
45 ml (3 T) butter

Preheat the oven to 190 °C. Grease a 20 cm square ovenproof glass dish with butter, margarine or nonstick spray.

CAKE Whisk the eggs well and whisk in the sugar.
Heat the butter and milk until the butter has melted.
Sift the dry ingredients together and fold into the egg mixture, alternating with the milk mixture. Add the essences and mix lightly.
Turn the batter into the prepared dish and bake for about 20 minutes or until a testing skewer comes out clean when inserted into the centre of the cake.

SYRUP Meanwhile heat the golden syrup or honey and butter together until the butter has melted and pour the hot syrup over the cake as soon as it comes out of the oven. Cut into squares and serve lukewarm.

MAKES 1 MEDIUM-SIZED CAKE.

Hazelnut tea cake

Nikki Young of Bellville is renowned for her interesting recipes. This white cake has a delicious chocolate, coconut and hazelnut filling.

90 ml (6 T) butter, at room temperature
160 ml (⅔ c) caster sugar
2 egg yolks
2 ml (½ t) vanilla essence
2 ml (½ t) caramel essence
pinch salt
350 ml self-raising flour, sifted
180 ml (¾ c) milk
4 egg whites
80 g baking chocolate, grated
45 ml (3 T) toasted and roughly
   chopped hazelnuts
60 ml (¼ c) toasted desiccated coconut
Amaretto or Frangelico liqueur
icing sugar for dusting

Preheat the oven to 180 °C and grease a 21 cm loose-bottomed cake tin with butter, margarine or nonstick spray.
Cream the butter and caster sugar together until light and fluffy. Add the egg yolks and vanilla and caramel essences and beat until well blended.
Sift the salt and self-raising flour together and fold the mixture into the butter mixture, alternating with the milk.
Whisk the egg whites until stiff peaks form and fold them into the batter. Spoon half the batter into the prepared tin.
Mix the chocolate and chopped nuts and scatter the mixture over the batter in the tin. Moisten the coconut with a little liqueur and scatter it over the chocolate and nuts. Spoon the remaining batter on top, levelling it with the back of a spoon.
Bake for 35–40 minutes or until done. Cool the cake slightly in the tin before carefully turning it out onto a wire rack. Serve lukewarm or cold. Dust with icing sugar just before serving.

MAKES 1 MEDIUM-SIZED CAKE.

Quick Rooibos tea cake

This moist, aromatic cake is ridiculously easy to make — simply sift and beat, that's it. We were sent the recipe by Christa Durant of Krugersdorp.

500 ml (2 c) cake flour
100 ml caster sugar
10 ml (2 t) ground ginger
10 ml (2 t) ground cinnamon
5 ml (1 t) baking powder
2 ml (½ t) salt
2 extra-large eggs, lightly whisked
250 ml (1 c) oil
250 ml (1 c) golden syrup
10 ml (2 t) bicarbonate of soda
250 ml (1 c) cold Rooibos tea

Preheat the oven to 190 °C and grease a small solid ring tin (not a loose-bottomed tin as the batter will run out) with butter, margarine or nonstick spray.
Sift the flour, caster sugar, spices, baking powder and salt together.
Whisk the eggs, oil and golden syrup together. Dissolve the bicarbonate of soda in the tea and add the mixture to the egg mixture. Add this mixture to the dry ingredients, mix well and turn the batter into the prepared tin.
Bake for 1 hour or until a testing skewer comes out clean when inserted into the centre of the cake. Serve lukewarm or cold.

MAKES 1 MEDIUM-SIZED CAKE.

Poppy seed streusel cake

The spicy topping for this rich cake bakes into the batter.

STREUSEL TOPPING

45 ml (3 T) sugar

45 ml (3 T) cake flour

30 ml (2 T) butter

2 ml (½ t) ground ginger

1 ml (¼ t) ground cinnamon

CAKE

330 ml (1⅓ c) cake flour

7 ml (1½ t) baking powder

5 ml (1 t) bicarbonate of soda

4 ml (¾ t) ground ginger

1 ml (¼ t) salt

160 ml (⅔ c) butter, at room temperature

280 ml sugar

2 extra-large eggs

125 ml (½ c) sour cream

125 ml (½ c) strong Rooibos tea

60 ml (¼ c) orange juice

10 ml (2 t) finely grated orange zest

5 ml (1 t) vanilla essence

80 ml (⅓ c) poppy seeds

Preheat the oven to 180 °C and grease a 22 cm loose-bottomed tin with butter, margarine or nonstick spray.

STREUSEL TOPPING Mix the ingredients for the topping until moist lumps form. Chill until needed.

CAKE Sift the dry ingredients, spices and salt and set aside.
Cream the butter and sugar together until light and fluffy.
Add the eggs one at a time, beating well after each addition. Add the sour cream, tea, orange juice and zest and vanilla essence. Add the dry ingredients and mix well. Add the poppy seeds and mix.
Turn the batter into the prepared tin, spreading it evenly (the batter will fill the tin only halfway).
Bake for 30 minutes and scatter over the topping mixture.
Bake for another 30 minutes or until a testing skewer comes out clean when inserted into the centre of the cake.
Leave the cake to cool in the tin for a few minutes before running a knife along the inside of the tin to loosen the cake. Carefully transfer the cake to a cake platter.

MAKES 1 MEDIUM-SIZED CAKE.

Spicy yoghurt cake

This moist, melt-in-the-mouth cake with its crunchy caramelised coconut topping doubles as a deliciously decadent dessert.

CAKE

450 ml (generous 1¾ c) cake flour

1 ml (¼ t) salt

10 ml (2 t) baking powder

5 ml (1 t) bicarbonate of soda

3 ml (generous ½ t) mixed spice

2 ml (½ t) ground ginger

5 ml (1 t) ground cinnamon

3 extra-large eggs

310 ml (1¼ c) soft brown sugar

125 g butter, melted

250 ml (1 c) plain yoghurt

TOPPING

50 ml cream

70 ml butter

125 ml (½ c) soft brown sugar

160 ml (⅔ c) desiccated coconut

½ packet (50 g) mixed nuts, finely chopped

Preheat the oven to 160 °C. Grease a 23 cm square cake tin with butter, margarine or nonstick spray. Line it with greased baking paper.

CAKE Sift the dry ingredients and spices together and set aside.
Whisk the eggs and sugar together. Add the melted butter while whisking continuously. Stir in the yoghurt.
Add the egg mixture to the dry ingredients and mix well.
Turn the batter into the prepared tin and bake for 45–60 minutes until done and a testing skewer comes out clean when inserted into the centre of the cake.

TOPPING Meanwhile slowly heat the ingredients for the topping until the sugar has melted. Bring the mixture to the boil and simmer for 1 minute. Remove the cake from the oven when done. Heat the oven grill and spoon the topping over the cake. Put the cake under the heated oven grill and heat until the topping begins to caramelise. Leave the cake to cool in the tin before turning it out.

MAKES 1 MEDIUM-SIZED CAKE.

German streusel cake

This traditional cake is also covered with a layer of plums and a crumb topping.

CAKE
60 ml (¼ c) sugar
180 g butter or margarine
2 extra-large eggs
500 ml (2 c) cake flour
10 ml (2 t) baking powder
pinch salt
310 ml (1¼ c) milk

CRUMB TOPPING
1 can (460 g) plums, drained, halved
 and pitted
180 ml (¾ c) cake flour
60 ml (¼ c) sugar
7 ml (1½ t) ground cinnamon
180 g cold butter, diced

Preheat the oven to 180 °C. Grease a 22 cm square cake tin with butter, margarine or nonstick spray and line it with greased baking paper.

CAKE Cream the sugar and butter or margarine together until light and fluffy. Add the eggs one at a time, beating well after each addition.
Sift the flour, baking powder and salt together and stir the mixture into the butter mixture, alternating with the milk.
Turn the batter into the prepared tin, spreading it evenly.

CRUMB TOPPING Arrange the fruit neatly on top of the batter. Mix the flour, sugar and cinnamon in a mixing bowl. Add the diced butter to the flour mixture and gently rub it in until the mixture becomes crumbly. Scatter the mixture over the fruit and batter. Bake for 30–35 minutes or until a testing skewer comes out clean when inserted into the cake. Serve with whipped cream.

MAKES 1 MEDIUM-SIZED CAKE.

Bee sting cake (Bienenstich)

German Bienenstich or bee sting cake is traditionally made with yeast.

CAKE
450 ml (generous 1¾ c) cake flour
15 ml (1 T) baking powder
2 ml (½ t) salt
120 g butter
160 ml (⅔ c) sugar
2 extra-large eggs
5 ml (1 t) vanilla essence
90 ml (6 T) milk

TOPPING
125 ml (½ c) almond splinters
80 ml (⅓ c) sugar
60 g butter
15 ml (1 T) milk or cream
15 ml (1 T) cake flour
50 ml flaked almonds

FILLING
3 egg whites
pinch salt
2 ml (½ t) almond essence
310 ml (1¼ c) thick custard

Preheat the oven to 190 °C. Grease a 22 cm springform tin or rectangular tin with butter, margarine or nonstick spray.

CAKE Sift the cake flour, baking powder and salt together and set aside. Cream the butter and sugar together until light and fluffy. Add the eggs one at a time, beating well after each addition. Stir in the vanilla essence. Add the flour mixture to the egg mixture in three batches, alternating each batch with the milk. Stir until just blended. Turn the batter into the prepared tin (the batter will be fairly stiff).

TOPPING Heat the almond splinters, sugar, butter and milk or cream over low heat until the sugar has dissolved. Sprinkle the flour over the batter in the tin and press it down gently with the back of a spoon. Evenly pour the hot almond mixture over the batter. Scatter over the almond flakes and bake for 25 minutes or until the cake is done. Leave the cake to cool in the tin for 10 minutes before turning it out onto a wire rack to cool completely.

FILLING Beat the egg whites until frothy, add the salt and beat until stiff peaks form. Fold the egg whites and essence into the custard. Cover the custard mixture with a sheet of wax paper and leave it in the fridge to chill. Halve the cake horizontally. Put the bottom layer on a cake platter and cover it with the custard filling. Put the remaining cake layer on top and chill the cake before serving.

MAKES 1 LARGE CAKE.

Bee sting cake

CAKES FOR WEIGHT-WATCHERS

Cakes are taboo if you're trying to shake off a few kilograms or cutting down on fat and sugar. Cake flour and sugar also cause blood-sugar levels to seesaw.

If you're watching your diet but want to treat yourself to the odd slice of cake, a few kilojoule-cutting tips come in handy. But it's not that easy: when baking, sugar, butter and flour must be used in the right proportions to avoid flops. You can't simply omit or substitute these ingredients.

In the following recipes we reduced the sugar, shortening and flour by partially substituting fruit for the sugar, nuts or cottage cheese for the shortening and among others maize meal and oat bran for the flour. In some instances vegetables such as carrots and sweet potatoes give the cakes a lovely moist texture.

Blueberry and cottage cheese cake

Creamed cottage cheese is used instead of butter to make this delicious cake.

4 eggs, separated
180 ml (¾ c) light brown sugar
1 tub (250 g) creamed
  cottage cheese
250 ml (1 c) cake flour
10 ml (2 t) baking powder
2 ml (½ t) salt
250 ml (1 c) semolina or coarse
  maize meal
500 ml (2 c) blueberries
30–60 ml (2–4 T) yellow sugar
60 ml (¼ c) flaked almonds
extra blueberries to decorate
  (optional)

Preheat the oven to 180 °C. Grease a 23 cm round or rectangular cake tin.

Whisk the egg yolks slightly, add the sugar and whisk until light and creamy. Add the cream cheese and mix.

Sift the flour, baking powder and salt together and sift the mixture over the cottage cheese mixture. Gently fold in the semolina.

Fold in the berries. Whisk the egg whites until stiff and fold them into the cake mixture.

Turn the batter into the prepared cake tin, spreading it evenly. Mix the sugar and almond flakes and sprinkle the mixture over the cake.

Bake for about 1 hour or until a testing skewer comes out clean when inserted into the centre of the cake. Scatter over extra blueberries just before serving if desired.

MAKES 1 LARGE CAKE.

Carmen says
- Don't expect these cakes to rise much. They also have a denser texture than conventional soft-crumb cakes.
- If you're trying to cut down on sugar, substitute it partially or with the same quantity Sugalite, a sweetener that's suitable for diabetics and for baking (most other sweeteners lose their sweetness when heated).
- See also recipes for lower-fat unbaked cheesecakes (p. 148–150), variation for baked cheesecakes (p. 73) and low-GI scones (p. 180).

Blueberry and cottage cheese cake

Venetian carrot cupcakes

These tasty cupcakes are made with carrots and sweet potatoes, which help to reduce the glycemic index.

CUPCAKES
160 ml (⅔ c) soft brown sugar
125 ml (½ c) oil
5 ml (1 t) vanilla essence
3 extra-large eggs
375 ml (1½ c) cake flour
15 ml (1 T) baking powder
pinch salt
2 ml (½ t) ground cinnamon
    or nutmeg
500 ml (2 c) finely grated carrots
250 ml (1 c) finely grated
    sweet potatoes
125 ml (½ c) sultanas
250 ml (1 c) almond splinters or
    chopped walnuts
finely grated zest of ½ lemon
15 ml (1 T) lemon juice

ICING
200 g low-fat cottage cheese
45 ml (3 T) icing sugar
5 ml (1 t) vanilla essence

Preheat the oven to 180 °C. Use a muffin tin with 12 hollows and line each hollow with a paper cup.

CUPCAKES Beat the sugar and oil together until creamy. Beat in the vanilla essence and eggs. Sift over the cake flour, baking powder, salt and spices and fold in. Add the remaining cupcake ingredients and mix. Fill the paper cups three-quarters of the way.

Bake for 30–40 minutes or until a testing skewer comes out clean when inserted into the centre of the cupcakes. Turn out onto a wire rack and leave to cool completely.

ICING Mix the ingredients and spread over the cupcakes just before serving.

MAKES 12 CUPCAKES.

Carmen says
- Use the recipe to bake one large cake, in which case bake it for 40–50 minutes or until done.
- Substitute part of the cake flour with oat bran. Use about 125 ml (½ c).

Hazelnut and pear loaf

The batter for this quick and easy loaf cake is mixed in a food processor. The loaf, which contains very little butter, has a dense texture and is packed with nuts.

375 ml (1½ c) hazelnuts
10 ml (2 t) grated orange zest
125 ml (½ c) cake flour
125 ml (½ c) sugar
40 g butter
1 extra-large egg plus
    1 egg white
15 ml marsala or any other
    fortified wine
6 fresh pears

Preheat the oven to 180 °C. Grease a 32 x 11 x 2 cm loose-bottomed loaf tin.
Blitz the hazelnuts in a food processor until fine and add the remaining ingredients one at a time, except 4 of the pears. Blitz until well blended. Press the mixture into the tin. Thinly slice the remaining pears and arrange them on top of the cake.
Bake for 50–60 minutes or until firm. Leave the loaf to cool and cut into slices.
Decorate with dried pear slices if desired (see p. 213).

MAKES 1 LOAF.

Polenta and yoghurt cake with fresh fruit

This cake, which contains no butter or flour, is packed with almonds and is topped with poached fruit. Celebrity TV chef Aldo Zilli discovered it while on holiday in Florence in Italy.

FRUIT TOPPING
2 pears, peeled, cored and sliced
160 ml (⅔ c) dry white wine
160 ml (⅔ c) water
60 ml (¼ c) caster sugar
1 whole clove
½ cinnamon stick

CAKE
6 extra-large eggs, separated
200 ml caster sugar
200 ml plain yoghurt
grated zest of 1 orange
160 ml (⅔ c) fine polenta or
    yellow maize meal
1¾ packets (175 g) ground almonds

TO FINISH
juice of 1 orange
45 ml (3 T) honey

FRUIT TOPPING Put the pear slices, wine, water, sugar and spices in a saucepan and cover the ingredients with a sheet of wax paper so it lies flat on the pear slices so they don't discolour. Slowly bring the ingredients to the boil, reduce the heat and simmer for 15 minutes or until the pear slices are soft. Leave the pears to cool in the syrup.

CAKE Preheat the oven to 180 °C and grease a 20 cm cake tin with butter, margarine or nonstick spray.
Whisk the egg yolks and sugar in a large mixing bowl until the mixture is thick and creamy. Stir in the yoghurt and orange zest. Using a large metal spoon, fold in the polenta and ground almonds. Whisk the egg whites until stiff peaks begin to form and fold them into the polenta mixture.
Turn the batter into prepared tin and bake for 30 minutes or until golden and firm to the touch. Leave to cool in the tin for a few minutes before turning out onto a cake platter.

TO FINISH Drain the pear slices and arrange them on the warm cake. Heat the orange juice and honey and pour the syrup over the pear slices. Leave to cool before serving.

MAKES 1 MEDIUM-SIZED CAKE.

Carmen says
Substitute fruit such as apples, nectarines, plums, oranges or grapes for the pears.

Whole orange cake

I came across this interesting recipe years ago in an overseas magazine. The cake, made with cooked oranges, contains no flour (so is gluten-free) or butter and is fairly flat. Served with thick Greek yoghurt or mascarpone cheese it makes a lovely dessert.

CAKE
2 large or 3 fairly small oranges
6 extra-large eggs
250 ml (1 c) caster sugar
300 g ground almonds
5 ml (1 t) baking powder
45 ml (3 T) cornflour

SYRUP
250 ml (1 c) fresh orange or
    lemon juice
60 ml (¼ c) caster sugar or honey
1 vanilla pod or 3 cardamom pods

TO SERVE
thick Greek yoghurt or
    mascarpone cheese

Preheat the oven to 180 °C. Grease a 23 cm loose-bottomed tin with butter, margarine or nonstick spray and line the bottom with greased baking paper.

CAKE Put the unpeeled oranges in boiling water and cook until soft. Drain the oranges, remove the pips and finely chop the flesh, preferably in a food processor.
Whisk the eggs and caster sugar together until light and fluffy. Combine the almonds, baking powder and cornflour and fold into the egg mixture, alternating with the chopped oranges.
Turn the batter into the tin and bake for 40–50 minutes or until golden and done.

SYRUP Bring the ingredients to the boil and cook for 10 minutes or until the mixture is syrupy. Prick the cake as soon as it comes out of the oven and pour over the hot syrup. Leave the cake to cool in the tin before transferring it to a cake platter. Serve with thick Greek yoghurt or mascarpone cheese.

MAKES 1 MEDIUM-SIZED CAKE.

VARIATION
Substitute 125 ml (½ c) chopped pistachios, 125 ml (½ c) desiccated coconut, 125 ml (½ c) flaked almonds and 125 ml (½ c) polenta for the ground almonds to make a syrupy citrus polenta cake.

Carmen says
This cake freezes well.

Mocha squares

I find cakes with a low glycemic index don't always taste that nice but these squares with their delicate coffee flavour are an exception. The recipe comes from Liesbet Delport and Gabi Steenkamp's book, **Eating for Sustained Energy 3.**

CAKE

375 ml (1½ c) cake flour
20 ml (4 t) baking powder
2 ml (½ t) salt
125 ml (½ c) oat bran
125 g soft margarine
130 ml (generous ½ c) caster sugar
2 extra-large eggs
1 egg white
250 ml (1 c) pie apples
5 ml (1 t) vanilla essence
60 ml (¼ c) skim milk
45 ml (3 T) instant coffee powder,
    dissolved in 15 ml (1 T)
    boiling water
80 ml (⅓ c) walnuts

ICING

15 ml (1 T) soft margarine
80 ml (⅓ c) cocoa
30 ml (2 T) instant coffee powder
60 ml (¼ c) boiling water
45 ml (3 T) icing sugar
90 g dark chocolate shavings (optional)

Preheat the oven to 180 °C. Grease a 20 cm square cake tin with nonstick spray.

CAKE In a mixing bowl, sift the flour, baking powder and salt together. Add the oat bran and mix with a spoon.

Cream the margarine and caster sugar together with a wooden spoon. Add the eggs and egg white one at a time, alternating with 15 ml (1 T) of the flour mixture. Beat for about 1 minute after each addition.

Blitz the apples, essence, milk and coffee in a food processor for 20 seconds or until the mixture is just smooth. Add it to the margarine mixture, alternating with the remaining flour mixture. Fold in the nuts and turn the batter into the prepared tin.

Bake for 50–60 minutes or until a testing skewer comes out clean when inserted into the centre of the cake. Cool the cake in the tin for a few minutes before turning it out onto a wire rack and cutting it into squares.

ICING Mix all the icing ingredients, except the chocolate, and spoon the mixture over the squares. Decorate with chocolate shavings if desired.

MAKES 16 SQUARES.

Carmen says

For a cake recipe that contains less fat and sugar and that's suitable for cupcakes, see the recipe for egg-free oven-pan chocolate cake (p. 56).

MICROWAVE CAKES

If you need to make a cake in a hurry these recipes for microwave cakes will come in handy. Don't, however, expect prize-winning results. Not all recipes are suitable for the microwave oven; I find quick and instant cake recipes that call for plenty of liquid and where you beat everything together work best. Experiment with the times as there are many factors that influence how long the cakes should be microwaved and consequently also the result.

Microwave chocolate cake

This is the quickest and easiest chocolate cake ever, says Renché van der Merwe of Saldanha. It takes her only 20 minutes to make this cake from start to finish.

CAKE
250 ml (1 c) cake flour
250 ml (1 c) sugar
15 ml (1 T) baking powder
1 ml (¼ t) salt
45 ml (3 T) cocoa
5 ml (1 t) vanilla essence
250 ml (1 c) boiling water
60 ml (¼ c) oil
2 extra-large eggs, whisked

ICING
200 g dark chocolate, chopped
2 ml (½ t) vanilla essence
70 ml water

Line the bottom of a 2 litre ice-cream container with paper towels.

CAKE Sift the dry ingredients together. Mix the vanilla essence, boiling water, oil and eggs in a large mixing bowl.
Add the dry ingredients, beating until well blended.
Turn the mixture into the prepared container and put it on an inverted saucer or microwave oven stand. Microwave on 100 per cent power for 12–15 minutes or until the cake is springy to the touch. Leave the cake to stand for 5 minutes.

ICING Put all the ingredients in a glass bowl and microwave until the chocolate has melted. Stir at 30-second intervals or the chocolate pieces will retain their shape even if they melt. Whisk until smooth and pour the icing over the hot cake. Leave to cool before cutting into squares.

MAKES 1 MEDIUM-SIZED CAKE.

Carmen says
■ Do not microwave the cake for too long or the centre will be burnt. Rather microwave the cake for a few seconds more if necessary. Remember, the cake also cooks while standing.
■ The microwave times given are approximate. Adjust the times according to your microwave oven's wattage.

Microwave carrot cake

You can even bake ever-popular carrot cake in a microwave oven.

CAKE
2 extra-large eggs
125 ml (½ c) oil
125 ml (½ c) light brown sugar
250 ml (1 c) cake flour
250 ml (1 c) grated carrots
250 ml (1 c) mashed banana
10 ml (2 t) baking powder
5 ml (1 t) bicarbonate of soda
10 ml (2 t) ground cinnamon

ICING
1 tub (250 g) cream cheese
100 ml caster sugar
80 ml (⅓ c) icing sugar
roughly chopped walnuts to decorate

Grease a 30 cm microwave-proof ring tin with butter, margarine or nonstick spray and line the bottom with paper towels.

CAKE Whisk the eggs, oil and sugar together. Stir in the remaining ingredients and turn the batter into the prepared tin. Put it on an inverted saucer or microwave oven stand and microwave on 100 per cent power (high) for 9–10 minutes. Leave the cake to stand for 2 minutes before turning out.

ICING Mix all the ingredients for the icing, except the walnuts. Cover the cake with the icing and scatter the walnuts on top.

MAKES 1 MEDIUM-SIZED RING CAKE.

Rooibos tea cake

A deliciously moist, quick and easy cake made with Rooibos tea and a little oil so it's not too rich, writes Nicolene Swanepoel of Secunda. The cake must be enjoyed while fresh.

CAKE
250 ml (1 c) strong Rooibos tea
   (use 1 bag)
5 ml (1 t) vanilla essence
60 ml (¼ c) oil
2 extra-large eggs, whisked
250 ml (1 c) cake flour
250 ml (1 c) caster sugar
20 ml (4 t) baking powder
pinch salt

ICING
375 ml (1½ c) fresh cream, chilled
60 ml (¼ c) caster sugar
5 ml (1 t) vanilla essence
sugar crystals or hundreds and
   thousands to decorate (optional)

Line the bottom of a 30 cm microwave-proof ring tin with paper towels.
Whisk the Rooibos tea, vanilla essence, oil and eggs together. Sift the dry ingredients together. Add the tea mixture and mix well.
Turn the batter into the tin. Put paper towels in the microwave oven in case the cake batter drips and put the tin on an inverted saucer or microwave oven stand.
Microwave on 100 per cent power (high) for 6–7 minutes. Leave the cake in the tin for 5 minutes before turning out onto a cake platter. Leave to cool completely.

ICING Whip the cream, caster sugar and vanilla essence together until the mixture is stiff. Cover the cake with the cream mixture and decorate with sugar crystals or hundreds and thousands. Serve immediately.

MAKES 1 MEDIUM-SIZED CAKE.

Versatile microwave cake

Mrs MM Lean of Ifafa often bakes this easy cake, which is made with mayonnaise instead of oil.

CAKE
2 extra-large eggs
250 ml (1 c) sugar
15 ml (1 T) mayonnaise
500 ml (2 c) cake flour
10 ml (2 t) baking powder
pinch salt
5 ml (1 t) vanilla essence
250 ml (1 c) boiling water
1 can (115 g) granadilla pulp

ICING
100 g white chocolate, broken into
   squares
25 ml (5 t) granadilla pulp

Line the bottom of a microwave-proof ring tin with paper towels.

CAKE Whisk the eggs, sugar and mayonnaise together.

Sift the dry ingredients together and stir the mixture into the egg mixture along with the vanilla essence. Add the boiling water and granadilla pulp and mix well.

Turn the batter into the prepared tin. Place on an inverted saucer or microwave stand and microwave on 100 per cent power (high) for 6–7 minutes or until the cake just begins to shrink from the inside of the tin and is springy to the touch. Leave the cake to cool in the tin before turning it out onto a cake platter.

ICING Melt the chocolate in the microwave oven and stir in the granadilla pulp. Spoon the mixture over the cake.

MAKES 1 MEDIUM-SIZED CAKE.

VARIATION
Mocha cake: Substitute 20 ml (4 t) coffee powder for the granadilla pulp in the cake. Omit the granadilla pulp in the icing and add 25 ml (5 t) plain yoghurt and 1 ml (¼ t) coffee powder. Alternatively, decorate the cake with caramel condensed milk.

Carmen says
When making a microwave cake always put it on an inverted saucer or microwave stand so the cake is raised and cooks evenly underneath. Remember, the cake cooks from the inside out so take care not to microwave the cake for too long. Rather microwave it for a shorter time, test it for doneness and microwave it a little longer if necessary. Cake tins are always lined with paper towels and not baking paper. The paper towels absorb moisture otherwise the cake will be heavy and dense underneath.

Versatile microwave cake

Cupcakes

Cupcakes should really be called mini-bites because each one is a perfect heavenly mouthful. These delightful confections are becoming increasingly popular as wedding cakes, dessert or tea-time treats to take along to the office. This is probably because they look so beautiful with their festive decorations and you can dispense with plates and forks when serving them.

Versatile cupcakes

These deliciously rich cupcakes are made with butter cake batter.

BASIC BATTER
125 g butter, softened
200 ml sugar
5 ml (1 t) vanilla essence
2 extra-large eggs
500 ml (2 c) cake flour
10 ml (2 t) baking powder
1 ml (¼ t) salt
160 ml (⅔ c) milk
butter icing (see p. 204)
silver or gold balls

Preheat the oven to 190 °C. Line the hollows of a deep muffin tin with paper cups.

Cream the butter and sugar together until light and fluffy. Add the vanilla essence and eggs and beat well.

Sift the cake flour, baking powder and salt together three times.

Fold the dry ingredients into the butter mixture, alternating with the milk.

Divide the batter among the paper cups and bake for 15–20 minutes or until done and a testing skewer comes out clean when inserted into the centre of the cupcakes. Leave to cool before decorating with butter icing and gold or silver balls.

MAKES 12 CUPCAKES.

VARIATIONS

Almond: Add 50 g toasted flaked almonds and 3 ml (generous ½ t) almond essence to the basic batter. Divide the batter among the paper cups. Decorate with butter icing, a scattering of toasted flaked almonds and a dusting of icing sugar.

Granadilla: Substitute 1¾ cans (200 g) granadilla pulp for the milk. Cut the tops off the baked cupcakes, halve and secure them with butter icing to make wings. Decorate with a dusting of icing sugar and a little extra granadilla pulp just before serving.

Orange: Substitute freshly squeezed orange juice for the milk in the basic batter and fold in the finely grated zest of 1 orange. Decorate the cupcakes with a butter icing to which the grated zest of 1 orange and a few drops orange juice have been added.

Coconut: Substitute coconut milk for the milk in the basic batter. Add 80 ml (⅓ c) desiccated coconut to the batter. Add just enough coconut milk to the icing sugar to make a drop icing and drizzle it over the cupcakes. Decorate with toasted desiccated coconut or fresh coconut shavings. Alternatively, decorate the cupcakes with 7-minute icing (see p. 205).

Lemon coconut: Use the coconut cupcake batter and instead of decorating the cupcakes with a drop icing moisten them with a lemon syrup.

Lemon syrup: Heat 125 ml (½ c) caster sugar, 60 ml (¼ c) water, 10 ml (2 t) grated lemon zest and 80 ml (⅓ c) lemon juice together and simmer for 2 minutes.

Chocolate chip: Add 250 ml (1 c) chocolate chips to the basic batter and decorate the cupcakes with butter icing mixed with 250 ml (1 c) chocolate chips.

Lemon meringue cupcakes

Toni Scorgie of The Tart in Johannesburg is not a muffin person but loves making these lemon meringue cupcakes. Her clients just love lemon meringue pie and these little cupcakes are a great alternative to the conventional pie.

BATTER
175 g butter
125 ml (½ c) milk
375 ml (1½ c) self-raising flour
pinch salt
3 extra-large eggs, separated
180 ml (¾ c) caster sugar
5 ml (1 t) vanilla essence

FILLING
1 can (385 g) condensed milk
3 egg yolks
juice and zest of 1 lemon

TO FINISH
6 egg whites
250 ml (1 c) caster sugar

Preheat the oven to 200 °C. Line 12 hollows of a muffin tin with paper cups.

BATTER Heat the butter and milk in a saucepan until the butter has melted. Leave the mixture to cool.
Sift the self-raising flour and salt together five times and set aside.
Whisk the egg yolks until frothy. Add the caster sugar by the spoonful, beating until the mixture is pale and thick.
Sift the self-raising flour over the egg yolk mixture and slowly beat in the butter mixture. Add the vanilla essence.
Whisk the egg whites in a clean glass bowl until stiff. Fold them into the batter.
Fill the paper cups three-quarters of the way and bake for 15–20 minutes or until golden and a testing skewer comes out clean when inserted into the cakes.

FILLING Whisk the condensed milk and egg yolks together. Add the lemon juice and zest and beat well.

TO FINISH Cut out a small hollow in the centre of each cupcake or make a hole with the back of a wooden spoon. Spoon a generous amount of the filling into each hollow. Whisk the egg whites and caster sugar together to make a stiff meringue. Spoon or pipe the meringue on top of the cupcakes and put them in a preheated oven until pale brown on top. Alternatively, brown the meringue with a gas flame.

MAKES 12 CUPCAKES.

Chocolate cupcakes

These cupcakes are regularly baked in our household.

1 x recipe for egg-free oven-pan
   chocolate cake (see p. 56)
yoghurt ganache (see p. 208)
gold and silver or coloured balls or
   decoration of choice

Line 24 muffin tin hollows with paper cups and fill them three-quarters of the way with the oven-pan cake batter.
Bake for 22–30 minutes or until done.
Prepare the ganache as described and spoon the mixture on top of the cupcakes.
Decorate as desired.

MAKES 24 CUPCAKES.

VARIATION
Pour the ganache icing over the cupcakes. Melt white chocolate and, using a thin nozzle, pipe names or messages on the cupcakes.

Mini rose cupcakes

Mini rose cupcakes

To make these cupcakes simply beat all the ingredients together in one bowl.

BATTER
250 ml (1 c) self-raising flour
125 g butter, at room temperature
125 ml (½ c) caster sugar
2 extra-large eggs
15 ml (1 T) rose-water

ICING
375 ml (1½ c) icing sugar
15 ml (1 T) glycerine
30-45 ml (2-3 T) rose-water
pink food colouring

DECORATION
12 pink rose petals
1 egg white
15 ml (1 T) caster sugar

Preheat the oven to 180 °C. Line 8–10 muffin tin hollows with paper cups.

BATTER Sift the flour into a bowl, add the butter, caster sugar, eggs and rose-water and beat with an electric beater until smooth.
Divide the batter among the paper cups and bake in the centre of the oven for 15–20 minutes or until done. Remove the cupcakes from the tin and leave them to cool on a wire rack.

ICING Sift the icing sugar into a mixing bowl and add the glycerine. Add just enough rose-water to make a soft mixture. Add a few drops food colouring and mix well. When the cupcakes have cooled completely spread a little of the icing on top and decorate each with a crystallised rose petal (see tip).

MAKES 8–10 CUPCAKES.

VARIATION
Dice Turkish delight and pile a little on top of the cupcakes.

Coffee and walnut butterfly cakes

CUPCAKES
1 x batter recipe for rose cupcakes but omit the rose-water
60 g walnuts, finely chopped
butter icing (see p. 204)
15 ml (1 T) strong coffee

Prepare the batter and fold in the walnuts.
Bake as described.
Mix the butter icing and coffee.
Cut the tops off the cupcakes when cooled.
Pipe a circle on the cupcakes with the icing.
Halve the tops of the cupcakes and press 2 halves into the icing on top of each cupcake to make wings. Pipe a rosette on top of each wing with the icing.

MAKES 8–10 BUTTERFLY CAKES.

Carmen says
Use the recipes for loaves (see p. 47) and versatile one-bowl cake (see p. 52) to bake cupcakes. Decorate as desired.

VARIATION
Mini rose cupcakes: Spoon the batter into mini cupcake tins. Bake for about 15 minutes. Stack on top of each other and drizzle with the icing. Decorate with rose petals.

To crystallise rose petals: Wash and dry the rose petals. Brush each rose petal with a thin layer of lightly whisked egg white and sprinkle with caster sugar. Put the petals on a sheet of baking paper and leave for 30 minutes or until dry.

Baked tarts

It's amazing how we associate carefree childhood memories with delicious baked tarts such as old-fashioned milk tart, tipsy tart and pumpkin tart. Nowadays we make tarts with real dark chocolate and loads of nuts and mix the shortcrust pastry in the food processor. We also love the tempting tang of lemon tart and the syrupy sweetness of adopted delicacies such as baklava.

Standard sweet shortcrust pastry

500 ml (2 c) cake flour
2 ml (½ t) salt
175 g cold butter, diced
15–30 ml (1–2 T) caster sugar
1 egg yolk
iced water if necessary

Sift the flour and salt together three times. Rub in the butter until the mixture resembles breadcrumbs.

Add the remaining ingredients and mix to form a soft dough.

Shape the dough into a ball and chill it for at least 2 hours.

Roll out the pastry, line the pie dishes/pie tins and bake it blind (see p. 122).

Rich sweet shortcrust pastry

This variation on rich French shortcrust pastry is ideal for fruit tarts and tartlets. It's quick and easy to mix in a food processor.

250 g butter
200 g icing sugar
pinch salt
500 g cake flour
4 egg yolks
60 ml (¼ c) iced milk or water

Blend the butter, icing sugar and salt in a food processor until creamy.

Add the cake flour and egg yolks and blitz until blended.

Add the milk or water drop by drop while the food processor is running.

Turn out the dough on a work surface and shape it into a ball. (Do not overhandle the dough.) Wrap the dough in clingfilm and chill it for 2 hours.

Roll out the pastry, line the pie dishes/pie tins and bake it blind (see p. 122).

MAKES ENOUGH PASTRY FOR 2 X 30 CM TARTS.

VARIATIONS
- Add the grated zest of 1 lemon or orange to the dough.
- Add 5 ml (1 t) vanilla essence to the dough.
- Add 125 ml (½ c) ground almonds or hazelnuts to the dough and increase the milk or water if necessary to make a soft dough.

IF YOU DON'T HAVE A FOOD PROCESSOR
Cream together the butter, icing sugar and salt with an electric beater. Add the flour and mix it with your hands or a wooden spoon if the dough becomes too stiff to use the beater. Add the egg yolks while mixing. Turn out the dough on a work surface and lightly shape it into a ball.

Carmen says
- The longer the dough is left to rest the better – the dough can be made up to four days in advance.
- Do not overhandle the dough or the pastry will be tough and hard. Lightly press the dough into a ball.
- It is important to leave the dough to rest to prevent it from shrinking while baking.

TIPS FOR MAKING SHORTCRUST PASTRY

HOW TO ROLL OUT PASTRY

Put the pastry on a lightly floured surface and roll it out gently with a rolling pin without rolling over the edges.
Roll out to a thickness of about 2 mm.

HOW TO LINE A PIE DISH

Carefully roll the pastry onto the rolling pin, put the rolling pin on the side of the dish and unroll the pastry over the dish.
Gently ease the pastry into the dish. Break off a small piece of pastry, dip it in cake flour and use it to neatly press the
pastry onto the inside of the dish.

WHEN YOU DON'T FEEL LIKE ROLLING OUT PASTRY

Shape the prepared dough into a long roll and chill it for at least 1 hour. Cut the roll into thin slices and arrange them on the
bottom and against the inside of the pie dish. Lightly press the pastry together and neaten the sides. Chill again for 1 hour.

HOW TO NEATEN THE EDGES

Gently roll the rolling pin over the dish or use a knife to neaten the edges.

HOW TO BAKE PASTRY BLIND

Line the pastry with baking paper and fill the dish with dried beans or uncooked rice. Bake at 200 °C for 10 minutes or until just
done and pale brown. Remove the baking paper and beans.

HOW TO BAKE PASTRY BLIND WITHOUT BAKING PAPER, RICE OR BEANS

Line the pie dish with the pastry and grease a cake tin that fits inside the pie dish with butter, margarine or nonstick spray.
Dust it with flour on the outside and rest it on the pastry. Bake until the edge of the pastry is pale brown. Remove the tin
and proceed with the recipe.

ALTERNATIVE TO BAKING BLIND

Brush the pastry with lightly whisked egg white and chill until the egg white is dry.

Delicious milk tart

This milk tart recipe has pride of place in her recipe collection, says cookery book writer Mariëtte Crafford. It's easy to make and the milk tart always looks fantastic when it comes out of the oven — puffed and a mottled brown. All it needs is a light dusting of cinnamon before she and her kids, Peter and Mariella, tuck in. Mariëtte says she leaves at least a quarter of the filling in the bowl for Mariella to lick. "One day you must say, 'Let's bake a milk tart,' but then you mustn't bake it; you must make a whole bowl of filling just for me," Mariella says wistfully every time they bake a milk tart.

CRUST
ready-made puff pastry or almond
    shortcrust pastry (see p. 126)

FILLING
150 ml cake flour
50 ml cornflour
50 ml custard powder
5 ml (1 t) baking powder
250 ml (1 c) sugar
1.25 litres (5 c) full-cream milk
2 large cinnamon sticks
3 extra-large eggs, separated
45 g butter
7 ml (1½ t) vanilla or almond essence
ground cinnamon

Preheat the oven to 200 °C. Grease two 23 cm pie dishes or a 30 cm springform tin with butter, margarine or nonstick spray.

CRUST Roll out the pastry and line the prepared dishes with it.

FILLING Combine the flour, cornflour, custard and baking powders and half the sugar. Stir in 125 ml (½ c) of the milk. Mix with a wire whisk to make a thin paste. Bring the remaining milk and cinnamon sticks to the boil. Add about 125 ml (½ c) of the hot milk to the flour paste, mix well and add the mixture to the remaining hot milk. Stirring continuously, heat the mixture until it thickens. (Alternatively make the filling in the microwave oven as for a white sauce.)
Remove the cinnamon sticks.
Whisk the egg yolks lightly and beat in the remaining sugar. Add a little of the hot milk mixture to the egg yolks, mix well and add to the milk mixture. Heat the mixture slowly, stirring it continuously with a wire beater until smooth and cooked. Stir in the butter and essence and leave to cool slightly.
Whisk the egg whites until soft peaks form and fold them into the filling.
Pour the filling into the unbaked pastry shells and bake for about 30 minutes or until the surface is a mottled brown. Dust the milk tart with ground cinnamon and serve it lukewarm.

MAKES 2 SMALL TARTS OR 1 LARGE TART.

Carmen says
If the filling sinks it may be due to one of the following: the filling is not thick enough, too little egg in the filling or the egg whites are overbeaten.

Erika's quick milk tart

Food editor of the magazine **Home**, Sonja Jordt, says her mom, Erika, is a natural when it comes to cooking and that she has always been her biggest inspiration. This quick and easy milk tart recipe is one of her mom's favourites.

CRUST

250 ml (1 c) cake flour
5 ml (1 t) baking powder
2 ml (½ t) salt
60 ml (¼ c) butter,
    at room temperature
60 ml (¼ c) sugar
1 extra-large egg
25 ml (5 t) milk

FILLING

1.5 litres (6 c) milk
60 ml (¼ c) butter
4 extra-large eggs, separated
200 ml sugar
100 ml cake flour
150 ml cornflour
2 ml (½ t) salt
ground cinnamon for sprinkling
    on top

Preheat the oven to 180 °C and grease two 23 cm pie dishes with butter, margarine or nonstick spray.

CRUST Sift the cake flour, baking powder and salt together.
Cream the butter and sugar together until the mixture is light and fluffy. Add the egg and beat well.
Add the dry ingredients to the creamed mixture, alternating with the milk. Beat until the mixture is spreadable. Divide the mixture between the two prepared pie dishes.
Spread the mixture on the bottom and along the inside of the pie dishes. Set aside until needed or chill.

FILLING Heat 1 litre (4 c) of the milk and butter until the butter has melted.
Whisk the egg yolks and sugar until thick and pale yellow.
Sift the cake flour, cornflour and salt together and add the remaining milk, beating until smooth. Add to the egg mixture and beat well.
Add a little of the hot milk to the egg mixture, mix and add the mixture to the hot milk in the saucepan. Heat slowly, stirring continuously until the mixture thickens and is cooked.
Whisk the egg whites until stiff peaks form and carefully fold into the filling. Pour the filling into the prepared crusts and bake for 30 minutes.
Remove from the oven, sprinkle with cinnamon and serve lukewarm.

MAKES 2 MEDIUM-SIZED TARTS.

Carrot tipsy tart

This tipsy tart made with carrots instead of dates is ideal for those who're not that fond of dates, writes Susan Wolmarans of Humansdorp.

TART

4 extra-large eggs
375 ml (1½ c) sugar
250 ml (1 c) oil
625 ml (2½ c) self-raising flour
7 ml (1½ t) bicarbonate of soda
1 ml (¼ t) salt
750 ml (3 c) grated carrots
5 ml (1 t) vanilla essence

SYRUP

375 ml (1½ c) sugar
375 ml (1½ c) water
125 g margarine
125 ml (½ c) brandy

Preheat the oven to 180 °C and grease a 30 cm square pie dish with butter, margarine or nonstick spray.

TART Whisk the eggs and sugar until thick and pale yellow. Add the oil and beat well.
Sift the self-raising flour, bicarbonate of soda and salt together three times and fold the mixture into the egg mixture. Fold in the carrots and essence. Turn the batter into the prepared dish and bake for 40 minutes or until golden brown and a testing skewer comes out clean when inserted into the centre of the tart.

SYRUP Heat the sugar, water and margarine together, stirring until the sugar has dissolved. Bring the mixture to the boil. Add the brandy and remove the mixture from the heat. Prick the hot tart and pour over the syrup. Serve cold with cream.

MAKES 1 LARGE TART.

Coconut and brandy tart

Served with cream or custard this delicious coconut tart, made with a generous shot of brandy, doubles as pudding, writes Leonie Jonker of Newcastle.

TART
2 extra-large eggs
250 ml (1 c) sugar
250 ml (1 c) lukewarm water
125 g margarine
250 ml (1 c) cake flour
15 ml (1 T) baking powder
1 ml (¼ t) salt
500 ml (2 c) desiccated coconut

SYRUP
250 ml (1 c) water
250 ml (1 c) sugar
60 ml (¼ c) brandy

Preheat the oven to 180 °C and grease a 25 x 18 x 3 cm ovenproof dish or 20 cm round pie dish with butter, margarine or nonstick spray.

TART Whisk the eggs, sugar, water and margarine together.
Sift the dry ingredients together, except the coconut, and add them to the egg mixture. Mix in the coconut.
Pour the mixture into the prepared dish and bake for about 30 minutes or until golden.

SYRUP Bring the water and sugar to the boil and simmer for 5 minutes.
Add the brandy and remove the saucepan from the heat. Pour the hot syrup over the tart as soon as it comes out of the oven. Serve lukewarm or cold.

MAKES 1 MEDIUM-SIZED TART.

Citrus tart

This is one of her standby recipes, writes Jeanette Ferreira of Oudtshoorn. Bake the tart in a pie dish or make individual tartlets for a splendid dessert.

TART
3 extra-large eggs
250 ml (1 c) caster sugar
180 ml (¾ c) milk
finely grated zest of 1 lemon
125 g butter or margarine
275 ml self-raising flour
5 ml (1 t) baking powder
2 ml (½ t) salt

SYRUP
250 ml (1 c) fresh orange juice
125 ml (½ c) sugar
10 ml (2 t) finely grated orange zest

Preheat the oven to 180 °C and grease a medium-sized ovenproof dish or 5–6 ramekins with butter, margarine or nonstick spray.

TART Whisk the eggs until frothy. Gradually add the sugar, beating until the mixture is thick and pale yellow.
Heat the milk, lemon zest and butter together, stirring until the butter has melted.
Sift the self-raising flour, baking powder and salt together and sift it over the egg mixture. Mix and stir in the milk mixture.
Pour the mixture into the prepared dish or ramekins and bake for about 40 minutes or until done.

SYRUP Bring the ingredients to the boil and simmer for 5 minutes. Remove the saucepan from the heat. Pour the hot syrup over the tart as soon as it comes out of the oven and leave it to cool slightly. Serve lukewarm with cream as a teatime treat or as a dessert with custard. (Invert each individual tartlet onto a side plate.)

MAKES 1 MEDIUM-SIZED TART OR 5–6 TARTLETS.

Nutty tart

This tart, with its caramel filling, is made with four different kinds of nuts.

CRUST
1 x recipe for sweet shortcrust
    pastry (see p. 121)

FILLING
6 extra-large eggs, whisked
180 ml (¾ c) golden syrup
60 ml (¼ c) butter, melted
125 ml (½ c) each chopped
    hazelnuts, walnuts,
    pecan and Brazil nuts
crème fraîche or cream to serve

Preheat the oven to 190 °C. Grease a 26 x 12 cm pie tin with butter, margarine or nonstick spray.

CRUST Line the tin with the shortcrust pastry and bake blind (see p. 122).

FILLING Mix all the filling ingredients, except the nuts and crème fraîche. Mix well and add the nuts. Spoon the filling into the prepared pastry shell and bake for 40–45 minutes or until the filling has set and is golden brown. Leave to cool before cutting into slices. Serve with a little crème fraîche or whipped cream.

MAKES 1 MEDIUM-SIZED TART.

Fig and pomegranate tart

Well-known cookery book author Mariëtte Crafford created this sublime tart. The filling is similar to a lemon meringue.

ALMOND SHORTCRUST PASTRY
190 g softened butter (not melted)
125 ml (½ c) caster sugar
5 ml (1 t) vanilla essence
70 g ground almonds
2 egg yolks
390 ml cake flour
pinch salt

CREAM CHEESE FILLING
1 tub (250 g) cream cheese
juice and finely grated zest
    of 3 lemons
1 can (398 g) condensed milk
50 ml poppy seeds
    (optional)

TOPPING
fresh figs, halved
pomegranate seeds

Preheat the oven to 180 °C. Line a 30 cm loose-bottomed pie tin with baking paper and grease with butter or margarine.

ALMOND SHORTCRUST PASTRY Cream the butter and sugar together until light and fluffy. Add the vanilla essence and ground almonds and mix well. Add the egg yolks, flour and salt and mix well for 1 minute to form a soft dough.
Shape the dough into a flat circle, wrap in clingfilm and rest in the fridge for 10 minutes.
Press the dough onto the bottom of the pie tin and prick.
Bake until golden. Leave the pastry base to cool completely on the loose bottom of the tin. Carefully remove the paper and store in an airtight container until ready to serve. (If the crust becomes soft, crisp it by heating it in a hot oven and leave to cool.)

CREAM CHEESE FILLING Mix the filling ingredients and chill until needed.

TOPPING Put the pastry shell on a large serving platter. Cover with the cream cheese filling and arrange the fig halves on top. Scatter the pomegranate seeds over the tart.

MAKES 1 LARGE TART.

VARIATIONS

Use fresh seasonal fruit such as gooseberries, diced mango and granadilla pulp and decorate with mint or lemon balm. Or pile whole strawberries and other berries on top and dust with icing sugar.

126

Lemon tart

Chef Nic van Wyk of Stellenbosch made this tart specially for us to celebrate the arrival of spring.

CRUST

1 x recipe for sweet shortcrust pastry (see p. 121)

FILLING

250 ml (1 c) caster sugar
4 extra-large eggs
250 ml (1 c) cream
250 ml (1 c) freshly squeezed lemon juice
zest of 1 lemon

MERINGUE

2 egg whites
60 ml (¼ c) caster sugar

Preheat the oven to 200 °C.

CRUST Prepare the pastry and use it to line a medium-sized pie tin or 5–6 smaller tartlet tins. Bake blind (see p. 122). Reduce the oven temperature to 140 °C.

FILLING Whisk the caster sugar, eggs, cream and lemon juice and zest together.
Pour the filling into the prepared pasty shell and bake for 10 minutes. Reduce the temperature to 90 °C and continue baking until the filling has just set but is still slightly soft inside. Remove the tart from the oven and leave it to cool.

MERINGUE Whisk together the egg whites and caster sugar until soft peaks form and spoon or pipe on top of the tart.
Bake at 200 °C for about 4 minutes or until the meringue starts to brown.

INSTANT VARIATION

Remove the tart from the oven and leave it to cool in a warm place (if it cools too rapidly the filling will crack. Dust the tart with a little caster sugar and heat with a gas flame until lightly caramelised.

MAKES 1 MEDIUM-SIZED TART OR 5–6 TARTLETS.

Carmen says
- Meringue must always be spooned onto a warm filling. If the meringue shrinks and draws too much moisture (it forms a syrupy layer between the meringue and filling) it could be that the oven temperature was too low, the meringue was spooned onto a cold filling, there was too much sugar in the meringue mixture or the sugar granules were too coarse.
- If the meringue forms golden syrupy droplets it could be that the sugar wasn't whisked with the egg whites until dissolved, the filling was too warm when the meringue was spooned on top of it or the oven temperature was too low.

Chocolate soufflé tart

Delicious chocolate tart

This delicious, easy-to-make tart is one of celebrity chef Jamie Oliver's standbys. It's easy to double the filling recipe to make two tarts. Alternatively freeze the remaining dough. The tart can be made a day in advance.

1 x recipe for rich sweet shortcrust pastry (see p. 121)

FILLING
140 g butter
150 g dark chocolate, broken into pieces
125 ml (½ c) cocoa
8 extra-large eggs
250 ml (1 c) caster sugar
45 ml (3 T) golden syrup
60 ml (¼ c) sour cream

DECORATION
fresh berries

Preheat the oven to 200 °C. Grease a 23 cm pie tin and line it with the prepared shortcrust pastry. Bake blind (see p. 122). Reduce the temperature to 150 °C.

FILLING In a fairly small saucepan heat the butter, chocolate and cocoa over very low heat, stirring slowly until the mixture is smooth. Remove the saucepan from the heat and leave the mixture to cool for a few minutes.

Whisk the eggs and caster sugar together until the mixture is light and fluffy. Beat in the golden syrup and sour cream. Add the cooled chocolate mixture to the egg mixture and mix well. Pour the filling into the pastry shell.

Bake for 45–50 minutes or until done. Carefully remove the tart from the oven and leave it to cool for at least 45 minutes. The filling will crack and sink slightly.

DECORATION Pile fresh berries on top of the tart just before serving and serve it with a little extra sour cream if desired.

MAKES 1 LARGE TART.

Chocolate soufflé tart

This recipe calls for hardly any flour, resulting in a deliciously moist, sticky tart.

80 ml (⅓ c) blanched almonds
45 ml (3 T) cake flour
85 g dark chocolate (with 70% cocoa solids), finely chopped
125 ml (½ c) cocoa, sifted
250 ml (1 c) caster sugar
150 ml boiling water
2 egg yolks
15 ml (1 T) brandy
4 egg whites
2 ml (½ t) cream of tartar
30–45 ml (2–3 T) icing sugar, or cocoa for dusting on top

Preheat the oven to 190 °C and grease a 20 cm springform cake tin with butter.
Line the bottom of the tin with baking paper and grease once more.
Blitz the almonds and flour in a food processor until fine. Mix the chocolate, cocoa and 190 ml of the caster sugar in a large mixing bowl. Add the boiling water and stir until the chocolate has melted and the mixture is smooth.
Whisk in the egg yolks and brandy.
Add the almond mixture to the chocolate mixture and mix well.
Whisk the egg whites and cream of tartar until soft peaks begin to form. Gradually add the remaining caster sugar and whisk until stiff.
Using a metal spoon, fold the egg whites into the chocolate mixture and turn the mixture into the prepared cake tin.
Bake for 30–35 minutes or until only a few moist crumbs stick to a testing skewer. Cool on a wire rack. Remove the cake tin and transfer the tart to a cake platter.
Dust with the icing sugar or cocoa and serve with cream if desired.

MAKES 1 MEDIUM-SIZED TART.

Pumpkin chiffon tart

Elizabeth Lotter of Irene says her grandmother's pumpkin tart is one of her fondest childhood memories. Everyone loved this old-fashioned treat.

CRUST
110 g butter
30 ml (2 T) caster sugar
30 ml (2 T) oil
1 extra-large egg
500 ml (2 c) cake flour
10 ml (2 t) baking powder
2 ml (½ t) salt

FILLING
125 ml (½ c) light brown sugar
4 extra-large eggs, separated
5 ml (1 t) ground cinnamon
2 ml (½ t) grated nutmeg
2 ml (½ t) ground ginger
2 ml (½ t) allspice
500 g cooked pumpkin, drained
125 ml (½ c) cream
100 g butter, melted
5 ml (1 t) white sugar
chopped nuts to serve
whipped cream to serve (optional)

Preheat the oven to 180 °C. Grease a 25 cm pie dish with butter, margarine or nonstick spray.

CRUST Beat the butter and sugar together until the mixture is thick and pale yellow. Add the oil and egg and mix well. **Sift** in the flour, baking powder and salt and mix well. Press the pastry into the prepared dish, prick the base and chill for 30 minutes. Bake the pastry shell for 10 minutes and leave it to cool before adding the filling.

FILLING Whisk the brown sugar, egg yolks and spices together. In a separate bowl mix the pumpkin, cream and melted butter. Fold the pumpkin mixture into the sugar mixture. Whisk the egg whites until soft peaks form. Sprinkle over the white sugar and continue whisking until stiff peaks begin to form. Fold the egg whites into the pumpkin mixture and spoon the mixture into the baked pastry shell. Bake for 40 minutes or until the filling is puffed and set. Leave the tart to cool and serve it with chopped nuts and whipped cream.

MAKES 1 LARGE TART.

Caramelised pear and yoghurt tart

The pastry crust is covered with a layer of honey-caramelised pears and yoghurt custard.

CRUST
1 x recipe for standard sweet shortcrust pastry (see p. 121)

FILLING
about 750 g firm, ripe pears
15 ml (1 T) light brown sugar
60 ml (¼ c) seedless raisins or sultanas
5 ml (1 t) ground cinnamon
10 ml (2 t) extra light brown sugar
25 ml (5 t) honey
2 egg yolks
250 ml (1 c) plain drinking yoghurt
25 ml (5 t) extra honey
10 ml (2 t) cornflour
cream or crème fraîche to serve

Preheat the oven to 200 °C. Grease a 34 x 11 cm or 23 cm round flan tin with butter, margarine or nonstick spray.

CRUST Prepare the pastry as described and roll it out. Line the tin with the pastry and chill while preparing the filling.

FILLING Peel, core and slice enough pears to make up 600 g.
Sprinkle the 15 ml (1 T) brown sugar in the bottom of the chilled pastry shell to prevent it becoming soggy.
Arrange the pear slices on the bottom of the pastry shell and scatter over the raisins or sultanas. Sprinkle with cinnamon and the extra brown sugar.
Drizzle 25 ml (5 t) honey over the fruit.
Whisk the egg yolks, yoghurt, extra honey and cornflour together.
Pour the egg mixture over the pears and bake the tart for 45 minutes or until the yoghurt mixture has just set. Leave to cool to room temperature and serve with whipped cream or crème fraîche.

MAKES 1 LARGE TART.

Baklava

A Middle Eastern sweet treat made with layers of phyllo pastry and nuts drenched in a sweet spicy syrup.

FILLING
100 g walnuts
50 g pistachio nuts, shelled,
  or pine nuts
50 g almonds
5 ml (1 t) ground cinnamon
2 ml (½ t) mixed spice
50 g caster sugar
1 packet (500 g) phyllo pastry
170 g butter, melted

SYRUP
250 ml (1 c) caster sugar
300 ml water
juice of ½ lemon
60 ml (¼ c) honey
15–30 ml (1–2 T) rose-water

Preheat the oven to 170 °C. Grease a 25 x 34 cm oven pan with butter, margarine or nonstick spray.

FILLING Roughly chop the nuts in a food processor, add the spices and caster sugar and mix.
Cut the phyllo pastry the same size as the tin. Cover the phyllo pastry with a damp tea towel to prevent it drying out. Arrange 10 layers of phyllo pastry, each brushed with melted butter, in the bottom of the tin. Sprinkle with a good helping of the nut mixture. Arrange 5 layers of phyllo pastry, each brushed with melted butter, on top and sprinkle with some of the nut mixture again. Repeat three more times, ending with a layer of phyllo pastry. Using a sharp knife, cut diamond patterns on the top layer of the baklava (do not cut all the way through).
Bake for 40 minutes.

SYRUP Slowly bring all the syrup ingredients, except the honey and rose-water, to the boil, stirring continuously until the sugar has dissolved. Simmer for about 10 minutes or until syrupy. Add the honey and rose-water. Pour the hot syrup over the baklava as soon as it comes out of the oven. Leave for at least 4 hours. Cut into diamond shapes and serve with Greek yoghurt.

MAKES 1 LARGE TART.

Apple crumble, apple upside-down tart, apple strudel — these are but a few
variations for universally popular apple tart.

Apple strudel

It's hard to resist a slice of delicious homemade apple strudel. This is a quick variation
on the traditional Austrian recipe — we've used phyllo pastry instead of strudel pastry.

FILLING

30 ml (2 T) butter

3 apples, cored, peeled
   and thinly sliced

80 ml (⅓ c) golden syrup

10 ml (2 t) ground cinnamon

5 ml (1 t) fresh lemon juice

45 ml (3 T) cornflour

60 ml (¼ c) water

30 ml (2 T) honey

60 ml (¼ c) currants

few drops almond essence

15 ml (1 T) vanilla essence

5 ml (1 t) grated lemon zest

PASTRY

6 sheets phyllo pastry

125 ml (½ c) melted butter

125 ml (½ c) finely chopped walnuts

60 ml (¼ c) caster sugar

5 ml (1 t) ground cinnamon

Preheat the oven to 200 °C and line a baking sheet with baking paper.

FILLING Put the butter, apple slices, golden syrup, cinnamon and lemon juice
in a saucepan and sauté the fruit for 2–3 minutes over medium heat or until soft.
Mix the cornflour and water and, stirring continuously, add the mixture to the
apples. Simmer slowly until the mixture thickens. Add the honey, currants,
essences and lemon zest. Remove from the heat and leave to cool.

PASTRY Brush each phyllo pastry sheet with the melted butter.
Mix the finely chopped walnuts and caster sugar and sprinkle the mixture over
the phyllo pastry sheets (reserve a little of the nut mixture for sprinkling on top).
Stack the phyllo pastry sheets on top of each other and spoon the apple mixture
over the length of the top sheet, leaving a 5 cm edge all around. Carefully roll up
the phyllo pastry sheets. Brush the top with butter and sprinkle with cinnamon and
the reserved nut mixture.
Put the strudel on the prepared baking sheet and bake for 20 minutes or until golden.
Leave to cool for a few minutes before cutting into slices, and serve.

SERVES 8.

Carmen says
- Sweet and crisp Cripps Pink apples are ideal for making a strudel
  (check the packaging or supermarket's price blackboard for apple varieties).
- Keep the phyllo pastry sheets moist while working by covering them
  with a damp tea towel.

Almond and apple tart

The recipe for this apple tart with its delicate almond flavour was sent in by Judy Munthree of Phoenix. Delicious!

FILLING
700 g (3–4 large) Granny Smith apples, peeled, cored and cut into wedges
5 ml (1 t) ground cinnamon
75 ml (6 T) light brown sugar

TOPPING
125 g butter, at room temperature
160 ml (⅔ c) light brown sugar
2 extra-large eggs
225 ml self-raising flour
3 ml (generous ½ t) almond essence
30 ml (2 T) milk
30 ml (2 T) flaked almonds
icing sugar

Preheat the oven to 180 °C. Grease a 27 cm ovenproof dish with butter, margarine or nonstick spray.

FILLING Arrange the apple wedges in the prepared ovenproof dish. Mix the cinnamon and brown sugar and sprinkle the mixture over the apples.

TOPPING Cream the butter and brown sugar together until the mixture is light and fluffy. Add the eggs one at a time, beating well after each addition.
Add the self-raising flour, almond essence and milk and mix.
Spoon the mixture over the apples, spreading it evenly.
Sprinkle the flaked almonds on top and bake for 50–60 minutes or until the topping is puffed and golden.
Mix a little icing sugar with a little water to make a drop icing. Drizzle the icing over the tart and serve it cut into squares with a scoop of ice cream if desired.

SERVES 8–10.

Apple crumble tartlets

Old-fashioned apple crumble is still one of the most delicious tarts you can make.

CRUMBLE
250 g butter
400 ml caster sugar
2 extra-large eggs
10 ml (2 t) vanilla essence
finely grated zest of 2 lemons
4 x 250 ml (4 c) cake flour
20 ml (4 t) baking powder

FILLING
4 cans (385 g each) pie apples
15 ml (1 T) ground cinnamon
60 ml (¼ c) caster sugar
160 ml (⅔ c) seedless raisins
30 ml (2 T) cake flour

Preheat the oven to 180 °C and grease 6–8 small aluminium foil pie tins with butter, margarine or nonstick spray.

CRUMBLE Cream the butter and sugar together. Add the eggs one at a time. Add the vanilla essence and lemon zest and beat well. Add half the cake flour and mix gently.
Add the remaining flour and baking powder, mixing to make a dough.
Divide the dough in half, wrap each half in clingfilm and chill. Roll out one half of the dough to a thickness of about 3 mm and cut out circles large enough to fit inside the tins.
Line the tins with the pastry circles.

FILLING Mix the filling ingredients and divide the mixture among the pastry shells. Grate the remaining dough over each tart. Bake for about 30 minutes or until golden. Dust with icing sugar and serve with whipped cream.

MAKES 6–8 TARTLETS.

Carmen says
The apple crumble can also be made in 2 larger pie tins.

VARIATION
Substitute oats for 250 ml (1 c) of the flour when making the crumble. Substitute berries or sultanas for the 160 ml (⅔ c) seedless raisins.

Norwegian apple tart

Sandy's apple tart

Sandra Geyer of Windhoek says her husband is so mad about this apple tart he's named it after her. The filling is made with a packet of instant vanilla pudding and the tart has a crust at the bottom and on top.

CRUST
1 x recipe for standard sweet shortcrust pastry (see p. 121)

FILLING
250 ml (1 c) seedless raisins
60 ml (¼ c) rum
juice of 1 lemon
2 kg (about 8 large) green apples, peeled, cored and diced
1 packet (90 g) instant vanilla pudding
750 ml (3 c) fresh cream
160 ml (⅔ c) sugar
1 egg yolk
milk
caster sugar

Preheat the oven to 200 °C and grease a deep oven pan or two 20 cm square cake tins with butter, margarine or nonstick spray.

CRUST Prepare the pastry as described and use three-fifths of the pastry to line the pan, pressing it halfway up the inside of the pan.
Bake blind as described (see p.122). Reduce the oven temperature to 180 °C.

FILLING Put the raisins in a bowl, pour over the rum and set aside.
Sprinkle the lemon juice over the apples and mix them with the soaked raisins. Spoon the mixture on the pastry base.
Mix the instant vanilla pudding powder with the cream and sugar. Heat slowly until the sugar has dissolved. Bring the mixture to the boil and simmer gently for 1 minute. Remove from the heat and spoon the mixture on top of the apple mixture.
Roll out the remaining pastry so it is large enough to cover the filling. Gently press the pastry on top of the filling and prick it with a fork. Bake for 1¼ hours or until done. Cover the tart with aluminium foil if the pastry browns too quickly. Whisk the egg yolk and a little milk and brush the pastry with the mixture 15 minutes before the end of the baking time. Dust with caster sugar and serve with cream.

MAKES 1 LARGE TART OR 2 MEDIUM-SIZED TARTS.

Norwegian apple tart

Mrs J.C. van Wyk of Clydesdale in Pretoria says she bakes four tartlets in aluminium foil tins at a time and freezes them.

250 ml (1 c) cake flour
10 ml (2 t) baking powder
pinch salt
375 ml (1½ c) sugar
2 extra-large eggs
10 ml (2 t) vanilla essence
250 ml (1 c) roughly chopped pecan nuts
4 medium-sized apples, peeled, cored and sliced

Preheat the oven to 180 °C. Grease a rectangular or a 22 cm round pie dish with butter, margarine or nonstick spray.
Sift the cake flour, baking powder and salt together. Add the sugar and mix well.
Whisk the eggs and vanilla essence together and add the dry ingredients. Add the pecan nuts and apples and mix.
Turn the mixture into the prepared pie dish and bake for about 30 minutes or until golden and done. Serve with cream.

MAKES 1 MEDIUM-SIZED TART.

Apple tarte Tatin with hazelnuts

This apple tarte Tatin is made with shortcrust pastry instead of traditional puff pastry. Hazlenuts are added to the apples.

PASTRY
310 ml (1¼ c) self-raising flour
5 ml (1 t) ground cinnamon
pinch mixed spice
30 ml (2 T) light brown sugar
100 g butter, diced
1 egg yolk
iced water

FILLING
½ packet (50 g) hazelnuts
5 small (about 400 g) apples,
    peeled and cored
juice and zest of 1 lemon
200 ml white sugar
200 ml water
80 ml (⅓ c) butter

VARIATION
Substitute pears for the apples and puff pastry for the shortcrust pastry.

Preheat the oven to 180 °C.

PASTRY Sift the flour and spices together and add the sugar.
Rub the butter into the flour mixture until the mixture resembles breadcrumbs.
Add the egg yolk and 15 ml (1 T) iced water. Mix gently to make a dough (add a little extra iced water if necessary) and shape into a ball. Chill until needed.

FILLING Toast the nuts in a heated pan until golden brown and set aside.
Cut the apples into wedges and sprinkle them with a little lemon juice to prevent discoloration.
Heat the sugar and water in a deep saucepan over low heat until the sugar has dissolved. Stir occasionally to ensure all the sugar crystals dissolve before the mixture comes to the boil. Bring to the boil and heat without stirring until the syrup just begins to change colour. Add the butter and heat until the syrup turns a light caramel colour.
Reduce the temperature to low, add the apples and sprinkle over the lemon zest. Slowly cook the mixture for about 8 minutes or until the apples begin to soften and the syrup thickens slightly. Remove the saucepan from the heat and leave it to cool for a few minutes. Spoon the filling mixture into a 23 cm cake tin with a solid base (not a loose-bottomed tin). Sprinkle the nuts over.
Remove the pastry from the fridge beforehand and roll it into a circle slightly bigger than the tin. Put the pastry circle on top of the apple filling, gently pressing it against the inside of the tin. Bake the tart for about 20 minutes or until the crust is done and golden.
Leave the tart to cool in the tin for a few minutes. Put a plate over the tin and invert it rapidly so the filling is on top. Work carefully as the syrup is very hot.
Serve the tart lukewarm with vanilla ice cream or cream.

MAKES 1 MEDIUM-SIZED TART.

WHAT IS THE ORIGIN OF TARTE TATIN?

The tart was apparently first baked in 1889 at the Hotel Tatin in Lamotte-Beuvron in France. The hotel was owned by the Tatin sisters, Stéphanie and Caroline.

There are many versions to the story but it's said Stéphanie, who did most of the cooking, was overworked. While making an ordinary apple tart she overcooked the apples in the butter and sugar. In an attempt to save the tart she laid the pastry on top of the apples, put the pan in the oven for a few minutes then inverted the tart onto a plate and served it. Amazingly the hotel patrons raved about the upside-down tart and it immediately became one of the hotel's specialities.

The recipe not only became famous in the region but spread to Paris where it was one of the standard items on the menu at the famous restaurant, Maxim's. Today the recipe has spread worldwide. In America the tart is made with Gold Delicious apples, a variety that's never used for traditional American apple pie.

Apple tarte Tatin with hazelnuts

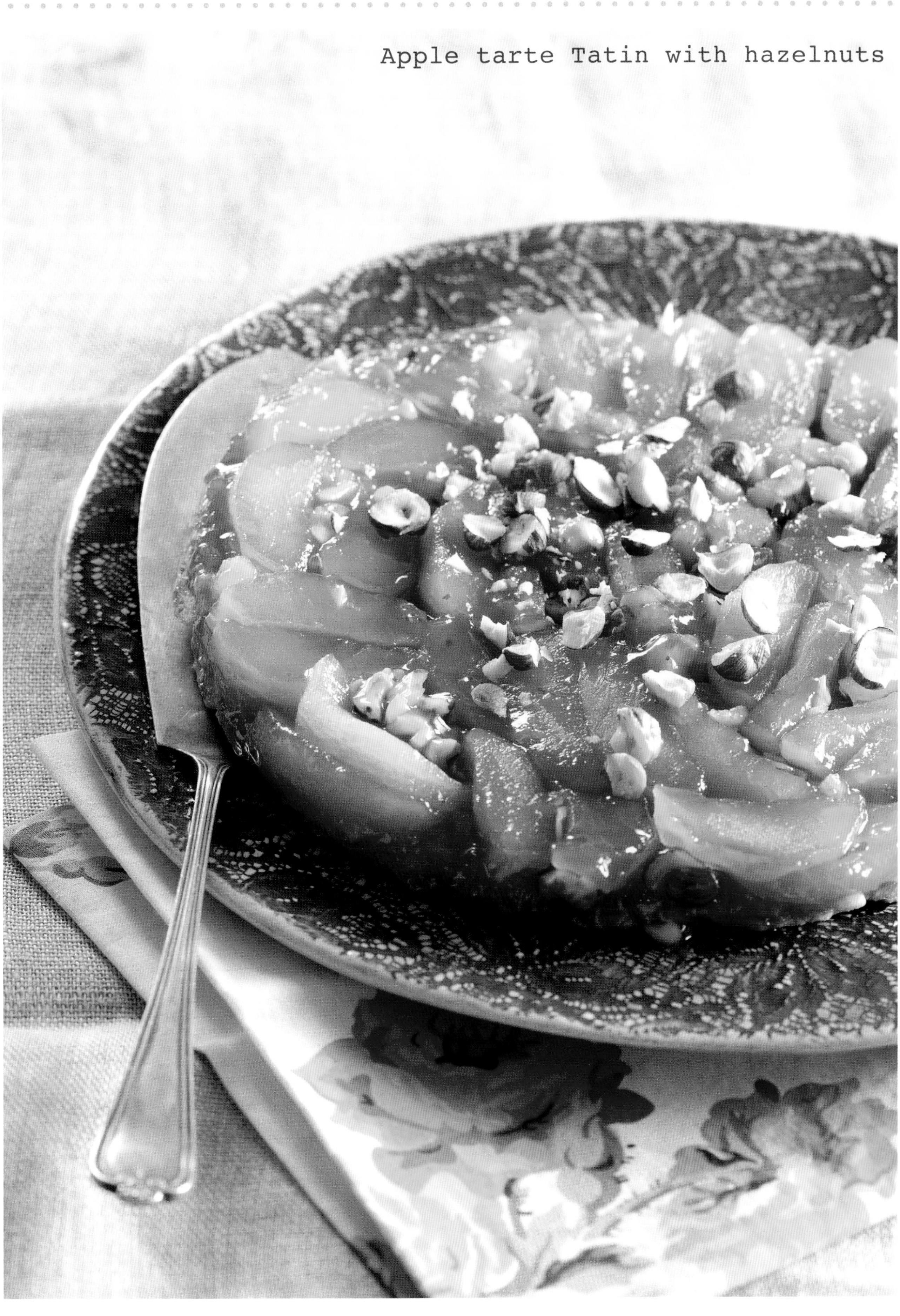

Blueberry cream tartlets

TARTLETS

Delicate tartlet shells with a fruit filling arranged on a silver platter always look festive. For a more rustic look envelop fruit in shortcrust pastry or drizzle a syrup over cake batter baked in muffin tins.

Blueberry cream tartlets

The pastry for these pretty tartlets isn't rolled out. Simply spoon a little bit into the tins and it will rise slightly along the sides while baking. Instead of the usual custard filling we've saved time by mixing mascarpone cheese with a little lemon curd and topping the filling with blueberries. Simply delicious! Remember, don't use too much mascarpone cheese or it will overpower the berries.

TARTLET SHELLS
100 g butter, softened
125 ml (½ c) caster sugar
100 g hazelnuts, toasted and ground

BLUEBERRY TOPPING
30 ml (2 T) caster sugar
15 ml (1 T) water
250 g blueberries

FILLING
250 g mascarpone cheese
30–45 ml (2–3 T) milk
45 ml (3 T) lemon curd (see p. 206)

VARIATION
Fill the tartlet shells with confectioner's custard (see below) and top with fresh fruit of your choice.

Preheat the oven to 180 °C and lightly grease 20 hollows of two small cupcake tins with butter, margarine or nonstick spray.

TARTLET SHELLS Beat the butter and sugar together until the mixture is soft and creamy. Mix in the hazelnuts.
Spoon generous teaspoonfuls of the mixture into each hollow.
Bake for about 10 minutes or until golden and slightly puffed along the edges.
Leave the shells to cool in the tins for 5 minutes or until firm enough to remove with a knife. Put the tartlet shells on paper towels to absorb the excess fat.

BLUEBERRY TOPPING Heat the sugar and water over low heat until the sugar has dissolved. Turn up the heat and simmer for about 30 seconds until syrupy. Remove from the heat and gently stir in the blueberries without breaking them. Leave to cool.

FILLING Beat the mascarpone and just enough milk to make a soft, creamy mixture with the consistency of whipped cream. Gently stir in the lemon curd, leaving yellow swirls for a pretty effect.
Spoon a little of the filling into each tartlet shell and top with a few of the syrupy blueberries.

MAKES 20 TARTLETS.

CONFECTIONER'S CUSTARD
Bring 500 ml (2 c) milk to just below boiling point. In a glass bowl whisk 6 egg yolks and 200 ml sugar together over a saucepan with boiling water. (Take care that the bowl doesn't touch the water.) Blend 75 ml (5 T) cornflour with a little of the hot milk and, using a wooden spoon, stir the paste into the egg yolk mixture. Add a pinch salt and stir in the milk. Heat, stirring continuously, until the mixture is thick and cooked. Remove from the heat and stir in 5 ml (1 t) vanilla essence. Cover the top of the custard with greased baking paper so it doesn't form a skin.
MAKES 625 ML (2 ½ C)

Maureen's Van der Spuytjies

Wilma Howells, co-author of the book **Entertain** and a former YOU test kitchen staffer, was given this recipe by her mom, Maureen, who used to bake the tartlet shells over walnut shell halves. We used the backs of cupcake tins instead.

TARTLET SHELLS
250 ml (1 c) cake flour
5 ml (1 t) baking powder
3 ml (generous ½ t) salt
60 ml (¼ c) butter
60 ml (¼ c) sugar
1 extra-large egg
melted butter
cinnamon sugar

FILLING
250 ml (1 c) cream
10 ml (2 t) caster sugar
125 ml (½ c) mixed nuts,
   finely chopped

Preheat the oven to 180 °C. Grease the backs of a few small cupcake tins with butter, margarine or nonstick spray.

TARTLET SHELLS Sift the cake flour, baking powder and salt together in a large mixing bowl.
Rub the butter and sugar into the flour mixture until the mixture resembles fine breadcrumbs.
Whisk the egg and add it to the pastry mixture. Mix until a fairly firm dough is formed. Knead gently and shape the pastry into a ball. Leave it to rest for 30 minutes before rolling out on a lightly floured surface to a thickness of about 2 mm.
Cut out circles with a small cookie cutter (the circles must fit over the backs of the greased cupcake tins). Put the cut-out pastry circles on the inverted cupcake tins.
Brush the pastry with melted butter and sprinkle with cinnamon sugar.
Bake for 10–12 minutes or until the pastry shells just begin to brown. Carefully remove them while still slightly warm or they will stick to the tins and break.

FILLING Whip the cream and caster sugar until thick and carefully fold in the finely chopped nuts. Spoon or pipe the filling into the cooled tartlet shells.

MAKES 30–35 TARTLETS.

Cheesecake tartlets in phyllo pastry

Your guests will love these individual little cheesecakes.

1 packet (500 g) phyllo pastry, thawed
melted butter for brushing
½ x recipe for cheesecake filling
   (see p. 73)
smooth apricot jam
glacé orange slices (see p. 210)

Preheat the oven to 160 °C and grease the hollows of a deep muffin tin.
Brush 4 phyllo pastry sheets with melted butter and stack them on top of each other. Cut the pastry sheets into large squares and line the muffin tin hollows with them.
Prepare the cheesecake filling as described and spoon the mixture into the pastry-lined hollows, filling each three-quarters of the way.
Bake for about 40 minutes or until the filling is done. Spread a little apricot jam on top of each tartlet and leave them to cool in the oven.
Decorate with a glacé orange slice.

MAKES 12–16 TARTLETS.

General Smuts tartlets

Most of us know Hertzog tartlets, made with coconut and jam and named after the Anglo-Boer War general and former South African prime minister. These tartlets, also named after a South African general and politician, are made without coconut.

PASTRY
750 ml (3 c) cake flour
250 g cold butter, grated
250 ml (1 c) sugar
pinch salt
10 ml (2 t) baking powder
2 extra-large eggs, whisked
15–20 ml (3–4 t) milk

FILLING
smooth apricot jam

TOPPING
60 ml (¼ c) sugar
60 ml (¼ c) butter
2 extra-large eggs, whisked
60 ml (¼ c) cake flour
5 ml (1 t) baking powder

Preheat the oven to 200 °C. Grease 2–3 cupcake tins with butter, margarine or nonstick spray.

PASTRY Sift the cake flour and rub in the butter until the mixture resembles breadcrumbs. Add the sugar, salt and baking powder and mix well. Add the eggs and just enough milk to make a stiff dough that is easy to roll out.
Roll out the dough on a floured surface to a thickness of about 3 mm. Cut out circles large enough to line the hollows of the cupcake tins and line the hollows with the pastry circles.

FILLING Spoon a teaspoonful of the jam into each pastry shell.

TOPPING Cream the sugar and butter together until the mixture is light and fluffy. Add the eggs and beat well.
Sift the cake flour and baking powder together and mix with the egg mixture.
Spoon 5 ml (1 t) of the topping mixture into each pastry shell and bake for 10–15 minutes or until the tartlets are done. Leave the tartlets to cool in the tins for a few minutes before carefully transferring them to a wire rack to cool completely.

MAKES 36 SMALL OR 24 LARGE TARTLETS.

> **Carmen says**
> Because these jam tartlets aren't made with perishable ingredients
> they will keep well for a few weeks if stored in an airtight container.

Syrupy lemon tartlets

These tartlets contain a little coconut and are moistened with a delicious lemon syrup.

BATTER
625 ml (2½ c) self-raising flour
250 ml (1 c) desiccated coconut
250 ml (1 c) caster sugar
15 ml (1 T) grated lemon zest
125 g butter, melted
250 ml (1 c) milk
2 extra-large eggs, whisked

SYRUP
125 ml (½ c) caster sugar
60 ml (¼ c) water
10 ml (2 t) grated lemon zest
80 ml (⅓ c) lemon juice

Preheat the oven to 180 °C. Line the hollows of deep muffin tins with paper cups or grease them with butter, margarine or nonstick spray.

BATTER Combine the self-raising flour, coconut, caster sugar and lemon zest.
Beat the butter, milk and eggs together and add to the flour mixture. Mix well.
Spoon the batter into the paper cups and bake for 20 minutes or until a testing skewer comes out clean when inserted into the centre of the tartlets.

SYRUP Slowly bring the caster sugar, water and lemon zest and juice to the boil and simmer for 2 minutes. Pour the syrup over the tartlets as soon as they come out of the oven and leave them to cool.

MAKES 12 TARTLETS.

Gooseberry, apple and berry tartlets

The pastry for these rustic tartlets is folded around the fruit filling so
it peeks out. Served lukewarm with custard or cream these tartlets make
a lovely dessert.

PASTRY
330 ml cake flour
125 g chilled butter, diced
60–75 ml (4–5 T) sour cream

FILLING
2 apples, peeled, cored and chopped
250 g mixed fresh or frozen berries
150 g gooseberries, washed
125 ml (½ c) caster sugar
1 egg yolk
15 ml (1 T) milk
15 ml (1 T) caster sugar for
   sprinkling on top

Preheat the oven to 180 °C. Grease a large baking sheet and lightly dust
it with flour.

PASTRY Sift the flour and rub in the butter until the mixture resembles
coarse breadcrumbs. Add just enough sour cream to combine the
ingredients. Shape the dough into a ball, cover with clingfilm and chill for
20 minutes.
Divide the pastry into 6 even parts and roll each part out on a lightly floured
surface. Put the pastry circles on the prepared baking sheet.

FILLING Mix the fruit in a mixing bowl and stir in the caster sugar. Spoon a little
of the fruit mixture in the centre of each pastry circle. Fold the edge of each pastry
circle over the filling to make a round tartlet. Leave an opening in the centre of
each tartlet so the filling peeks out.
Mix the egg yolk and milk and brush the pastry with the mixture. Sprinkle the
tartlets with the caster sugar and bake them for 30 minutes or until the pastry is
crisp and golden and the fruit is soft. Carefully transfer the tartlets to side plates
and serve them lukewarm.

MAKES 6 FAIRLY LARGE TARTLETS.

Peach tartlets

These tartlets are similar to caramelised apple tart. The individual tartlets make
a lovely dessert but if desired you can bake a large tart instead. The recipe was
sent in by Joey Fourie of Noordeinde.

BATTER
2 extra-large eggs
250 ml (1 c) sugar
500 ml (2 c) self-raising flour
pinch salt
10 ml (2 t) bicarbonate of soda
1 can (410 g) peaches
10 ml (2 t) lemon juice

SYRUP
250 ml (1 c) sugar
1 small can (170 g) evaporated milk
50 ml butter
5 ml (1 t) caramel essence

Preheat the oven to 180 °C and grease 2 muffin tins with butter, margarine
or nonstick spray.

BATTER Whisk the eggs and sugar together until thick and pale yellow.
Sift the self-raising flour, salt and bicarbonate of soda together and add the
mixture to the egg mixture.
Drain the peaches but reserve the syrup. Add the lemon juice to the syrup and
set the mixture aside. Chop the peaches and add them to the batter along with the
syrup mixture. Mix and spoon the batter into the greased muffin tins, filling each
hollow three-quarters of the way. Bake for 15 minutes or until well risen and golden.

SYRUP Heat all the ingredients, except the caramel essence, over low heat until
the sugar has melted. Bring the mixture to the boil and simmer for about
5 minutes. Spoon the syrup over the tartlets as soon as they come out of the
oven. Serve lukewarm or at room temperature with whipped cream.

MAKES 17 TARTLETS.

Gooseberry, apple and berry tartlets

Fridge tarts and cheesecakes

If baking's not your thing you can always fall back on fridge tarts. They make excellent desserts or teatime treats. Experience has taught me that fridge tarts, along with fudge, are also the first things teens want to learn to make when they start pottering in the kitchen.

Before you try these recipes, first read the information on gelatine. Remember, if you let gelatine come to the boil the tart won't set. Also keep in mind not all tarts set firm; some are fairly soft so take care when serving them.

Unbaked cheesecakes are my favourite kind of fridge tart. They're not too rich because the cottage cheese (use the creamed variety) provides all the smoothness without the extra kilojoules. We've also included several recipes for lower-fat tarts.

Cassata

Besides well-known cassata ice cream, the Italians also make a classic cassata cake with ricotta and candied fruit. It's traditionally covered with a layer of brightly coloured marzipan but we simply dusted the cake with icing sugar instead.

75 g mixed candied peel, chopped
75 g red glacé cherries, chopped
90 ml (6 T) sherry or muscadel
2 x 20 cm sponge cakes
500 g ricotta cheese
125 ml (½ c) caster sugar
2 ml (½ t) vanilla essence
50 g unsalted pistachio nuts, chopped
juice and finely grated zest of 1 lemon
icing sugar for dusting on top

Soak the peel and cherries in 45 ml (3 T) of the sherry or muscadel for 15 minutes.
Line the bottom and inside of a 20 cm loose-bottomed cake tin with wax paper and put one of the sponge cakes in the bottom of the tin. Sprinkle over the remaining 45 ml (3 T) sherry or muscadel.
Mix the ricotta, sugar, vanilla essence, pistachio nuts and lemon juice and zest.
Drain the candied peel and cherries but reserve the liquid.
Mix the fruit with the ricotta mixture and spoon it over the sponge base. Cover with the other sponge layer and sprinkle over the reserved sherry or muscadel.
Chill until firm. Carefully unmould the cake on a serving platter and dust with icing sugar.

MAKES 1 MEDIUM-SIZED TART.

Ricotta fridge tart

This fridge tart, made with low-fat ricotta cheese layered with Tennis biscuits, is similar to the Italian dessert tiramisu. Jill van Graan of Benoni, who sent us the recipe, says the tart can be made well in advance, preferably the day before so it can chill overnight.

2 packets (200 g each) Tennis biscuits
150 ml caster sugar
2 extra-large eggs, separated
500 g ricotta cheese
10 ml (2 t) instant coffee powder
50 ml rum
2 ml (½ t) vanilla essence
250 ml (1 c) cream, chilled
cocoa for dusting on top

Grease a 20 x 30 cm pie dish with butter, margarine or nonstick spray. Arrange a layer of Tennis biscuits in the bottom of the dish.
Whisk the caster sugar and egg yolks together until thick and pale yellow.
Add the ricotta cheese, pressing it through a sieve to break up the pieces. Mix well.
Dissolve the coffee powder in the rum and mix with the ricotta mixture. Add the vanilla essence and mix.
Whisk the egg whites until stiff peaks form. Whip the cream until stiff and fold into the egg whites. Fold the cream mixture into the ricotta mixture.
Spoon half the ricotta mixture over the biscuit layer. Arrange another layer of biscuits on top followed by the remaining ricotta mixture. Crush the remaining biscuits and sprinkle the crumbs over the tart. Chill overnight and dust with cocoa just before serving.

MAKES 1 LARGE TART.

> **Carmen says**
> This tart is soft and cannot be cut into neat squares as with a set fridge tart. You can also substitute creamed cottage cheese for the ricotta cheese.

Tiramisu freezer tart

This tart is like a frozen tiramisu and must be made the day before so it can be left in the freezer overnight.

15 ml (1 T) instant coffee powder
60 ml (¼ c) boiling water
45 ml (3 T) coffee liqueur
2 extra-large eggs, separated
80 ml (⅓ c) caster sugar
1 tub (250 g) creamed cottage cheese
60 ml (¼ c) sherry
5 ml (1 t) vanilla essence
100 ml grated chocolate
12–16 sponge fingers

Line a 22 x 13 cm loaf tin with a double layer of baking paper.
Dissolve the instant coffee in the boiling water and add the coffee liqueur. Set aside.
Whisk the egg whites until stiff peaks form. Add the sugar and whisk until thick.
Whisk the cottage cheese, egg yolks, sherry and vanilla essence together. Whisk a little of the egg white mixture into the cottage cheese mixture and carefully fold in the rest. Add the chocolate.
Arrange half the sponge fingers lengthways in the loaf tin with the sugared sides facing down (you may have to cut the biscuits to size). Sprinkle two-thirds of the coffee liqueur mixture over the sponge fingers. Spoon the cottage cheese mixture on top, spreading it evenly.
Arrange the remaining sponge fingers on top of the cottage cheese mixture and sprinkle over the remaining coffee liqueur mixture.
Cover the loaf tin and freeze for at least 5 hours or preferably overnight. Turn out onto a serving platter. Carefully peel away the baking paper and cut the tart into slices.

MAKES 1 MEDIUM-SIZED TART.

COOKING WITH GELATINE

Gelatine is one of those finicky ingredients that is often avoided because things can easily go wrong if you use just a little too much or too little. Also, gelatine doesn't set with pineapple or pawpaw. Follow our tips for making perfect gelatine dishes (see p. 148).

Citrus and ricotta cheesecake

200 g digestive biscuits, crushed
100 g unsalted butter, melted
180 ml (¾ c) sugar
12 ml (2½ t) gelatine
60 ml (¼ c) water
2 extra-large eggs, at room temperature and separated
5 ml (1 t) vanilla essence or ½ vanilla pod
650 g fresh ricotta cheese
15 ml (1 T) grated orange zest
15 ml (1 T) grated lemon zest
15 ml (1 T) fresh lemon juice
pinch salt
250 ml (1 c) cream, chilled

Mix the crushed biscuits, melted butter and 60 ml (¼ c) of the sugar and press the mixture onto the bottom of a 20 cm springform tin.
Sprinkle the gelatine over the 60 ml (¼ c) water and set it aside for 5 minutes to sponge. Melt the gelatine over a saucepan with boiling water.
Whisk the egg yolks, remaining sugar and vanilla essence together until the mixture is thick and pale yellow.
Add the ricotta cheese, orange and lemon zest, lemon juice, salt and gelatine mixture, stirring until smooth.
Whip the cream until stiff peaks begin to form and fold it into the ricotta mixture.
Whisk the egg whites until stiff peaks form and carefully fold them into the ricotta mixture. Pour the mixture into the crust and chill the tart for about 3 hours or until set. Serve with citrus vanilla compote (see p. 211).

MAKES 1 LARGE CHEESECAKE.

HOW MUCH GELATINE SHOULD I USE?

Usually 15 ml (1 T) gelatine powder or 6 gelatine sheets are used to set 500 ml (2 c) liquid. If, however, beating the gelatine mixture to increase its volume or if the mixture is very acidic the amount of gelatine must be increased.

Rich chocolate cheesecake

This unbaked cheesecake is made with caramelised chocolate-flavoured condensed milk.

2 packets (200 g each) chocolate biscuits, crushed
125 ml (½ c) butter, melted
1 can (380 g) caramel condensed milk (chocolate flavour)
1 tub (250 g) creamed cottage cheese
250 ml (1 c) thick cream
45 ml (3 T) cocoa, sifted
60 ml (¼ c) boiling water
25 ml (5 t) gelatine
30 ml (2 T) water
cocoa or chocolate curls

Grease a 24 cm loose-bottomed tin with butter, margarine or nonstick spray.
Mix the biscuits and melted butter and press the mixture onto the bottom and along the inside of the prepared cake tin. Chill until needed.
Whisk the condensed milk, cottage cheese and cream together.
Mix the cocoa and boiling water to make a paste and add the mixture to the cottage cheese mixture.
Sprinkle the gelatine over the cold water and melt it over a saucepan with boiling water or in the microwave oven (do not let it come to the boil).
Whisk the gelatine into the chocolate mixture and carefully pour the filling into the crumb crust.
Chill for at least 24 hours or until firmly set. Remove from the tin and dust with cocoa or decorate with chocolate curls.

MAKES 1 LARGE CHEESECAKE.

Fridge cheesecake

The recipe for this easy cheesecake made with instant pudding was sent in by Sussie Liebenberg of Halfway House.

CRUST
2 packets (200 g each) coconut or Marie biscuits, crushed
100 ml melted butter

FILLING
250 ml (1 c) cream, chilled
1 packet (90 g) instant vanilla pudding
1 tub (175 ml) plain yoghurt
1 tub (250 g) creamed cottage cheese

TOPPING
1 can (115 g) granadilla pulp
3 ml (generous ½ t) cornflour

CRUST Mix the biscuits and butter together and press the mixture onto the bottom of a 24 cm loose-bottomed cake tin. Chill.

FILLING Beat the cream and instant pudding together until the mixture thickens slightly.
Add the yoghurt and cottage cheese and beat until blended.
Pour the mixture into the crust and chill until firm.

TOPPING Mix the granadilla pulp and cornflour and heat until the mixture thickens. Leave the mixture to cool until firm and spoon over the set cheesecake. Store the cheesecake in the fridge.

MAKES 1 MEDIUM-SIZED CHEESECAKE.

BASIC PROPORTIONS FOR USING GELATINE

TYPE OF DISH	GELATINE	LIQUID
plain jelly	15 ml (1 T)	500 ml
individual moulds	20 ml (4 t)	500 ml
jelly with sweet fruit	20 ml (4 t)	500 ml
jelly with acidic fruit	25 ml (5 t)	500 ml
jelly with whipped cream	15–20 ml (3–4 t)	500 ml
jelly with whisked egg white	25 ml (5 t)	500 ml

Apricot cheesecake for diabetics

Mrs M. Hobbs, a diabetic living in East London, enjoys making this unbaked cheesecake with its homemade cake layers for special occasions.

CAKE
125 ml (½ c) low-fat milk
15 ml (1 T) margarine
2 extra-large eggs, separated
30 ml (2 T) sugar
250 ml (1 c) cake flour
10 ml (2 t) baking powder
pinch salt

COTTAGE CHEESE MIXTURE
15 ml (1 T) gelatine
25 ml (5 t) cold water
80 ml (⅓ c) boiling water
1 can (410 g) light evaporated milk
1 tub (250 g) smooth cottage cheese
45 ml (3 T) artificial sweetener powder
30 ml (2 T) custard powder
1 can (410 g) sugar-free apricots,
   drained but reserve the syrup
125 ml (½ c) water
apricot jam for diabetics
granadilla pulp
gooseberries
mint leaves

Preheat the oven to 180 °C and grease a 22 cm loose-bottomed tin with butter or nonstick food spray.

CAKE Bring the milk and margarine to the boil. Remove from the heat and leave to cool.

Whisk the egg whites until stiff peaks form. Add the egg yolks, followed by the sugar, beating until thick and light.

Sift the cake flour, baking powder and salt together. Fold the flour mixture into the egg mixture, alternating with the milk mixture, until well blended.

Turn the batter into the prepared cake tin and bake for 15–20 minutes or until done and a testing skewer comes out clean when inserted into the centre of the cake. Cool completely.

Halve the cake layer horizontally. The layers must be very thin. Sandwich the two layers together with a little of the apricot jam and return them to the cake tin, pressing down slightly to completely cover the base.

COTTAGE CHEESE MIXTURE Sprinkle the gelatine over the cold water and leave to sponge. Add the boiling water and stir until dissolved.

Mix the evaporated milk, cottage cheese, sweetener and gelatine and set aside.

Mix the custard powder with a little of the apricot syrup to form a paste.

Bring the remaining syrup and water to the boil and add the custard powder paste. Cook, stirring continuously, until the mixture is fairly thick.

Cool for a few minutes and stir a little of the cottage cheese mixture into the custard mixture.

Add the remaining cottage cheese mixture.

Turn the mixture into the prepared tin and chill until set, preferably overnight.

Arrange the apricots on top and glaze with slightly heated apricot jam.

Decorate with granadilla pulp, gooseberries and mint leaf strips.

MAKES 1 MEDIUM-SIZED CHEESECAKE.

6 TIPS FOR FLOP-PROOF GELATINE DISHES

- Soak the gelatine powder or sheets in cold water for a few minutes.
- The soaked gelatine can be stirred into a hot mixture. Do not allow the mixture to come to the boil after adding the gelatine – it will affect the taste and prevent setting.
- Use a metal spoon to stir the mixture so you can easily tell when the gelatine has dissolved.
- Before adding soaked gelatine to a cold mixture, heat it over boiling water to dissolve completely.
- Mix a little of the cold mixture with the dissolved gelatine before adding it to the remaining cold mixture.
- Cook pineapple, pawpaw and figs before mixing them with gelatine.

Fruity low-fat cheesecake

Petro van Zyl of Upington uses any combination of fruit and fruit yoghurt to make this low-fat cheesecake.

2 packets (200 g each) bran or
 Marie biscuits, crushed
125 ml (½ c) melted low-fat
 margarine
10 ml (2 t) custard powder
1 can (410 g) light evaporated milk
1 sachet (40 g) low-kilojoule
 granadilla jelly
125 ml (½ c) boiling water
500 ml (2 c) low-fat granadilla
 yoghurt
1 tub (250 g) fat-free cottage cheese
1 can (115 g) granadilla pulp
5 ml (1 t) custard powder

Mix the crushed biscuits and margarine and press the mixture onto the bottom of a flat 35 x 20 cm dish.

Mix the 10 ml (2 t) custard powder with the evaporated milk and bring the mixture to the boil. Heat until thick.

Dissolve the jelly in the boiling water and mix with the custard, yoghurt and cottage cheese.

Spoon the mixture onto the crumb crust and chill until set.

Mix the granadilla pulp and 5 ml (1 t) custard powder and bring the mixture to the boil. Heat until slightly thick and done. Cool for a few minutes and spread over the cold cheesecake. Chill until set before serving.

MAKES 1 LARGE CHEESECAKE.

Fruit and cottage cheese Swiss roll tart

The recipe for this tart, with its layer of fruit under the condensed milk and cottage cheese layer, was sent in by Jacomina Scheepers of Weenen in KwaZulu-Natal.

1 ready-made Swiss roll
1 large can (800 g) fruit, such as
 cherries, gooseberries or peach
 slices in syrup
45 ml (3 T) custard powder
45 ml (3 T) caster sugar
½ x 397 g can condensed milk
45 ml (3 T) lemon juice
1 tub (250 g) creamed
 cottage cheese
10 ml (2 t) gelatine
30 ml (2 T) cold water
180 ml (¾ c) cream, stiffly whipped

Grease a 20 x 30 cm pie dish. Cut the Swiss roll into 1 cm thick slices and arrange them in the pie dish.

Drain the fruit and reserve the syrup.

Cut the fruit into smaller pieces if necessary and heat with the syrup.

Mix the custard powder and caster sugar with a little water to make a paste.

Mix the custard paste with a little of the hot syrup and add the mixture to the fruit mixture in the saucepan.

Bring the mixture to the boil and, stirring continuously, simmer until the syrup thickens slightly. Spoon the mixture over the Swiss roll.

Whisk together the condensed milk and lemon juice and mix in the cottage cheese. Sprinkle the gelatine over the cold water and leave to sponge. Melt the gelatine over a saucepan with boiling water or in the microwave oven but do not let it come to the boil. Stir the gelatine into the cottage cheese mixture.

Fold in the cream and spread the mixture over the fruit.

Chill until set.

MAKES 1 MEDIUM-SIZED TART.

One-of-everything cottage cheese tart

It's easy to measure the ingredients for this tart because you use one packet or can of everything. It's a great standby for when you have unexpected guests, writes Mrs A.E. Bloom of Pretoria North.

FILLING

1 packet (250 ml) artificial cream, such as Orley Whip, chilled
1 can (398 g) condensed milk
1 tub (250 g) smooth cottage cheese
1 sachet (15 g) gelatine
125 ml (½ c) boiling water

CRUST

1 packet (200 g) Tennis biscuits, crushed
125 ml (½ c) melted butter

TOPPING

1 can (410 g) mixed berries
5 ml (1 t) cornflour

FILLING Whip the artificial cream until stiff.

Mix the condensed milk and cottage cheese until just blended and fold in the artificial cream.

Dissolve the gelatine in the slightly cooled boiling water.

Mix the gelatine with a little of the cottage cheese mixture and add the mixture to the remaining cottage cheese mixture.

CRUST Mix the crushed biscuits and butter.

Press the mixture onto the bottom of a 20 x 30 cm pie dish. Spoon the cottage cheese mixture into the crust and leave the tart in the fridge to set.

TOPPING Drain the berries and thicken the juice with a little cornflour. Cut the tart into squares and serve with the berries.

MAKES 1 LARGE TART.

Carmen says
If you don't have Tennis or Marie biscuits on hand to make a pie crust use cornflakes instead: substitute 750 ml (3 c) cornflakes for a 200 g packet of biscuits. Crush the cornflakes and mix with 80 ml (⅓ c) melted butter or margarine and 20 ml (4 t) sugar.

Peppermint Crisp tart

For this lower-fat variation of popular Peppermint Crisp tart the filling is made with a cocoa and cornflour paste instead of cream. Lee-Ann van Geems of Panorama sent us the recipe.

500 ml (2 c) boiling water
375 ml (1½ c) sugar
30 ml (2 T) butter
125 ml (½ c) cornflour
60 ml (¼ c) cocoa
1 ml (¼ t) salt
200 ml cold water
20 ml (4 t) vanilla essence
1½ packets (300 g) Tennis biscuits
1 large Peppermint Crisp, finely chopped

Grease a 30 x 20 cm glass dish with butter, margarine or nonstick spray.

Heat the boiling water, sugar and butter together until the sugar has dissolved.

Mix the cornflour, cocoa, salt and water together to make a smooth paste.

Stir the cocoa paste into the sugar mixture and, stirring continuously, bring the mixture to the boil. Simmer over low heat until the mixture thickens and is cooked. Remove the mixture from the heat and stir in the vanilla essence.

Arrange a layer of biscuits in the bottom of the glass dish and cover them with a layer of the chocolate mixture. Repeat until everything has been used, ending with a layer of the chocolate mixture. Sprinkle the chopped Peppermint Crisp over the tart and chill until firm.

MAKES 1 LARGE TART.

Instant milk tart

Her family loves this unbaked milk tart, writes Anna Vrey
of Oudtshoorn.

CRUST

1 packet (200 g) Tennis biscuits,
    crushed
60 ml (¼ c) butter or margarine,
    melted

FILLING

1 can (397 g) condensed milk
700 ml boiling water
15 ml (1 T) butter
80 ml (⅓ c) cornflour
45 ml (3 T) iced water
2 extra-large eggs, separated
5 ml (1 t) vanilla essence
pinch salt
ground cinnamon

Grease a 25 cm pie dish with butter, margarine or nonstick spray.

CRUST Mix the crushed biscuits and butter or margarine and press the mixture onto the bottom and along the inside of the pie dish. Chill until needed.

FILLING Bring the condensed milk, boiling water and butter to the boil and simmer gently for 5 minutes.

Blend the cornflour and iced water to make a paste, add the egg yolks and mix well. Stirring continuously with a wire beater, slowly add the cornflour mixture to the milk mixture in a thin stream. Bring the mixture to the boil and simmer until it thickens and is cooked. Remove the mixture from the heat, add the essence and leave it to cool for a few minutes.

Whisk the egg whites and salt until stiff peaks form and fold them into the filling mixture.

Pour the filling into the biscuit crust and chill until firm. Dust with cinnamon.

MAKES 1 LARGE TART.

Caramel fridge tart

Rich, creamy and delicious — this more-ish fridge tart, made with sponge fingers,
a mixture of cocoa, toffees and nuts — is perfect for special occasions.

200 ml milk
30 ml (2 T) coffee liqueur
2 packets (125 g each) sponge fingers
45 ml (3 T) butter
125 ml (½ c) icing sugar, sifted
30 ml (2 T) cocoa powder
2 egg yolks
30 ml (2 T) brandy
375 ml (1½ c) cream, chilled
10 ml (2 t) instant coffee powder
15 ml (1 T) water
8 ml (generous 1½ t) gelatine
½ packet (50 g) pecan nuts,
    chopped
1 packet (125 g) soft toffees
    (Sunrise), cut into small pieces
chocolate curls (see p. 209)
    to decorate

Line the bottom of a 20 x 23 cm loaf tin with wax paper.

Mix the milk and coffee liqueur and dip the sponge fingers in the mixture. Arrange a row of biscuits on the bottom of the loaf tin.

Cream the butter and icing sugar together until light and fluffy. Sift in the cocoa powder, add the egg yolks and beat well.

Add the brandy to the cream and whip until stiff. Fold the cream mixture into the butter mixture.

Dissolve the coffee in the water and sprinkle over the gelatine. Leave until spongy and melt over boiling water or in the microwave oven, taking care not to let it come to the boil. Stir the gelatine mixture into the butter mixture.

Mix the nuts and toffees and set aside. Spoon one-third of the cream mixture over the biscuit layer in the tin and scatter over a layer of the nut mixture.

Repeat the layers twice more, ending with a layer of sponge fingers that have been dipped in the milk mixture. Cover and chill overnight. Carefully loosen the sides with a spatula and turn out onto a serving platter. Peel away the wax paper.

Decorate the tart with chocolate curls.

MAKES 1 MEDIUM-SIZED TART.

Brownies and squares

Brownies, decadently dense and rich.
Cake squares, wholesome, moist and sticky.
Delicious! Brownies and cake squares don't
require much work: in most cases you simply
mix everything together and bake it in an
oven pan or roasting tin. These quick bakes
are a hit with kids and ideal when you have
to rustle up something sweet in a hurry.

Chocolate brownies

These decadent brownies are crisp on top and moist and slightly sticky inside.

400 g dark chocolate
  (at least 55% cocoa solids)
325 g butter
6 extra-large eggs
2 egg yolks
300 g caster sugar
50 g cocoa
80 g cake flour

Preheat the oven to 180 °C. Line a 20 cm cake tin with baking paper so the paper is about 5 cm higher than the rim of the tin. Grease well with butter, margarine or nonstick spray.
Place a mixing bowl over a saucepan with boiling water, taking care the bottom of the bowl doesn't touch the water.
Break the chocolate into squares and put them in the mixing bowl along with the butter. Stirring continuously, heat until the chocolate and butter have melted and the mixture is smooth. Remove the bowl from the saucepan and leave the mixture to cool for a few minutes.
Whisk together the eggs, egg yolks and caster sugar with an electric beater set on high. Beat until the mixture is thick and double in volume. Fold in the melted chocolate mixture. Sift together the cocoa and flour and fold the mixture into the egg mixture, mixing well.
Pour the batter into the prepared tin and bake for 30 minutes or until the batter has risen up the sides of the tin. Leave the brownies to cool completely in the tin. Remove them from the tin by lifting out the paper. Cut into squares.

MAKES 16-20 SQUARES.

Carmen says
Add 160 ml (⅔ c) raisins that have been soaked in 125 ml (½ c) rum to the batter.

Christi's brownies

Towards the end of 2008 celebrity couple Nico and Christi Panagio treated us to Christmas dinner. Christi is mad about brownies so we specially developed this recipe for her in our test kitchen. The brownies are wonderfully moist and chock-a-block with nuts.

125 ml (½ c) butter
310 ml (1¼ c) caster sugar
2 extra-large eggs
5 ml (1 t) vanilla essence
10 ml (2 t) toffee liqueur or Amarula
200 g dark chocolate, melted
270 ml (generous 1 c) cake flour
5 ml (1 t) baking powder
30 ml (2 T) cocoa
300 g Brazil nuts, roughly chopped
icing sugar
ice cream

Preheat the oven to 180 °C and line a 20 cm square cake tin with baking paper. Grease with butter, margarine or nonstick spray.
Cream the butter and sugar together with an electric beater. Beat in the eggs one at a time.
Stir in the vanilla essence, liqueur and chocolate.
Sift the flour, baking powder and cocoa together and fold the mixture into the creamed mixture.
Fold in the nuts and turn the batter into the cake tin. Bake for 25 minutes or until done (see tip).
Leave the brownies to cool in the tin before removing and cutting into squares. Dust with icing sugar and serve for dessert with ice cream if desired.

MAKES ABOUT 12 SQUARES.

Carmen says
To test if the egg and sugar have been beaten long enough, switch off the mixer and lift it: the mixture should leave a trail for 1 to 2 seconds before dissolving into the rest of the mixture.

To test for doneness
Insert a cocktail stick into the brownies; a few moist crumbs should stick to it when removed. If the mixture is still runny leave it to bake for another few minutes.

155

Wholewheat chocolate brownies

Rebecca Looringh van Beeck of Newlands in Cape Town sent us the recipe for these budget-beating brownies. They contain no chocolate, only cocoa, and are packed with fibre, making them a healthier option than traditional brownies.

4 extra-large eggs
500 ml (2 c) soft brown sugar
330 ml (1⅓ c) oil
500 ml (2 c) wholewheat flour
125 ml (½ c) cocoa
5 ml (1 t) baking powder
250 ml (1 c) finely chopped
   nuts (optional)
10 ml (2 t) vanilla essence

Preheat the oven to 180 °C and grease a 25 cm square tin with butter, margarine or nonstick spray. Line the tin with baking paper and grease again.

Whisk the eggs until frothy. Add the sugar and oil and beat until fluffy and pale yellow.

Sift the flour, cocoa and baking powder together and fold the mixture into the egg mixture, alternating with the nuts if using. Add the vanilla essence. Turn the batter into the prepared tin and bake for 50–60 minutes or until firm.

Leave the brownies to cool in the tin before removing and cutting them into squares.

MAKES 20–25 BROWNIES.

Chocolate squares

We've been sent this popular recipe by several readers. The squares, packed with wholesome nuts, oats and coconut, are so easy to make you can leave it to the kids. We baked them in a roasting tin.

DOUGH
500 ml (2 c) cake flour
500 ml (2 c) oats
500 ml (2 c) desiccated coconut
250 ml (1 c) sugar
60 ml (¼ c) cocoa
10 ml (2 t) baking powder
375 g butter

ICING
500 ml (2 c) icing sugar, sifted
50 g butter
25 ml (5 t) cocoa
little hot water

Preheat the oven to 180 °C and grease a 20 x 30 cm oven pan or roasting tin with margarine, butter or nonstick spray.

DOUGH Combine the dry ingredients and rub in the butter until crumbly.

Turn the dough into the prepared pan, pressing it down to level it. Bake for 25–30 minutes or until a testing skewer comes out clean when inserted into the centre of the cake.

ICING Cream the sifted icing sugar and butter together. Add the cocoa and whisk until well blended. Add just enough hot water to the mixture to make a smooth and runny icing.

Drizzle the icing over the cake as soon as it comes out of the oven. Leave the cake to cool until the icing has nearly set. Cut the cake into squares.

MAKES 38–40 SQUARES.

Raisin and oat squares

FILLING
500 ml (2 c) seedless raisins
250 ml (1 c) white sugar
5 ml (1 t) cornflour
250 ml (1 c) water
125 ml (½ c) apple juice

DOUGH
625 ml (2½ c) cake flour
6 ml (1¼ t) bicarbonate of soda
3 ml (generous ½ t) salt
375 g butter
375 ml (1½ c) light brown sugar
1 extra-large egg
5 ml (1 t) vanilla essence
625 ml (2½ c) oats

Preheat the oven to 180 °C. Grease an 18 x 27 cm baking sheet with butter, margarine or nonstick spray. Line the sheet with baking paper and grease again.

FILLING Blitz the raisins with the sugar in a food processor until finely chopped. Pour the mixture in a saucepan.
Mix the cornflour, water and apple juice and add the mixture to the raisins. Stirring continuously, heat the mixture until it comes to the boil. Leave it to cool.

DOUGH Combine the flour, bicarbonate of soda and salt and set the mixture aside.
Cream the butter, add the sugar and beat until the mixture is pale and fluffy. Beat in the egg and vanilla essence. Add the flour mixture and oats, stirring until blended.
Press half the dough into the baking sheet and spread over the filling. Crumble the remaining dough on top. Bake for about 30 minutes or until golden. Leave to cool in the tray before cutting into squares.

MAKES 18–20 SQUARES.

Carmen says
Date and oat squares: Bring 250 g chopped dates, 30 ml (2 T) orange zest and 125 ml (½ c) orange juice to the boil and cook until the dates are soft. Leave the mixture to cool. Mix 200 ml cake flour, 350 ml oats, 175 ml brown sugar and 250 ml (1 c) melted butter together until crumbly. Press half the dough into an 18 cm square baking sheet, spread over the date mixture and crumble the remaining dough on top. Bake at 180 °C for 30 minutes.
MAKES ABOUT 20 SQUARES.

Easy chocolate and oat fingers

You don't even have to mix the ingredients — simply sprinkle them into a cake tin and bake. Quick, easy and delicious!

125 g margarine, melted
250 ml (1 c) oats
125 ml (½ c) chopped glacé cherries
125 ml (½ c) sultanas
50 g milk or baking chocolate
200 ml desiccated coconut
1 can (385 g) condensed milk

Preheat the oven to 180 °C.
Pour the melted margarine into a 20 x 30 cm cake tin and sprinkle over the oats, glacé cherries and sultanas. Grate the chocolate on top and sprinkle over the coconut.
Pour the condensed milk on top and bake for 25 minutes.
Leave the cake to cool in the tin before cutting it into fingers.

MAKES ABOUT 24 SQUARES.

Fruit 'n nut squares

The squares have a lovely caramel taste thanks to the brown sugar.

CRUST

80 ml (⅓ c) firmly packed
   soft brown sugar
90 g butter
310 ml (1⅓ c) cake flour
1 egg yolk

TOPPING

2 extra-large eggs
250 ml (1 c) firmly packed
   soft brown sugar
80 ml (⅓ c) self-raising flour, sifted
125 ml (½ c) sultanas
180 ml (¾ c) halved glacé cherries
310 ml (1¼ c) chopped mixed nuts
250 ml (1 c) desiccated coconut -1ps

Preheat the oven to 180 °C. Grease a 20 x 30 cm cake tin with butter, margarine or nonstick spray. Line the bottom of the tin with baking paper and grease again.

CRUST Heat the sugar and butter in a saucepan over medium heat, stirring until the butter has melted. Remove the saucepan from the heat and add the flour and egg yolk, stirring until mixed. Press the dough onto the bottom of the prepared tin and bake for about 10 minutes or until pale brown. Leave the crust to cool.

TOPPING Beat the eggs and sugar together until pale and fluffy. Gently fold in the sifted flour and stir in the remaining ingredients. Spread the topping over the cooled crust and bake for 30 minutes or until golden. Leave to cool in the tin and cut into squares.

MAKES 24 SQUARES.

Ginger squares

These squares, made with ginger preserve, are soft rather than crisp.

SQUARES

430 ml (1¾ c) cake flour
4 ml (¾ t) baking powder
4 ml (¾ t) bicarbonate of soda
15 ml (1 T) ground ginger
5 ml (1 t) ground cinnamon
2 ml (½ t) grated nutmeg
pinch ground cloves
1 ml (¼ t) salt
1 ml (¼ t) pepper
125 ml (½ c) butter
310 ml (1¼ c) soft brown sugar
1 extra-large egg
1 egg yolk
60 ml (¼ c) honey
180 ml (¾ c) seedless raisins
250 ml (1 c) ginger
   preserve, chopped

ICING

60 ml (¼ c) light brown sugar
30 ml (2 T) milk
30 ml (2 T) butter
5 ml (1 t) vanilla essence
250 ml (1 c) icing sugar

Preheat the oven to 180 °C. Grease an 18 x 27 cm baking sheet with butter, margarine or nonstick spray and line it with greased baking paper.

SQUARES Combine the dry ingredients and set the mixture aside.
Cream the butter and sugar together until the mixture is pale and fluffy. Beat in the egg, egg yolk and honey. Add the flour mixture to the egg mixture and mix well.
Add the raisins and half the chopped ginger preserve. Mix to make a stiff dough and spoon it onto the baking sheet, spreading it evenly. Bake for about 20 minutes or until firm to the touch. Leave to cool completely in the tray.

ICING Heat the brown sugar, milk and butter in a saucepan until the butter and sugar have melted.
Remove from the heat and beat in the vanilla essence and icing sugar. If the mixture is too thick add a few drops of milk; if too thin add a little extra icing sugar. Leave the icing to cool for a few minutes before spreading it over the cake layer. Leave for about 15 minutes so the icing can harden.
Scatter over the remaining chopped ginger preserve.

MAKES ABOUT 20 SQUARES.

Fruit 'n nut squares

Cookies

No home is complete without a supply
of cookies, especially if there are kids
around. I remember how we spent the December
holidays baking cookies so we had a plentiful
supply for visitors over the festive season.
The tins were filled with delights such as
ginger cookies, apricot squares and Romany
creams to name but a few. During the April
holidays the ritual was repeated, with the
added excitement of knowing the cookie tins
were being packed to take to the seaside.

Heart cookies

Isabella Niehaus of Langebaan made these cookies for her 50th birthday and for her son, Taro's 21st. "I cover them with a thick layer of caster sugar which melts and makes them extra delicious," she writes.

125 g butter
150 g caster sugar
1 extra-large egg yolk, whisked
225 g cake flour
finely grated zest of 1 lemon
1 extra-large egg white mixed
   with 15 ml (1 T) water
caster sugar for sprinkling on top

Preheat the oven to 180 °C and grease a few baking sheets.

Cream the butter and caster sugar together until the mixture is light and fluffy. Add the egg yolk and beat well. Add the cake flour and lemon zest and mix well. Knead the dough gently and shape it into a ball. Wrap in clingfilm and chill for about 30 minutes.

Roll out the dough to a thickness of about 5 mm and cut out various shapes and sizes as desired. Arrange the cookies on the prepared baking sheets and brush with the egg white. Sprinkle over a thick layer of caster sugar.

Bake the cookies for 15 minutes or until lightly browned. Leave to cool on the baking sheets for a few minutes before transferring the cookies to a wire rack.

MAKES 20–24 COOKIES

The secret to baking perfect cookies

- Preheat the oven to the required temperature. Put the cookies on a cold baking sheet so they retain their shape.
- When rolling out the dough put it between two layers of clingfilm; this makes the process easier. You don't need any extra flour and the dough is handled less, resulting in cookies with a finer texture.
- If putting more than one baking sheet in the oven at a time, swop them halfway through the baking time to ensure the cookies bake evenly.
- It's important to chill the dough before rolling it out; it will be easier to roll out and cut. Leaving the dough to rest also prevents the cookies shrinking while baking. Ensure the dough is completely covered with clingfilm before putting it in the fridge or it will dry out.
- Coat the cookie cutter with flour while cutting out shapes to prevent dough sticking to it.
- Leave the cookies to cool on the baking sheet for a few minutes before carefully removing them with a spatula. Leave them to cool on a wire rack before putting them in a tin to ensure they stay crisp and retain their flavour. Sprinkling a little cornflour or sugar in the tin absorbs moisture and prevents the cookies going soft. Put a sheet of wax paper between layers of delicate cookies to prevent them breaking.
- Remember, cookies will be soft when they come out of the oven even though they're baked through. To test for doneness turn the cookies over: they should be golden. If they are too dark underneath the baking trays may be old or they were put too close to the bottom element of the oven.

Ginger cookies

Remember, ginger cookies are inclined to spread while baking so space them far apart. We were sent this recipe by Marié Keuler of Florida, who was given it by a neighbour.

250 g butter
450 ml sugar
125 ml (½ c) smooth apricot jam
2 extra-large eggs
10 ml (2 t) bicarbonate of soda
15 ml (1 T) ground ginger
4 x 250 ml (4 c) cake flour
15 ml (1 T) mixed spice

Preheat the oven to 180 °C and grease a few baking sheets with butter, margarine or nonstick spray.
Cream the butter and sugar together until the mixture is light and fluffy.
Add the jam and beat well.
Beat the eggs and add the bicarbonate of soda. Add the egg mixture to the butter mixture, beating until well blended. Add the dry ingredients and mix to make a stiff dough.
Roll the dough into walnut-sized balls and arrange them on the baking sheets, leaving enough room for the cookies to spread. Flatten the balls slightly with your fingers or a fork.
Bake for 10 minutes or until golden and done.
Leave to cool before storing in airtight containers.

MAKES 90 COOKIES.

Stained-glass cookies

Nicolene Botha of Pellissier sent us this recipe early in the nineties. Boiled sweets give the cookies a pretty stained-glass effect in their centres. The cookies make original Christmas tree decorations too — remember to make a hole in each cookie so it can be hung up.

250 ml (1 c) softened butter
250 ml (1 c) sugar
80 ml (⅓ c) honey
60 ml (¼ c) water
2 ml (½ t) salt
3 ml (generous ½ t) baking powder
750 ml (3 c) cake flour, sifted
large packet Sparkles sweets

Preheat the oven to 170 °C and line 2 baking sheets with aluminium foil, shiny side facing down. Do not grease the aluminium foil.
Cream the butter, sugar and honey together until the mixture is light and fluffy. Add the water and beat until smooth.
Sift the salt, baking powder and flour together. Gradually add the dry ingredients to the butter mixture, mixing to form a dough. Knead until the dough feels like soft clay. Chill for about 10 minutes or until firm.
Sort the Sparkles according to colour and put the various colours in strong plastic bags. Use a meat mallet to break the sweets into pieces.
Roll out the dough to a thickness of 3 mm and cut out various shapes. Make a small hollow in the centre of each cookie with your thumb. Put the cookies on a baking sheet and bake them for 5–8 minutes.
Leave them to cool. Fill each cookie hollow with an even layer of sweet splinters, using one colour for each hollow.
Bake the cookies for another 5–8 minutes or until the sweet splinters have melted and begin to bubble. Leave the cookies to cool completely before removing them from the aluminium foil.

MAKES ABOUT 60 COOKIES.

Florentines

These fruit 'n nut cookies, which are very soft when they come out of the oven, are coated with chocolate when cool. The recipe was sent in by Yasmin Ebrahim of Brindhaven.

180 ml (¾ c) sultanas
500 ml (2 c) crushed cornflakes
180 ml (¾ c) roughly chopped unsalted peanuts
180 ml (¾ c) roughly chopped red glacé cherries
180 ml (¾ c) condensed milk
100 g dark chocolate, broken into squares

Preheat the oven to 180 °C and grease a few baking sheets with butter, margarine or nonstick spray. Dust the baking sheets with cornflour and knock out the excess.
Put all the ingredients, except the chocolate, in a mixing bowl and mix well.
Drop teaspoonfuls of the mixture onto the prepared baking sheets, leaving enough room for the cookies to spread.
Bake for 10–15 minutes. Leave the cookies to cool on the baking sheets before carefully removing them with a spatula.
Melt the chocolate in a glass bowl over a saucepan with boiling water or in the microwave oven, stirring occasionally.
Cover the flat sides of the cookies with a layer of the melted chocolate. Using a fork, make patterns in the chocolate. Leave until the chocolate has hardened and use the remaining chocolate to drizzle on top of the cookies.
Store in an airtight container.

MAKES 30–35 COOKIES.

Lemon and cream cheese cookies

Hayley Coelho of Brixton sent us the recipe for these deliciously tangy cookies that are sandwiched with a lemon icing.

COOKIES
250 g butter, softened
90 g cream cheese
250 ml (1 c) sugar
1 extra-large egg yolk
3 ml (generous ½ t) lemon essence
5 ml (1 t) finely grated lemon zest
625 ml (2½ c) cake flour
2 ml (½ t) salt

ICING
250 ml (1 c) icing sugar, sifted
juice and finely grated zest of 1 lemon

Preheat the oven to 180 °C and grease a few baking sheets with butter, margarine or nonstick spray.

COOKIES Cream the butter, cream cheese and sugar together until the mixture is light and fluffy.
Add the egg yolk, lemon essence and lemon zest. Beat until the mixture is light.
Sift the cake flour and salt together and add to the butter mixture. Mix to form a dough.
Using a cookie maker, press flower-shaped cookies onto the prepared baking sheets.
Bake for 7–10 minutes or until the cookies just begin to change colour.

ICING Make a spreadable icing with the icing sugar and lemon juice and zest. Sandwich the cookies with the icing. Leave them until the icing has hardened and store in airtight containers.

MAKES 30 COOKIES.

Walnut and coffee cookies

These cookies are a variation on ever-popular coffee cookies, except they're twice as good as they're sandwiched with a walnut filling and topped with coffee icing.

DOUGH
420 ml cake flour
pinch salt
125 g butter
60 ml (¼ c) sugar
1 extra-large egg
5 ml (1 t) instant coffee powder

FILLING
60 g butter
40 ml (8 t) icing sugar
20 ml (4 t) cocoa
125 g ground walnuts
20 ml (4 t) milk

ICING
375 ml (1½ c) icing sugar
15 ml (1 T) instant coffee powder
about 50 ml boiling water
5 ml (1 t) softened butter

Preheat the oven to 180 °C. Grease a baking sheet with butter, margarine or nonstick spray.

DOUGH Sift the cake flour and salt together and rub in the butter until the mixture resembles breadcrumbs. Add the sugar, egg and coffee powder and mix well. Transfer the dough to a lightly floured surface and knead gently. Roll out to a thickness of 5 mm. Using a 3 cm cookie cutter, cut out dough circles and put them on the prepared baking sheet. Bake the cookies for 10–12 minutes or until done. Leave them to cool on the baking sheet for a few minutes before carefully removing them to a wire rack to cool completely.

FILLING Cream the butter until soft. Add the icing sugar and cocoa and beat until well blended. Stir in the walnuts and milk. Sandwich the cookies together with the filling.

ICING Sift the icing sugar into a glass bowl over a saucepan of boiling water. Mix the coffee powder and boiling water and add the mixture to the icing sugar. Add the butter and beat the mixture until smooth. Add more boiling water if necessary. Dip each cookie halfway into the icing and leave them on a wire rack over a baking sheet to catch the excess icing. Store in an airtight container.

MAKES ABOUT 40 COOKIES.

Coffee and nut macaroons

Macaroons are similar to meringues in that they contain no butter or cake flour. Lionel Slabber of Benoni West sandwiches them with a coffee filling.

MACAROONS
2 large egg whites
125 ml (½ c) caster sugar
150 ml ground walnuts
45 ml (3 T) ground almonds
5 ml (1 t) cornflour
extra walnut pieces

FILLING
50 g butter or margarine
190 g icing sugar
15 ml (1 T) instant coffee powder
15 ml (1 T) vanilla essence

Preheat the oven to 160 °C and line a baking sheet with baking paper. Dust the paper with a little cornflour.

MACAROONS Whisk the egg whites until frothy. Add the caster sugar by the spoonful while beating continuously. Using a metal spoon, fold in the other ingredients, except the walnut pieces.
Drop small teaspoonfuls of the mixture onto the baking sheet, leaving enough space for the macaroons to spread. Decorate each macaroon with a walnut piece and bake them for about 40 minutes or until done. Leave the macaroons to cool on the baking sheet before transferring them to a wire rack.

FILLING Whisk together the ingredients and sandwich the macaroons together with the filling. Store them in an airtight container.

MAKES 15 COOKIES.

Coffee and nut macaroons

Almond coffee cookies

Koti Basson of Nuwerus loves baking these almond cookies, which she sandwiches with a creamy coffee filling.

DOUGH
800 ml cake flour
pinch salt
250 g butter
160 ml (⅔ c) sugar
½ packet (50 g) ground almonds
2 extra-large egg yolks
milk for mixing

FILLING
250 g butter
250 ml (1 c) sugar
250 ml (1 c) milk
30 ml (2 T) strong black coffee

Preheat the oven to 180 °C. Grease a few baking sheets.

DOUGH Sift the cake flour and salt together and rub in the butter until the mixture resembles fine breadcrumbs. Add the sugar and almonds and mix. Whisk the egg yolks and add them to the flour mixture. Add enough milk to make a stiff, manageable dough. Cover the dough with clingfilm and leave it to rest in the fridge for about 30 minutes. Remove the dough from the fridge and leave it until it reaches room temperature.

Roll out the dough on a lightly floured surface to a 3 mm thickness. Cut out shapes with a cookie cutter and put them on the prepared baking sheets. Bake for 7–10 minutes or until the cookies just begin to brown.

FILLING Put the ingredients in a medium-sized saucepan and, stirring continuously, heat slowly until the sugar has melted. Bring the mixture to the boil, reduce the heat and, stirring continuously, simmer until the filling thickens. Leave the filling to cool. Sandwich the cookies together with the cooled filling.

MAKES 40–50 COOKIES.

Nutty balls

These sticky Middle-Eastern cookies are packed with nuts and dried apricots and contain no butter or flour.

2 packets (100 g each) ground almonds
330 ml (1⅓ c) icing sugar
2 ml (½ t) vanilla essence
2 ml (½ t) almond essence
1 egg white, lightly whisked
1 packet (100 g) pistachio or walnuts,
    roughly chopped
24 dried apricots, finely chopped
icing sugar for rolling in

Preheat the oven to 180 °C. Grease a baking sheet with butter, margarine or nonstick spray.
Mix the almonds and icing sugar. Add the vanilla and almond essences and egg white and mix well. Add the nuts and apricots and mix. Shape the mixture into balls and bake them for about 15 minutes or until golden – the cookies will spread slightly. Using two teaspoons, reshape them into balls. Roll the balls in icing sugar while still hot.

MAKES ABOUT 24 BALLS.

Coconut cookies

The mixture for these cookies requires no rolling or cutting out. The dough is shaped into thin rolls that are rolled in caster sugar and coconut, which form a delicious coating around each cookie.

DOUGH
250 g butter or margarine, at
    room temperature
250 ml (1 c) sugar
3 egg whites
500 ml (2 c) desiccated coconut
125 ml (½ c) mixed nuts,
    finely chopped
2 ml (½ t) finely grated lemon zest
750 ml (3 c) cake flour
50 ml milk

TOPPING
1 egg white, lightly whisked
160 ml (⅔ c) desiccated coconut
60 ml (¼ c) sugar

Preheat the oven to 180 °C and grease a few baking sheets with butter, margarine or nonstick spray.

DOUGH Cream the butter and sugar together until the mixture is light and fluffy. **Whisk** the egg whites until stiff peaks form and fold in the coconut, nuts and lemon zest. Fold the egg white mixture into the butter mixture. **Sift** the cake flour and mix it with the coconut mixture, alternating with the milk. Shape the dough into rolls with a 3 cm diameter and chill them until firm.

TOPPING Brush each roll with the lightly whisked egg white. Mix the coconut and sugar and coat each roll in the mixture. Cut each roll into 7 mm rounds. Put the cookies on the prepared baking sheets and bake for 12–15 minutes or until they begin to brown. Leave the cookies to cool on the baking sheet for a few minutes before transferring to a wire rack to cool completely. Store in an airtight container.

MAKES ABOUT 60 COOKIES.

Yummy cookies

These cookies have been aptly named by Mareen de Wet of Villiersdorp because they are simply yummy.

250 g butter
500 ml (2 c) sugar
2 extra-large eggs
5 ml (1 t) vanilla essence
625 ml (2½ c) cake flour
10 ml (2 t) baking powder
pinch salt
500 ml (2 c) desiccated coconut
500 ml (2 c) oats
7 ml (1½ t) bicarbonate of soda,
    dissolved in a little milk
500 ml (2 c) breakfast cereal, such as
    Rice Krispies

Preheat the oven to 180 °C and grease a few baking sheets with butter, margarine or nonstick spray.
Cream the butter and sugar together until the mixture is light and fluffy. Add the eggs one at a time, beating well after each addition. Stir in the vanilla essence.
Sift the cake flour, baking powder and salt together and add to the creamed mixture along with the coconut and oats. Add the bicarbonate of soda and mix well. Add the cereal. Roll the mixture into walnut-sized balls and put them on the prepared baking sheets, flattening them slightly with a fork.
Bake the cookies for 20 minutes. Leave the cookies to cool on the baking sheets before transferring them to a wire rack to cool completely. Store in an airtight container.

MAKES ABOUT 70 COOKIES.

Speculaas

Speculaas are spicy cookies that are traditionally served on 6 December in Holland to celebrate the Festival of St Nicholas. The cookies are traditionally made in speculaas moulds but you can also use an ordinary cookie cutter.

100 g butter, at room temperature
150 ml sugar
1 extra-large egg
grated zest of ½ lemon
500 ml (2 c) cake flour
5 ml (1 t) baking powder
pinch salt
5 ml (1 t) ground cinnamon
2 ml (½ t) grated nutmeg
2 ml (½ t) ground cloves
1 ml (¼ t) ground cardamom
1 ml (¼ t) white pepper
1 ml (¼ t) ground ginger
125 ml (½ c) ground almonds

Cream the butter and sugar together until the mixture is light and fluffy. Beat in the egg and lemon zest.

Sift the flour, baking powder, salt and spices together.

Mix the almonds and half the flour mixture with the creamed mixture. Gradually add the remaining flour mixture, kneading to form a stiff dough. Wrap the dough in clingfilm and chill for 3–4 hours.

Preheat the oven to 200 °C. Grease a few baking sheets with butter, margarine or nonstick spray.

Roll out the chilled dough on a floured surface to a thickness of 5–6 mm. Cut out cookies with a cookie cutter. Alternatively cut out rectangles or shape the dough in greased speculaas moulds. Put the cookies on the baking sheets and bake for 10–15 minutes or until golden. Leave the cookies to cool on the baking sheets for a few minutes before transferring to a wire rack to cool completely.

Store in airtight containers.

MAKES 45 SPECULAAS COOKIES.

Currant and rum cookies

Joy Purdon of Bathurst in the Eastern Cape says these cookies, which are rolled in crushed cornflakes before they're baked, keep well if stored in an airtight container.

225 g butter or margarine
375 ml (1½ c) sugar
2 extra-large eggs
finely grated zest of 1 lemon
2 ml (½ t) rum essence
750 ml (3 c) cake flour
5 ml (1 t) bicarbonate of soda
5 ml (1 t) cream of tartar
2 ml (½ t) baking powder
1 ml (¼ t) salt
180 ml (¾ c) currants
500 ml (2 c) crushed cornflakes

Preheat the oven to 180 °C and grease a few baking sheets with butter, margarine or nonstick spray.

Cream the butter and sugar until the mixture is light and fluffy. Add the eggs one at a time, beating well after each addition. Add the lemon zest and rum essence.

Sift the dry ingredients together and add the currants. Add the flour mixture to the creamed mixture and mix to make a stiff, manageable dough. (If the dough is too soft add a little cake flour.)

Roll the dough into walnut-sized balls and roll the balls in the crushed cornflakes. Arrange the balls on the prepared baking sheets, flattening them slightly with a fork. Bake for 5–7 minutes or until golden. Leave the cookies to cool on the baking sheets before transferring to a wire rack to cool completely. Store in airtight containers.

MAKES 50–55 COOKIES.

Currant and rum cookies

Chocolate chip cookies

American chocolate chip cookies are equally popular in South Africa. This recipe was sent in by Lisa Moody of Cape Town.

160 g butter, at room temperature
160 g margarine, at room temperature
250 ml (1 c) soft brown sugar
250 ml (1 c) white sugar
2 extra-large eggs
10 ml (2 t) vanilla essence
875 ml (3½ c) cake flour
3 ml (generous ½ t) salt
5 ml (1 t) baking powder
500 ml (2 c) dark chocolate chips
250 ml (1 c) chopped pecan nuts

Preheat the oven to 180 °C and grease a few baking sheets.

Beat the butter and margarine together. Add the brown and white sugars and cream the mixture until light and fluffy. Add the eggs one at a time, beating well after each addition. Add the vanilla essence and beat well.

Sift the dry ingredients together and add them to the creamed mixture, alternating with the chocolate chips and nuts. Mix well.

Roll the mixture into walnut-sized balls and arrange them on the prepared baking sheets, leaving enough room for the cookies to spread. Flatten the balls slightly with your fingertips.

Bake the cookies for about 10 minutes or until they just begin to brown. Leave the cookies to cool on the baking sheets for a few minutes before transferring them to wire racks to cool completely. Store the cookies in airtight containers.

MAKES ABOUT 90 COOKIES.

Oat and coconut chocolate chip cookies

She always bakes plenty of these cookies when her grandchildren come to visit, writes Mrs M.B. Lubbe of Yzerfontein.

250 g butter or margarine
375 ml (1½ c) sugar
15 ml (1 T) milk
7 ml (1½ t) vanilla essence
2 extra-large eggs, whisked
375 ml (1½ c) cake flour
7 ml (1½ t) bicarbonate of soda
5 ml (1 t) salt
5 ml (1 t) ground cinnamon
1 ml (¼ t) grated nutmeg
1 ml (¼ t) ground cloves
750 ml (3 c) oats
350 ml desiccated coconut
375 ml (1½ c) chocolate chips

Preheat the oven to 180 °C. Line a few baking sheets with baking paper and grease with butter, margarine or nonstick spray.

Cream the butter and sugar together.

Add the milk, vanilla essence and eggs and beat well.

Sift the cake flour, bicarbonate of soda, salt and spices together. Add the oats, coconut and chocolate chips and mix well.

Drop half-teaspoonfuls of the mixture on the prepared baking sheets, spacing the cookies so they can spread. Bake for 7–10 minutes or until baked through. Leave the cookies to cool on the baking sheets before transferring them to a wire rack to cool completely. Store in airtight containers.

MAKES 120 COOKIES.

Foam cookies

Precilla Jackson sent us the recipe for these economical cookies in 2000. She was given it by her mom, Mrs L.L. van Blerk of East London. The cookies contain no eggs and are perfect for dunking in tea.

4 x 250 ml (4 c) cake flour
pinch salt
250 g butter
375 ml (1½ t) caster sugar
5 ml (1 t) bicarbonate of soda
90 ml (6 T) milk
5 ml (1 t) vanilla essence

Preheat the oven to 180 °C and grease a few baking sheets with butter, margarine or nonstick spray.
Sift the flour and salt together in a large mixing bowl. Rub in the butter until the mixture resembles coarse breadcrumbs.
Mix the caster sugar and bicarbonate of soda in a saucepan. Add the milk and heat slowly until the mixture forms a white foam. Do not let the mixture come to the boil. Remove the saucepan from the heat and add the vanilla essence. Leave the mixture to cool for a few minutes. Add the flour mixture and mix to make a manageable dough.
Roll the dough into balls and arrange them on the baking sheets, flattening them slightly with a fork. Alternatively use a cookie maker. Chill the cookies for 30 minutes. Bake for 10 minutes or until golden and done.
Leave the cookies to cool on the baking sheets before transferring to wire racks to cool completely. Store in airtight containers.

MAKES 100 COOKIES.

Jam cookies

The recipe for these cookies, sent in by Meisie du Toit of Kroondal, is similar to that for popular spoon-handle cookies which appeared in **Wenresepte 1** from Huisgenoot.

500 g butter
250 ml (1 c) sugar
3 extra-large eggs
180 ml (¾ c) condensed milk
7 x 250 ml (7 c) cake flour
35 ml (7 t) baking powder
pinch salt
7 ml (1½ t) cream of tartar
125 ml (½ c) smooth apricot jam
250 ml (1 c) desiccated coconut

Preheat the oven to 180 °C and grease a few baking sheets with butter, margarine or nonstick spray.
Cream the butter and sugar together until the mixture is light and fluffy. Add the eggs one at a time, beating well after each addition. Add the condensed milk, beating until just blended.
Sift the cake flour, baking powder, salt and cream of tartar together. Add the flour mixture to the creamed mixture and mix to make a dough.
Roll the dough into small balls and arrange them on the prepared baking sheets. Using the back of a wooden spoon, make a hole in each cookie and fill it with a little jam. Sprinkle the cookies with the coconut and bake them for 12–15 minutes or until golden.
Leave the cookies to cool before storing in airtight containers.

MAKES 148 COOKIES.

Lemon and coconut squares

Elizabeth Avenant of Montana was given this recipe by a neighbour who worked for a home-industry business. These cookies are similar to apricot squares with a layer of jam and crumb topping.

DOUGH
500 ml (2 c) cake flour
5 ml (1 t) baking powder
5 ml (1 t) ground cinnamon
10 ml (2 t) finely grated lemon zest
30 ml (2 T) desiccated coconut
30 ml (2 T) caster sugar
150 g butter
60 ml (¼ c) honey
30 ml (2 T) lemon juice

FILLING
180 ml (¾ c) desiccated coconut
130 g butter, at room temperature
1 can (397 g) condensed milk
125 ml (½ c) lemon juice

Preheat the oven to 180 °C. Grease an 18 x 28 cm baking sheet with butter, margarine or nonstick spray.

DOUGH Sift the cake flour, baking powder and cinnamon together in a large mixing bowl. Add the lemon zest, coconut and sugar. Set aside.

Heat the butter, honey and lemon juice together in a saucepan until the butter has melted. Leave the mixture to cool to room temperature.

Mix the butter mixture with the dry ingredients to form a dough.

Cut off a third of the dough, wrap in clingfilm and chill until firm.

Press the remaining dough into the greased baking sheet and bake it for about 10 minutes or until pale brown. Leave to cool while preparing the filling.

FILLING Mix the filling ingredients and leave the mixture to stand for about 2 minutes.

Spread the filling evenly over the cookie layer in the baking sheet. Using the coarse side of the grater, grate the remaining dough over the filling.

Bake for 25 minutes or until pale brown. Cut into squares while lukewarm and leave to cool in the tray. Store in an airtight container.

MAKES 20–25 SQUARES.

Sticky oat squares

These squares are similar to old-fashioned crunchies but include Rice Krispies, nuts, coconut and cherries to make them even more delicious. The recipe was sent in by Ursula Bezuidenhout of Austerville.

860 ml cake flour
15 ml (1 T) baking powder
pinch salt
250 ml (1 c) oats
250 ml (1 c) sugar
250 ml (1 c) desiccated coconut
125 ml (½ c) halved glacé cherries
250 ml (1 c) breakfast cereal, such
    as Rice Krispies
250 ml (1 c) chopped nuts
250 g butter
250 ml (1 c) golden syrup
1 extra-large egg, whisked

Preheat the oven to 180 °C. Grease an oven pan or roasting tin with butter, margarine or nonstick spray.

Sift the flour, baking powder and salt together. Add the oats, sugar, coconut, cherries, cereal and nuts and mix well.

Heat the butter and golden syrup together until the butter has melted. Leave the mixture to cool for a few minutes, then add the egg. Slowly add the butter mixture to the dry ingredients, mixing well.

Spoon the mixture into the prepared pan, pressing it down firmly. Bake for 30–35 minutes or until golden and done. Cut into squares and leave to cool in the pan. Remove carefully and store in an airtight container.

MAKES 30 SQUARES.

Muesli cookies

These fibre-rich cookies are quick and easy to make. The recipe was sent in by Itani Magabo of Louis Trichardt.

250 ml (1 c) muesli
250 ml (1 c) desiccated coconut
250 ml (1 c) oats
160 ml (⅔ c) self-raising flour
110 ml soft brown sugar
75 ml (5 T) sesame seeds
15 ml (1 T) honey
1 extra-large egg, whisked
200 g butter or margarine, melted

Preheat the oven to 180 °C and lightly grease a few baking sheets.

Combine the muesli, coconut, oats, self-raising flour, brown sugar and sesame seeds in a large mixing bowl.

Mix the honey, egg and butter and add to the dry ingredients. Drop teaspoonfuls of the mixture onto the prepared baking sheets, leaving enough space for the cookies to spread.

Bake for 7–10 minutes or until golden. Leave the cookies to cool on the baking sheets for a few minutes before transferring them to a wire rack to cool completely. Store in airtight containers.

MAKES ABOUT 100 COOKIES.

Currant and oat triangles

These delicious cookies are similar to traditional crunchies except that currants are added to the mixture. Anja van der Westhuizen of Stellenbosch sent us the recipe.

50 ml golden syrup
450 g butter or margarine
3 extra-large eggs, whisked
4 x 250 ml (4 c) cake flour
2 ml (½ t) salt
15 ml (1 T) bicarbonate of soda
750 ml (3 c) sugar
4 x 250 ml (4 c) oats
250 ml (1 c) currants

Preheat the oven to 180 °C. Grease an oven pan or roasting tin with butter, margarine or nonstick spray.

Heat the golden syrup and butter together until the butter has melted. Leave the mixture to cool. Add the eggs and mix.

Sift the cake flour, salt and bicarbonate of soda together. Add the sugar, oats and currants and mix well. Add the syrup mixture and mix well. Press the mixture into the prepared oven pan.

Bake for 12–15 minutes or until golden and done. Cut into triangles and leave them to cool. Use a spatula to transfer the cookies to a wire rack to cool completely. Store in an airtight container.

MAKES 48 TRIANGLES.

SHORTBREAD

Rich, crisp shortbread is so more-ish it's hard to stop once you've tasted one of these delicious cookies. Served with coffee they're the perfect end to a meal.

In Scotland, where shortbread originates from, it's traditionally served for New Year. Shortbread is basically a variation on shortcrust pastry: butter is rubbed into flour and the mixture is generously sweetened with sugar.

Traditional shortbread doesn't have to be rolled out; simply rapidly press the pastry into a pan and sprinkle it with caster sugar. Alternatively copy the Greeks and Italians by rolling the shortbread in icing sugar as soon as it comes out of the oven.

Lavender shortbread

We were given this recipe by well-known food writer Phillippa Cheifitz. The shortbread is decorated with lavender flowers.

500 ml (2 c) cake flour
60 ml (4 T) cornflour
pinch salt
160 ml (⅔ c) caster sugar
250 g butter, diced
16 lavender flowers
icing sugar for dusting on top

Preheat the oven to 160 °C. Grease 2 loose-bottomed 15–18 cm cake or pie tins with butter.

Sift the flour, cornflour and salt together. Mix in the caster sugar and, using a knife, cut the butter into the flour mixture. Lightly rub the mixture with your fingertips to make a dough. Press the dough into the prepared cake tins. Cut the pastry into 8 wedges and make an even pattern on the surface of the pastry by pricking it with a fork. Insert a lavender flower into each wedge. Chill the pastry in the freezer for at least 15 minutes.

Bake the shortbread for 45 minutes or until pale brown. Cut into wedges and leave to cool completely in the tins. Remove the shortbread from the tins and dust with icing sugar. Scatter fresh lavender flowers over the shortbread if desired.

MAKES 16 SHORTBREAD WEDGES.

Carmen says
The cornflour ensures the shortbread is wonderfully light and crisp. Always use real butter and not margarine to make shortbread.

Milky Bar shortbread

Rabia Khan of Benoni melts a slab of white chocolate and spreads it over the shortbread as soon as it comes out of the oven.

225 g butter, softened
180 ml (¾ c) caster sugar
125 ml (½ c) oil
5 ml (1 t) baking powder
500 ml (2 c) toasted desiccated coconut
5 ml (1 t) vanilla essence
about 700 ml cake flour
1 slab (100 g) white chocolate, broken into squares

Preheat the oven to 180 °C and grease a 22 cm square cake tin with butter, margarine or nonstick spray.
Cream the butter and caster sugar together until the mixture is light and fluffy.
Beat in the oil. Mix in the remaining ingredients, except the chocolate. Add just enough flour to make a stiff, manageable dough. Press the dough into the prepared tin and bake for 20 minutes or until golden.
Melt the chocolate in a glass bowl over a saucepan with boiling water or in the microwave oven. Spread the melted chocolate over the shortbread and cut into squares while still slightly warm. Leave to cool in the tin. Store in an airtight container.

MAKES 24 SQUARES.

Greek shortbread

When we made this recipe sent in by Mrs R. Watson of Pinetown we ate the shortbread straight from the oven they were so delicious.

250 g butter, softened
100 ml caster sugar
1 egg yolk
25 ml (5 t) brandy
5 ml (1 t) vanilla essence
800 ml cake flour
125 g blanched almonds, finely chopped
icing sugar

Preheat the oven to 160 °C. Line 2 large baking sheets with baking paper and grease them with butter, margarine or nonstick spray.
Cream the butter and sugar together until the mixture is light and fluffy. Beat in the egg yolk, brandy and vanilla essence.
Add the flour and almonds and knead to make a soft dough. Roll the mixture into balls, flatten them slightly and arrange them on the baking sheets. Chill for 15–20 minutes.
Bake for 30 minutes or until done but still pale brown. Put the shortbread in a bowl with icing sugar while still hot and leave to cool. Store in an airtight container.

MAKES 85 COOKIES.

VARIATION
Italian shortbread: Add 30 ml (2 T) honey while creaming the butter and sugar. Sprinkle the balls with almond splinters and flatten them slightly. Proceed as described.

Scones and muffins

We'd hardly started school when we had our first baking lesson in my mom's kitchen - making scones! We had to rub in the butter until there was not a speck visible; the mixture had to be as fine as maize meal. We used a bone-handle knife for mixing the dough and when it came to rolling it out the scrubbed top of the kitchen table and roller were ceremoniously dusted with flour and the rolling was done with a firm, but light hand. With the leftover dough we created our own masterpieces, which were then baked to perfection according to our own set of criteria.

My mom was an excellent teacher, especially when it came to figures and explaining. She also knew children don't have much patience, which is why she probably started us on scones. After only 15 minutes in the oven we could enjoy the fruits of our labour.

A proper scone made according to the rubbing-in method rises beautifully and has soft sides and a golden dome. Sometimes it also has stretch marks on the sides, as if the top rose too quickly.

Instant scones, where everything is mixed together in one go, aren't as handsome. They're flatter with a coarser texture, nearly like muffins.

We distinguish between breakfast and tea scones. Breakfast scones are made without sugar and have a coarser texture than tea scones, which are often brushed with a little milk and egg yolk to give them lovely golden crusts.

Breakfast scones

Use the basic recipe and ring the changes by adding savoury ingredients as desired. Breakfast scones should be substantial in size so use a glass to cut them out or fashion them into large, rustic, round shapes.

500 ml (2 c) cake flour
20 ml (4 t) baking powder
3 ml (generous ½ t) salt
60 ml (¼ c) butter
1 extra-large egg
about 160 ml (⅔ c) buttermilk
   or sour milk
milk for brushing on top

Preheat the oven to 220 °C and dust a baking sheet with cake flour.

Sift the cake flour, baking powder and salt together in a large mixing bowl and rub in the butter until the mixture resembles coarse breadcrumbs.

Whisk the egg lightly and add enough buttermilk or sour milk to make up 180 ml (¾ c). Add the egg mixture to the flour mixture and, using an ordinary knife, cut in to make a soft dough. Take care not to overmix the dough.

Gather the dough into a ball and put it on a floured surface. Gently flatten the ball slightly so it's about 2 cm thick and cut out large scones with a glass or large scone cutter. Arrange the scones on the baking sheet, leaving enough space for the scones to rise. Brush with a little milk.

Bake the scones for 10–15 minutes or until they have risen and are golden on top.

MAKES 4–6 LARGE SCONES.

Carmen says

- Scones made with sour milk have a lovely soft texture. If you don't have buttermilk or sour milk on hand add about 10 ml (2 t) lemon juice to fresh milk to sour it.
- To make deliciously rich scones use cream or sour cream instead of buttermilk.

VARIATIONS

Cheese scones: Add 100 ml grated mature Cheddar cheese and 5 ml (1 t) paprika to the dry ingredients for the basic recipe.

Scone wheels with sun-dried tomatoes and feta cheese: Add 80 ml (⅓ c) fresh shredded basil leaves and 4–6 chopped sun-dried tomatoes to the liquid for the basic recipe. Proceed as described. Shape the dough into a large circle and mark off wedges but do not cut all the way through. Crumble 2 rounds of feta cheese over the scones. Bake for about 20 minutes or until done.

Olive scones: Add 125 ml (½ c) chopped calamata olives to the dry ingredients for the basic recipe and proceed as described.

Tea scones: Add 15 ml (1 T) sugar to the buttermilk mixture, roll out the dough to a thickness of about 5–7 mm and cut out scones using a smaller scone cutter than for breakfast scones. Brush the tops with milk and egg.

Tips for baking scones

- Ensure that the butter is thoroughly rubbed into the flour; there should be no visible pieces of butter and the mixture should resemble coarse maize meal.
- Use a spatula or ordinary table knife to mix in the liquid so the dough is handled as little as possible. Mix until the dry ingredients are just moistened and the dough is coarse rather than smooth. Mix only until there is no visible dry flour.
- Don't knead the dough or the scones won't rise to their full extent and will have tunnels inside. The scones will also be tough and coarse.
- Add just the right amount of liquid; the dough must be soft but not slack and must be easy to roll out.
- Don't add too much baking powder or the scones will have an unpleasant aftertaste.
- Scones must be baked at a high temperature so they can rise rapidly to their full extent.

Troubleshooting: Scones

	PROBLEMS	CAUSES
APPEARANCE	Uneven shape	Dough handled carelessly Uneven oven temperature
	Crust pale	Oven temperature too low Work surface overfloured Not brushed with milk Dough too stiff
	Crust too dark	Oven temperature too high Overbaked
	Crust unevenly browned	Uneven oven temperature Shape uneven
	Flat and heavy	Dough too stiff Incorrect proportions used for ingredients Overmixed Oven temperature too low Not baked through
	Low volume	Dough too stiff Not mixed enough
TEXTURE	Hard and dry	Incorrect proportions used for ingredients Overbaked
	Coarse	Dough too slack Oven temperature too low Ingredients not mixed enough
	Dense	Too much or too little leavening agent Incorrect mixing method Poor-quality ingredients
	Crisp and crumbly	Too much shortening
TASTE	Soapy aftertaste	Too much leavening agent

Cheese and apple scones

The apple and oat bran ensure the scones have a much lower GI (glycemic index) than their plain white-flour counterparts. These scones are also suitable for diabetics.

400 ml self-raising flour
5 ml (1 t) baking powder
2 ml (½ t) salt
50 g butter
50 g oat bran
5 ml (1 t) sugar (optional)
125 g Cheddar cheese, diced
1 Granny Smith apple, peeled, cored
  and chopped
100–150 ml buttermilk
extra buttermilk for brushing on top

Preheat the oven to 200 °C. Lightly grease a baking sheet with butter, margarine or nonstick spray, dust it with flour and knock out the excess.

Sift the self-raising flour, baking powder and salt together in a large mixing bowl.

Rub in the butter until the mixture resembles crumbs. Mix in the oat bran and sugar. Add the cheese and apple and mix. Add the buttermilk and mix, taking care not to overwork the dough.

Gather the dough into a ball and roll it out on a floured surface to a thickness of 2–3 cm.

Cut out scones with a 4–5 cm round cookie cutter and put the scones on the prepared baking sheet. Brush the tops with the extra buttermilk and bake them for 15 minutes or until nicely risen and golden.

Serve the scones with grated cheese, tomato jam or fruit spread.

MAKES 15–18 SCONES.

Carmen says
■ For low-GI baking mix the ingredients as little as
possible. The more you handle the ingredients and the
more processed or refined the ingredients you're using
become, the higher the GI will be.

Cheese and apple scones

Quick tea scones

Maureen Theron of Port Elizabeth came across this recipe for feather-light scones while visiting Australia. They're made with only four ingredients and contain no butter or eggs.

750 ml (3 c) self-raising flour
pinch salt
250 ml (1 c) cream
250 ml (1 c) lemonade

Preheat the oven to 220 °C. Lightly grease a baking sheet with oil or nonstick spray and dust it with flour.
Sift the self-raising flour and salt together and make a well in the centre. Mix the cream and lemonade and pour the liquid into the well.
Cut the liquid in with a knife to make a soft dough. Turn the dough out on a floured surface and flatten it slightly.
Cut out scones and arrange them on the baking sheet. Bake for 12–15 minutes or until golden and done. Serve with jam and whipped cream.

MAKES 12 SCONES.

Instant scones

We were treated to these scones at Fynbos guesthouse in Riversdale. The sprinkling of sesame seeds makes them extra special.

500 ml (2 c) cake flour
20 ml (4 t) baking powder
2 ml (½ t) salt
5 ml (1 t) mustard powder
250 ml (1 c) grated Cheddar cheese
1 extra-large egg
80 ml (⅓ c) oil
150 ml milk
paprika and sesame seeds for
   sprinkling on top

Preheat the oven to 220 °C. Grease 12 hollows of a muffin tin with butter, margarine or nonstick spray.
Sift the dry ingredients together and add the cheese. Whisk the egg, oil and milk together and add the mixture to the flour mixture. Cut in lightly with a knife until just mixed. Spoon the mixture into the prepared muffin tin.
Sprinkle with a little paprika and sesame seeds. Bake for 10–15 minutes or until a testing skewer comes out clean when inserted into the centre of the scones.
Serve straight from the oven with butter and jam.

MAKES ABOUT 12 SCONES.

Cheddar and maize meal scones

The maize meal gives these scones a lovely nutty taste.

250 ml (1 c) maize meal
250 ml (1 c) cake flour
15 ml (1 T) baking powder
5 ml (1 t) salt
3 ml (generous ½ t) bicarbonate of soda
1 ml (¼ t) cayenne pepper
250 ml (1 c) buttermilk
90 ml (6 T) melted butter
1 extra-large egg
250 ml (1 c) grated Cheddar cheese

Preheat the oven to 220 °C. Grease 12 hollows of a muffin tin with butter, margarine or nonstick spray. Line the hollows with paper cups.
Mix the dry ingredients in a mixing bowl. Whisk the buttermilk, butter and egg together until blended. Add the dry ingredients to the buttermilk mixture, stirring gently until just blended. Fold in the grated cheese. Fill each muffin tin hollow three-quarters of the way. Bake the scones for about 20 minutes or until a testing skewer comes out clean when inserted into the centre of the scones. Leave the scones to cool in the tin for 10 minutes. Serve lukewarm with butter, cheese and jam.

MAKES 12 SCONES.

MUFFINS

Muffins originate from England where they were originally shaped like a flat bread roll and made with yeast, writes food fundi Peter Veldsman in his book **Teatime Favourites**. During the eighteenth century they became lighter and were halved, toasted and served with butter and jam during winter. In Victorian England muffins were sold by street vendors who rang a bell to advertise their wares. Muffins are divided into breakfast (not very sweet), tea (sweet), savoury and health muffins.

Tips for baking muffins

- Preheat the oven before you start making the muffins.
- Grease the tins, even the nonstick kind.
- Muffins can also be baked in paper cups.
- Scone dough is firm enough to be rolled out while muffins are made with a stiff batter that can be spooned into muffin tin hollows.
- Do not overmix the batter; it should be slightly lumpy. Overmixing the batter will result in muffins with huge holes and crusts that are smooth and flat instead of coarse.
- Muffins can be frozen for three months.

Troubleshooting: Muffins

	PROBLEMS	CAUSES
APPEARANCE	Crust forms a high point	Overmixed Tin too full Uneven heat distribution Batter too stiff Oven too hot
	Pale	Overmixed Oven temperature too low
	Smooth crust	Overmixed
TEXTURE	Hard crust	Overbaked Oven temperature too high
	Risen at an angle with large holes	Overmixed Batter too stiff
	Flat with heavy, dense texture	Not mixed enough Too little raising agent
	Tough	Overmixed Incorrect proportions used for ingredients
	Dry, hard texture	Batter too stiff Overbaked

Savoury muffins

Use the basic savoury muffin mixture to bake various kinds of delicious savoury muffins.

BASIC SAVOURY MUFFINS
500 ml (2 c) cake flour
15 ml (1 T) baking powder
5 ml (1 t) salt
2 extra-large eggs
50 ml oil
150–175 ml milk

Preheat the oven to 180 °C. Grease the hollows of deep muffin tins or line them with paper cups.

Sift the flour, baking powder and salt together. Whisk the eggs, oil and milk together and, using a knife, cut the mixture into the dry ingredients until just mixed. Add any of the ingredients for the variations and mix gently. Spoon the mixture into the muffin tins, filling the hollows three-quarters of the way.

Bake for 20 minutes or until golden and a testing skewer comes out clean when inserted into the centre of the muffins. Serve lukewarm as is or with butter.

MAKES 6–8 MUFFINS.

VARIATIONS

Parmesan, sage and chive: Divide 100 g freshly grated Parmesan cheese in half and add 10 ml (2 t) chopped fresh sage and half a bunch chopped chives to the one half. Fold the mixture into the muffin mixture and spoon it into the muffin tins. Brush with whisked egg and sprinkle over the remaining Parmesan cheese. Put a fresh sage leaf on top of each muffin and bake for 20 minutes.

Bacon, olive, feta and thyme: Fry 125 g chopped bacon until crisp. Add 50 g pitted, chopped calamata olives and leave the mixture to cool. Then add 1 finely crumbled round of feta cheese with 10 ml (2 t) chopped fresh thyme and mix. Gently fold the bacon mixture into the basic muffin mixture and proceed with the basic recipe. Top each muffin with a sprig of fresh thyme before putting them in the oven.

Cheese, onion and rosemary: Sauté 1 roughly chopped red onion and 1 crushed clove garlic in oil until soft. Cover and cool completely. Add 50 g crumbled soft cheese and 10 ml (2 t) finely chopped fresh rosemary. Fold the mixture into the muffin mixture and proceed with the basic recipe.

Quick idea for muffins
Banana muffins: Mash 4 ripe bananas and mix with 200 ml caster sugar and 1 whisked extra-large egg. Stir in 80 ml (⅓ c) melted butter. Sift 375 ml (1½ c) cake flour, 5 ml (1 t) bicarbonate of soda, 5 ml (1 t) baking powder and a pinch of salt together. Add the banana mixture to the dry ingredients and stir until just mixed. Spoon into greased muffin tins and bake at 180 °C for 20 minutes or until done. Leave to cool for a few minutes before turning out.

Health muffins

As the name indicates these substantial muffins are packed with wholesome ingredients. The mixture can be varied as desired and will keep in the fridge for up to two weeks to use as needed. We used large 180 ml (¾ c) muffin cups but you can get similar size muffins by filling the hollows of a deep muffin tin to the top.

125 ml (½ c) oil
2 extra-large eggs
250–375 ml (1–1½ c) soft brown sugar
5 ml (1 t) vanilla essence
250 ml (1 c) milk
250 ml (1 c) plain yoghurt or
    buttermilk
5 ml (1 t) salt
12 ml (2½ t) bicarbonate of soda
750 ml (3 c) wholewheat flour
375 ml (1½ c) cake flour
125 ml (½ c) oats
500 ml (2 c) bran

Preheat the oven to 180 °C and grease 10–12 large muffin cups or the hollows of large muffin tins with butter, margarine or nonstick spray.

Whisk the oil, eggs, sugar, vanilla essence, milk, yoghurt and salt together.

Dissolve the bicarbonate of soda in a little of the egg mixture and add to the remaining mixture.

Combine the dry ingredients and add to the yoghurt mixture, mixing lightly until just blended. Spoon the mixture into the prepared muffin cups, filling them three-quarters of the way.

Bake the muffins for 20–25 minutes or until done. Leave the muffins to cool in the cups for 4 minutes before turning them out carefully. Serve with butter, cheese and conserve.

MAKES 10–12 LARGE MUFFINS.

VARIATIONS

Apricot muffins: Soak 180 ml (¾ c) soft Turkish apricots in tea for a few minutes. Drain and chop them and add to 500 ml (2 c) of the basic mixture. Mix gently and spoon the mixture into large muffin cups. Bake as instructed.

Date and nut muffins: Add 125 ml (½ c) chopped mixed nuts and 125 ml (½ c) finely chopped soft dates to 500 ml (2 c) of the basic mixture. Mix gently and spoon into large muffin cups. Bake as instructed.

Green fig/citron preserve muffins: Add 250 ml (1 c) roughly chopped green fig or citron preserve to 500 ml (2 c) of the basic mixture (first drain the preserves on paper towels). Mix gently and spoon into large muffin cups. Bake as instructed.

Quick idea for muffins
Fruity muffins: These satisfying muffins are ideal for serving with tea or packing into school or office lunchboxes.
Sift 500 ml (2 c) cake flour, 10 ml (2 t) bicarbonate of soda and 10 ml (2 t) salt together. Stir in 310 ml (1¼ c) sugar. Add 125 ml (½ c) desiccated coconut, 125 ml (½ c) chopped raisins, 500 ml (2 c) grated carrots, 250 ml (1 c) grated apples and 125 ml (½ c) chopped nuts.
Whisk 3 eggs, 250 ml (1 c) oil and 5 ml (1 t) vanilla essence together and add to the flour mixture, stirring until just mixed. Spoon into muffin tin hollows and bake at 180 °C for 25 minutes or until done. Cool the muffins in the tin for a few minutes before turning them out.

Breakfast muffins

These muffins have a marmalade centre and are topped with a sprinkling of nuts, seeds and raisins.

MUFFINS
100 g dried apricots, chopped
60 ml (¼ c) orange juice
2 extra-large eggs
140 ml plain yoghurt
100 ml oil
125 ml (½ c) soft brown sugar
625 ml (2½ c) self-raising flour
5 ml (1 t) baking powder
125 ml (½ c) chopped mixed nuts and seeds
12 heaped teaspoons marmalade

TOPPING
50 g soft brown sugar or light caramel sugar
30 ml (2 T) oil
125 ml (½ c) mixture chopped nuts, seeds and raisins

Preheat the oven to 190 °C. Grease a muffin tin with deep hollows or muffin cups with butter, margarine or nonstick spray.

MUFFINS Soak the apricots in the orange juice. Whisk the eggs, add the yoghurt, oil and sugar and beat well. Add the soaked apricots along with the orange juice.
Sift the self-raising flour and baking powder together and add to the apricot mixture along with the seed mixture. Mix gently until just blended and still slightly lumpy.
Spoon the mixture into the greased muffin tin hollows. Make a slight hollow in each muffin and spoon a little marmalade into each.

TOPPING Mix all the ingredients together and sprinkle over the muffins. Bake for 25–30 minutes or until nicely risen and a testing skewer comes out clean when inserted into the muffins. Serve lukewarm with butter.

MAKES 6–8 LARGE MUFFINS.

Carmen says
■ Substitute apricot jam for the marmalade if desired.

Orange and Rooibos upside-down muffins

Make these delicious muffins for a special breakfast or tea party, suggests Mrs K Wilke of Wolmaransstad.

50 ml honey
50 ml light brown sugar
1 orange, unpeeled, thinly sliced and quartered
500 ml (2 c) cake flour
20 ml (4 t) baking powder
2 ml (½ t) salt
60 ml (¼ c) white sugar
1 extra-large egg
50 ml oil
200 ml strong Rooibos tea
20 ml (4 t) orange juice
finely grated zest of 1 orange

Preheat the oven to 190 °C and grease 12 hollows of a muffin tin with butter, margarine or nonstick spray.
Mix the honey and brown sugar and divide the mixture among the muffin tin hollows. Put the orange slices on top of the honey mixture. Sift the flour, baking powder and salt together.
Add the white sugar to the dry ingredients and mix. Whisk the egg and oil together. Add the tea and orange juice and zest and mix. Add the egg mixture to the dry ingredients and stir until just mixed.
Spoon the batter into the muffin tin hollows and bake for about 20 minutes or until a testing skewer comes out clean when inserted into the centre of the muffins. Serve upside-down, with the orange slices facing up.

MAKES 12 MUFFINS.

Quick idea for muffins
Date muffins: This muffin mixture can be made a day in advance and stored in the fridge. Mix 500 ml (2 c) cake flour, 500 ml (2 c) milk, 125 ml (½ c) oil, 3 ml (generous ½ t) salt, 10 ml (2 t) bicarbonate of soda, 375 ml (1½ c) crushed All Bran flakes, 250 ml (1 c) caster sugar, 250 ml (1 c) chopped dates and 2 extra-large eggs. Spoon into greased muffin tins and bake at 180 °C for 15–20 minutes or until done.

Apple and cinnamon muffins

The recipe for deliciously spicy muffins comes from Anneka Manning's book, **Good Food.**

580 ml (2⅓ c) cake flour
15 ml (1 T) baking powder
10 ml (2 t) ground cinnamon
180 ml (¾ c) firmly packed soft
   brown sugar
2 Golden Delicious apples, peeled,
   cored and diced
180 ml (¾ c) sultanas
125 g butter, melted and cooled
2 extra-large eggs, lightly whisked
180 ml (¾ c) milk

Preheat the oven to 190 °C and grease 12 hollows of a muffin tin with butter, margarine or nonstick spray.

Sift the flour, baking powder and cinnamon together in a large mixing bowl. Add the brown sugar, apples and sultanas. Lightly whisk the melted butter, eggs and milk together and fold the mixture into the dry ingredients with a large metal spoon, taking care not to overmix the ingredients; the flour should just be moistened.

Spoon the mixture into the prepared muffin tin hollows and bake for 12–15 minutes or until a testing skewer comes out clean when inserted into the centre of the muffins. Serve with butter.

MAKES 12 MUFFINS.

Banana muffins

Date muffins

Rusks

Rusks are the ideal any-time snack:
they're great for dunking with your early-
morning coffee, packing into school and
office lunchboxes or stilling late-night
hunger pangs. In fact no home should be
without a supply of homemade rusks.

Carmen says
- Brush melted butter between the balls of dough when packing them in the tins; this will make them easier to separate once they're baked.
- Keep the tin at an angle when packing it with the balls of dough; this will ensure they fit snugly into the pan.
- Leave the rusks to cool completely before breaking or cutting them into pieces or they will crumble and the sides will be doughy. It's preferable to break rather than cut rusks into pieces; use a fork for this task.
- If cutting the rusks into fingers use a serrated bread knife or an electric knife or the rusks will crumble, especially if they contain plenty of roughage.
- When drying the rusks arrange them in a single layer on a baking sheet, leaving a little space between them. Rusks that haven't been completely dried won't be crisp and delicious, nor will they last very long.

Bran and seed rusks

These are my favourite kind of rusks — they're packed with bran and seeds and not too rich. This is probably the easiest way to ensure your family enjoys wholesome goodness. Vary the bran and seeds in this recipe as desired and according to what you have on hand.

1 kg self-raising flour
15 ml (1 T) baking powder
5 ml (1 t) salt
160–250 ml (⅔–1 c) sugar
250 ml (1 c) wheat bran
250 ml (1 c) oat bran
250 ml (1 c) oats
375 ml (1½ c) seeds, such as linseed
   and sesame, pumpkin and
   sunflower seeds
125 ml (½ c) sultanas or cranberries
2 extra-large eggs, lightly whisked
625–750 ml (2½–3 c) buttermilk
200–400 g butter or margarine,
   melted and cooled

Preheat the oven to 180 °C and grease a large oven pan, roasting tin that comes with the oven or 3 loaf tins with butter, margarine or nonstick spray.

Sift the self-raising flour, baking powder and salt together in a large mixing bowl.

Add the sugar, bran, oats, seeds and sultanas and mix well.

Whisk the eggs, buttermilk and melted butter or margarine together and add the mixture to the dry ingredients. Mix well.

Spoon the mixture into the pan, roasting tin or loaf tins, spreading it evenly.

Bake for 45 minutes or until a testing skewer comes out clean when inserted into the centre of the rusks. Leave the rusks to cool in the pan for 5 minutes before carefully turning them out onto a wire rack to cool completely. Cut into neat fingers and leave in a 90 °C oven until completely dry. Store the rusks in airtight containers.

MAKES ABOUT 100 RUSKS.

Carmen says
To make rusks for diabetics substitute Sugalite for half the sugar.
Use the lesser amount of shortening, substituting it with low-fat margarine.

HOW TO DRY RUSKS

Preheat the oven to 90 °C. Arrange the rusks on large baking sheets and leave them in the oven for 3–4 hours or until completely dry inside.

Nutty wholewheat rusks

These rusks are ideal if you have a lactose or egg intolerance. They contain pecan nuts that give both flavour and texture.

375 ml (1½ c) cake flour
10 ml (2 t) baking powder
5 ml (1 t) bicarbonate of soda
5 ml (1 t) salt
500 ml (2 c) wholewheat flour
180 ml (¾ c) sugar
375 ml (1½ c) bran flakes
   (All Bran flakes)
250 ml (1 c) oats
250 ml (1 c) chopped pecan nuts
180–250 g margarine, melted
325 ml (1⅓ c) water
15 ml (1 T) vinegar

Preheat the oven to 180 °C and grease an oven pan or roasting tin with butter, margarine or nonstick spray.

Sift the flour, baking powder, bicarbonate of soda and salt together in a large mixing bowl. Add the remaining dry ingredients and nuts and mix well.

Whisk the margarine, water and vinegar together and add to the dry ingredients. Mix well and turn the dough into the prepared pan, spreading it evenly.

Bake for 50–60 minutes or until golden and a testing skewer comes out clean when inserted into the centre of the rusks. Turn out onto a wire rack and leave to cool. Cut into neat fingers.

Leave in a 90 °C oven until completely dry, cool and store in airtight containers.

MAKES 60–80 RUSKS.

> Carmen says
> Substitute oat bran for 125 ml (½ c) of the bran flakes or some of the oats. Use seeds or cranberries instead of the pecan nuts if desired.

Aniseed rusks

These rusks are similar to Italian biscotti.

125 g butter
250 ml (1 c) sugar
45 ml (3 T) brandy
5 ml (1 t) aniseed, crushed
3 extra-large eggs
750 ml (3 c) cake flour
10 ml (2 t) baking powder
250 ml (1 c) chopped walnuts,
   almonds or pecan nuts

Preheat the oven to 190 °C and grease 2 baking sheets with butter, margarine or nonstick spray.

Cream the butter and sugar together until light and fluffy. Beat in the brandy and aniseed. Add the eggs one at a time, beating well after each addition.

Sift the flour and baking powder together and fold into the butter mixture, alternating with the nuts. Chill the dough for 2 hours.

Divide the dough into 4 equal parts and shape each part into a long oval. Put 2 ovals on each baking sheet.

Bake for about 20 minutes or until golden and a testing skewer comes out clean when inserted into the centre of the rusks.

Leave to cool on the baking sheets. Cut into diagonal 2 cm thick slices.

Arrange the slices in a single layer on the baking sheets and bake at 190 °C for about 10 minutes or until completely dry. Leave to cool and store in airtight containers.

MAKES ABOUT 60 RUSKS.

Nutty wholewheat rusks

Super rusks

These rusks are made with a sponge so require more work than rusks made with, for instance, baking powder. It's worth the effort though as the rusks are deliciously light.

SPONGE
20 ml (4 t) active dry yeast (not instant yeast)
45 ml (3 T) sugar
750 ml (3 c) lukewarm water
45 ml (3 T) maize meal

RUSKS
225 g hard margarine
30 ml (2 T) butter
500 ml (2 c) sugar
750 ml (3 c) milk
3 extra-large eggs, whisked
2.25 kg cake flour
15 ml (1 T) salt
sugar water for brushing

SPONGE Mix the yeast, 15 ml (1 T) of the sugar and 125 ml (½ c) of the lukewarm water and leave the mixture to stand for 20 minutes. Pour it into a large jar and stir in the remaining sugar and water and the maize meal. Seal the jar and leave it to stand for about 30 minutes or until the mixture has formed air bubbles.

RUSKS Meanwhile heat the margarine, butter, sugar and milk until the mixture is lukewarm. Stir until the sugar has dissolved and the margarine has melted. In a large mixing bowl mix the sponge and lukewarm milk mixture. Add the eggs and 900 g of the flour and mix to form a slack batter. Cover the bowl with clingfilm and a warm blanket. Leave the dough to rise for 1–1 ½ hours.

Add the remaining flour and salt to the dough and mix until if forms a manageable dough. Knead the dough for 15 minutes or until it is smooth and elastic. Cover the dough and leave it to rise again for 1–1 ½ hours or until it is double in volume. Meanwhile grease 3 large (28 x 9 cm) loaf tins.

Preheat the oven to 200 °C. Shape the dough into small balls (do not knock down the dough) and arrange them in the greased tins, packing them tightly together.

Cover the tins with clingfilm and a warm blanket and leave the rusks to rise for 50–90 minutes or until the tins are full.

Bake the rusks in the preheated oven for 20 minutes. Reduce the oven temperature to 190 °C and bake the rusks for another 25–30 minutes. Brush the rusks with sugar water as soon as they come out of the oven. Remove them from the tins and leave them to cool. Separate and leave the rusks in a 90 °C oven to dry completely.

MAKES ABOUT 100 RUSKS.

Bran buttermilk rusks with semolina

Grace Barrett of Montagu writes that she once accidentally added semolina to her usual rusk mixture. Now she never bakes rusks without it.

750 g margarine
4 x 250 ml (4 c) sugar
15 ml (1 T) salt
3 small packets (500 g each) self-raising flour
250 ml (1 c) desiccated coconut
1 packet (500 g) semolina
8 x 250 ml (8 c) bran
35 ml (7 t) baking powder
1 litre (4 c) buttermilk
5 extra-large eggs

Preheat the oven to 180 °C and grease 2 oven pans or roasting tins.

Heat the margarine and sugar together until melted.

Combine the salt, self-raising flour, coconut, semolina, bran and baking powder.

Add the margarine mixture and mix well.

Whisk the buttermilk and eggs together and add the mixture to the flour mixture, stirring until well blended.

Turn the mixture into the prepared tins, spreading it evenly, and bake for 30 minutes. Reduce the temperature to 160 °C and bake for another 20 minutes or until done and a testing skewer comes out clean when inserted into the centre of the rusks.

Leave the rusks to cool slightly in the tins. Turning them out onto a wire rack to cool completely. Separate and leave the rusks in a 90 °C oven to dry completely.

MAKES 120 RUSKS.

Egg-free buttermilk rusks

These white buttermilk rusks, made with boiling water, contain no eggs, making them ideal for those who are allergic to eggs.

1.5 kg self-raising flour
10 ml (2 t) cream of tartar
7 ml (1½ t) salt
15 ml (1 T) aniseed (optional)
200 ml yellow sugar
200 ml white sugar
375 g butter or margarine
250 ml (1 c) boiling water
500 ml (2 c) buttermilk

Preheat the oven to 180 °C and grease 4 loaf tins.

Combine the self-raising flour, cream of tartar, salt and aniseed in a large mixing bowl. Make a well in the centre of the mixture.

Mix the yellow and white sugars, butter or margarine and boiling water, stirring until the butter or margarine has melted. Add the buttermilk.

Pour the liquid into the well in the dry ingredients and mix to make a smooth dough. Turn the dough out onto a floured surface and knead until completely smooth and elastic.

Roll pieces of dough into golf ball-size balls and put them in the greased tins, packing them tightly together.

Bake for 40 minutes or until the rusks have risen and a testing skewer comes out clean when inserted into the centre of the rusks. Leave the rusks to cool in the tins for a few minutes before turning them out onto a wire rack to cool completely. Separate the rusks or cut them into fingers and leave in a 90 °C oven until completely dry. Store in airtight containers.

MAKES 60–80 RUSKS.

Farm-style rusks

This is one of her standby recipes, Mrs E van der Linde of Pretoria North wrote in 2001. She was given the recipe many years ago by a friend from Groblersdal.

3 kg cake or white bread flour
15 ml (1 T) salt
2 sachets (10 g each) instant yeast
250 ml (1 c) sugar
250 g butter or margarine
1 litre (4 c) milk
2 extra-large eggs, whisked
500 ml (2 c) mashed potato
about 500 ml (2 c) lukewarm water

Grease three 24 cm square cake tins with butter, margarine or nonstick spray.

Sift the flour and salt together. Sprinkle over the instant yeast and mix well.

Heat the sugar, butter or margarine and milk together in a large heavy-bottomed saucepan until the sugar and butter have melted. Remove from the heat and leave to cool. Add the egg and mashed potato to the milk mixture and mix well.

Add the milk mixture to the dry ingredients and mix well, adding just enough lukewarm water to make a dough that is easy to knead.

Knead the dough until smooth and elastic and it no longer sticks to your hands. Lightly brush the dough with oil and leave it to stand for about 15 minutes. Knock down the dough, break off pieces and roll into balls. Arrange the balls in the prepared tins. Cover the tins and leave the dough to rise in a warm place until doubled in volume.

Preheat the oven to 180 °C. Bake for 40–60 minutes or until a testing skewer comes out clean when inserted into the centre of the rusks. Turn out the rusks on a wire rack and leave them to cool. Separate the rusks and arrange them on baking sheets and leave in a 90 °C oven to dry completely. Store in airtight containers.

MAKES 120 RUSKS.

193

Koeksisters, cream puffs, pancakes and flapjacks

Koeksisters with tea, pancakes on a cold, rainy day and cream puffs for dessert — who can say no to these irresistible traditional treats?

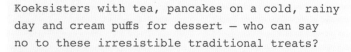

Lemony koeksisters

A dash of lemon juice added to the syrup for koeksisters turns this South African delicacy into a special treat. Charmaine Bothma of Elarduspark sent us the recipe.

SYRUP
6 x 250 ml (6 c) sugar
600 ml water
300 ml lemon juice
zest of 3 lemons, cut into strips

DOUGH
5 x 250 ml (5 c) cake flour
50 ml (10 t) baking powder
2 ml (½ t) salt
60 ml (4 T) butter
2 extra-large eggs
375 ml (1½ c) cold water
 or buttermilk
enough oil for deep-frying

SYRUP Heat the sugar and water over low heat, stirring until the sugar has dissolved. Bring the mixture to the boil and simmer gently for about 10 minutes. Add the lemon juice and zest. Pour the syrup into a large bowl and chill it in the freezer. (The syrup can be made a day in advance and left in the fridge to ensure it's ice cold.)

DOUGH Sift the cake flour, baking powder and salt together and rub in the butter until the mixture resembles fine breadcrumbs. Whisk the eggs and water or buttermilk together and, using a knife, cut the mixture into the flour mixture until well blended and a soft dough forms.

Knead the dough for 4–5 minutes or until smooth and elastic. Put it in a floured bowl and chill for at least 30 minutes.

Roll out the dough on a floured surface until 5 mm thick and cut into 80 x 40 mm rectangles. Cut each rectangle into 3 strips but do not cut all the way through at the top. Loosely plait the strips and press the ends together. Cover the pastry plaits with a damp cloth to prevent them drying out.

Heat the oil for deep-frying until very hot. Fry a few koeksisters at a time until golden on the outside and cooked inside. Remove from the oil with a slotted spoon and immediately dunk them in the ice-cold syrup, submerging them so they can absorb the syrup. Drain the koeksisters on a wire rack. Store uncovered in the fridge for a day or two. Alternatively freeze the koeksisters in airtight containers; they defrost quickly and will be ready to serve 5–10 minutes after removing them from the freezer.

MAKES 50–60 KOEKSISTERS.

Troubleshooting: Koeksisters

	PROBLEMS	CAUSES
	Oil foams	Oil too cold Dry flour or pieces of dough that break off in the oil Too much water or egg in the recipe
APPEARANCE	Uneven colour	Oil too hot
	Dull crust with crystals	Syrup not acidic enough
TEXTURE	Dense	Dough too firm Not puffed enough or too little leavening agent
	Doughy in parts	Oil too hot and koeksisters removed before cooked through
	Soft	Syrup used with koeksisters made with baking powder not ice cold
	Oily	Oil too cold Dough too slack Not drained enough Dough tooo rich
TASTE	Too sweet	Syrup not acidic enough

Coconut balls

These Indian treats, made with powdered milk, are rapidly deep-fried, dunked in a lemon syrup and rolled in coconut. They're similar to Malayan koesisters.

SYRUP
500 ml (2 c) sugar
300 ml boiling water
100 ml lemon juice
thick strip lemon zest

DOUGH
500 ml (2 c) powdered milk
  (not coffee creamer)
180 ml (¾ c) self-raising flour
about 115 ml milk
oil for deep-frying
desiccated coconut for rolling in

SYRUP Slowly heat the sugar, water and lemon juice together until the sugar has melted. Bring the mixture to the boil and simmer for 2 minutes. Leave to cool to room temperature and chill until ice cold, preferably overnight.

DOUGH Sift the powdered milk and self-raising flour together and add the milk. Mix to form a stiff dough. Roll pieces of the dough into small balls.
Heat enough oil for deep-frying in a deep-fryer or saucepan until very hot. Fry the balls until puffed, cooked and golden. Remove with a slotted spoon and immediately dunk them in the ice-cold syrup. Submerge the balls for a few seconds so they can absorb the syrup. Put the balls on a wire rack to drain and immediately roll them in coconut.

MAKES 40 BALLS.

Spitsroken

Marié du Plessis of Gardens in Cape Town was given this Dutch recipe by her sister about 40 years ago. Teaspoonfuls of puff (choux) pastry are deep-fried in oil and then dunked in syrup.

SYRUP
5 x 250 ml (5 c) sugar
1 litre (4 c) water
7 ml (1½ t) almond essence

PASTRY
300 ml water
125 g butter
300 ml cake flour
pinch salt
4 extra-large eggs
oil for deep-frying

SYRUP Slowly heat the ingredients for the syrup until the sugar has dissolved. Stir frequently. Bring the mixture to the boil and simmer rapidly for 15–20 minutes or until syrupy. Leave to cool to room temperature and chill until ice cold.

PASTRY Bring the water and butter to the boil and heat until the butter has melted. Reduce the heat to very low and add the flour and salt at once, stirring rapidly with a wooden spoon until the mixture forms a ball in the saucepan. Remove the saucepan from the heat and leave the paste to cool. Beat in the eggs one at a time, beating well after each addition.
Deep-fry half-teaspoonfuls of the pastry in hot oil until golden. (It takes 10–15 minutes.) Remove the puffs with a slotted spoon and immediately dunk them in the ice-cold syrup. Submerge the puffs for a few seconds so they can absorb the syrup. Remove the puffs with a slotted spoon and drain them on a wire rack over a tray.

MAKES 50–60 BALLS.

VARIATION
Instead of dunking the puffs in syrup dust them generously with icing sugar.

Puffs and éclairs

Choux pastry is used to make delectable treats such as cream puffs and éclairs. To make éclairs, 10 cm long fingers of pastry are piped onto a baking sheet.

250 ml (1 c) water
115 g butter
250 ml (1 c) cake flour
1 ml (¼ t) salt
4 extra-large eggs
250 ml (1 c) cream, whipped
1 slab (100 g) chocolate, melted

Carmen says
Baked cooked puffs will last well in an airtight container for up to three weeks. They also freeze well for up to one month.

Preheat the oven to 200 °C and grease a baking sheet with butter, margarine or nonstick spray.

Bring the water and butter to the boil in a medium-sized saucepan. Add the flour and salt at once, stirring the mixture with a wooden spoon until it forms a paste and no longer sticks to the bottom or inside of the saucepan. Remove the saucepan from the heat and leave the paste to cool for about 5 minutes.

Add the eggs one at a time, beating well after each addition. The pastry must be stiff and shiny – use only 3 eggs if necessary. Leave the choux pastry to cool.

Drop teaspoonfuls of the choux pastry on the baking sheet, spacing the puffs at 4 cm intervals. Alternatively pipe the pastry onto the baking sheet.

Sprinkle them with a little water to create steam. Bake for 15 minutes, reduce the temperature to 180 °C and bake them for another 15 minutes. Leave to cool.

Cut a slit in each puff just big enough so you can insert a piping-bag nozzle into the slit. Fill the puffs with the whipped cream and dip them in melted chocolate. Leave until the chocolate has hardened before serving.

MAKES ABOUT 50 PUFFS.

VARIATIONS
Fill the puffs with lemon curd mixed with a little whipped cream. Alternatively fill them with confectioner's custard (see p. 139).
To make savoury puffs fill them with herbed cottage cheese or mascarpone cheese, smoked salmon or snoek and thin slices of cucumber.

Troubleshooting: Puffs

	PROBLEMS	CAUSES
APPEARANCE	Pastry falls flat in the oven	Batter too slack
	Puffs don't puff up during the baking process	Too much water, batter too slack to retain steam, too much water has evaporated so not enough left to form steam Too little or too much shortening Not beaten long enough after adding eggs
	Poorly formed hollow	Batter not heated long enough Eggs added too soon Too much shortening Not baked long enough
	Shortening runs out during the baking process	Too little liquid due to excessive moisture evaporation Proportion of shortening to flour too great after moisture has evaporated
	Pastry has a split appearance after the eggs have been added	Too much moisture has evaporated

PANCAKES

A runny batter is used to make both pancakes and flapjacks. The difference between them is in the consistency of the batter, their shape and how much leavening agent is used. A very runny batter, the consistency of thick cream, is used to make pancakes while flapjack batter is slightly thicker.

Pancakes

Pancakes with cinnamon sugar are the best kind in my book. But pancakes can be served in numerous ways and are the ideal wraps for sweet or savoury fillings.

THIN PANCAKE BATTER
2 large eggs
200 ml milk
20 ml (4 t) oil
5 ml (1 t) lemon juice or brandy
250 ml (1 c) cake flour
1 ml (¼ t) salt
200 ml water
cinnamon sugar for sprinkling on top

Whisk the eggs. Add the milk, oil, lemon juice or brandy, flour and salt and beat until the mixture is smooth. Add the water and mix well. Leave the batter to stand for at least 30 minutes. Pour a little oil in a pan and heat the pan until very hot. Pour out the excess oil and spoon just enough batter into the pan to cover the bottom. Tilt the pan in all directions so the batter covers the entire surface of the pan. Heat the pancake until the sides begin to lift slightly. Flip the pancake and heat until the other side is cooked and brown. Stack the pancakes on top of each other over a saucepan with boiling water. Sprinkle with cinnamon sugar and serve with lemon slices or fill them with a sweet or savoury filling (see below).

MAKES 15 PANCAKES.

Carmen says
- When filling pancakes ensure they are cold before adding the filling.
- Pancakes freeze well. Put a sheet of wax paper between the pancakes and stack them on top of each other.

SWEET FILLINGS
Fill the pancakes with lemon curd or flavoured cream and serve them with any of the fruit compotes such as citrus vanilla, ginger strawberry, poached fruit or spicy fruit (see p. 211). Fresh fruit such as strawberries with melted chocolate are also delicious.

SAVOURY FILLINGS
Spread the pancakes with a little herbed cottage cheese and fill with any of the following:
- Fried chicken livers with onions, mushrooms, grapes and a little sherry.
- Braised sheep's kidneys with bacon and onion.
- Bolognese sauce. Cover the pancakes with a white sauce, sprinkle with cheese and bake them.
- Parma ham, Brie cheese and rocket.
- Smoked salmon, caviar and sour cream.
- Stir-fried chicken and vegetables with teriyaki sauce.

Pancakes filled with Parma ham, Brie cheese and rocket

Carmen says

- To make thin pancakes use a runny batter so it spreads quickly, forming a thin layer on the surface of a hot pan. Batters without leavening agents are usually thinner.
- The batter for thick pancakes is less runny and contains baking powder and stiffly whisked egg whites that are folded in, making it similar in consistency to flapjack batter.
- Use a heavy-based saucepan, heat it well and brush the bottom with good-quality oil. Pour out the excess oil. Greasing the pan again should not be necessary.
- The pan must be very hot when the batter is added. Use a measuring cup or soup ladle to pour the batter into the pan, adding just enough batter each time.
- Shake the pancake once the edges are firm and dry. Use a spatula or egg lifter to turn the pancake or, if you're feeling brave, flip it in the air. Leave the pancake to brown on the other side. Slide the cooked pancake onto a hot plate.
- Keep pancakes warm by stacking them on top of each other over a saucepan of boiling water. Put a sheet of wax paper between the pancakes. Pancakes become tough if kept warm in the oven.
- To make softer pancakes add brandy or lemon juice to the batter.

Bazaar pancakes

When baking pancakes in large quantities there's no time to struggle with batter that sticks to the bottom of the pan. That's when a recipe that contains plenty of oil comes in handy. The batter can be made in advance and kept in the fridge until needed.

5 extra-large eggs
1.25 litres (6 c) milk
5 ml (1 t) salt
500 ml (2 c) oil
15 ml (1 T) vanilla essence
4 x 250 ml (4 c) self-raising flour
oil for baking
cinnamon sugar

Whisk the eggs, milk, salt and oil together. Add the vanilla essence. Add the self-raising flour a little at a time, beating well until the mixture is smooth. Leave the batter to rest for at least 30 minutes.

Brush a heated pan with a little oil. Ladle just enough batter into the pan to cover the surface. Turn the pancake when bubbles appear on the surface. Bake until light-brown spots appear on both sides. Sprinkle with cinnamon sugar and roll up.

MAKES ABOUT 40 PANCAKES.

Gourmet pancakes

In 2007 we developed the recipe for these delicious pancakes. The pancakes are fairly thick but light and puffy, nearly like flapjacks. Pile them on top of each other in threes and serve with cream and a cherry sauce.

THICK PANCAKE BATTER
3 large eggs, separated
250 ml (1 c) cake flour
7 ml (1½ t) baking powder
200 ml milk
1 ml (¼ t) salt
oil for baking

CHERRY SAUCE
1 can (400 g) black cherries
60 ml (¼ c) sugar
30 ml (2 T) cornflour
30 ml (2 T) brandy
2 ml (½ t) almond essence

DECORATION
whipped cream
fresh cherries
chocolate curls or shavings
   (see p. 209)
fresh mint leaves

PANCAKES Whisk the egg yolks, flour and baking powder together and gradually add the milk, beating until the mixture is smooth and thick.
Whisk the egg whites and salt together until stiff peaks begin to form.
Fold the egg whites into the batter and leave it to stand for at least 30 minutes.
Pour a little oil into a pan and heat until very hot. Pour out the excess oil and spoon 125 ml (½ c) of the batter into the pan. Bake the pancakes.

CHERRY SAUCE Drain the cherries and reserve the syrup. Add enough water to the syrup to make up 250 ml (1 c). Pour the liquid into a saucepan and add the sugar and cornflour. Bring the mixture to the boil over low heat and simmer until the sauce has thickened slightly. Remove from the heat and add the drained cherries, brandy and essence. Stack 3 pancakes on top of each other, putting a dollop of cream between them. Spoon a little of the cherry sauce on top. Decorate with fresh cherries, chocolate curls, or shavings and mint leaves.

MAKES 10–12 SMALL PANCAKES.

Carmen says
■ Substitute blueberry sauce (see p. 213) for the cherry sauce.

FLAPJACKS

Flapjacks are made with a slightly thicker batter than that used for pancakes and it always contains a leavening agent such as baking powder or bicarbonate of soda. Flapjacks are made on a very hot, lightly greased stove plate or in a pan. Use oil to grease the plate or pan as butter will burn.

Flapjacks with bacon, banana, cheese and syrup

The sweet and savoury combination is unbelievably delicious. Serve them for breakfast.

FLAPJACKS
2 extra-large eggs
30 ml (2 T) sugar
250 ml (1 c) milk
30 ml (2 T) oil
500 ml (2 c) cake flour
20 ml (4 t) baking powder
2 ml (½ t) salt

FILLING
1 banana, thinly sliced
80 g Cheddar cheese, grated
150 g rashers bacon,
  crisply fried
maple syrup

Whisk the eggs and sugar together. Add 125 ml (½ c) of the milk and oil and mix gently.

Sift the cake flour, baking powder and salt together and add the mixture to the egg mixture. Whisk only until there are no more lumps. Gradually add the remaining milk to make a smooth mixture. Do not stir the mixture again and leave it to stand for at least 30 minutes.

Bake the flapjacks in miniature greased pans or drop spoonfuls of the mixture on a hot, greased stove plate. Grease the pan only once.

Turn the flapjacks with an egg lifter as soon as air bubbles appear on the surface and the flapjacks are firm. Lightly brown the other side.

Put banana and grated cheese on a flapjack and cover with another flapjack. Top with fried bacon rashers and drizzle with maple syrup. Repeat with the remaining ingredients.

MAKES ABOUT 16 FLAPJACKS.

Trimmings and toppings

Besides tasting delicious a cake should also be visually appealing. So it's important you choose the right decoration for your cake. The current trend is to keep it simple with fresh fruit and flowers. For rustic cakes a dusting of icing sugar is all that's needed, while a three-tier Victorian sandwich or chocolate cake festooned with a chocolate collar or shavings and flowers looks wonderfully festive. Let the kind of cake you bake determine how you should decorate it.

Carmen says
- Ensure the icing you choose for a cake complements the flavour of the cake. Coffee icing with an orange cake is out while a chocolate cake with coffee or chocolate icing is simply delicious. Candied orange peel is also excellent with chocolate cake, provided the cake also has an orange flavour. Nuts go with just about any cake while fruit preserve or rose petals are perfect with a cheesecake or plain sponge.
- Basic cakes such as sponges are transformed into something special if served with a fruit compote. Be creative when decorating a cake but ensure the flavours work well together.
- Keep an eye out for interesting decorations at your local supermarket and specialist baking and kitchenware stores.
- Chocolate vermicelli, silver balls, crystallised flowers and edible gold and silver glitter and foil turn a cake into a work of art.

UNCOOKED ICINGS

Drop icing

After a dusting of icing sugar, this is probably the easiest way to decorate a cake.

250 ml (1 c) icing sugar
25 ml (5 t) lemon juice or hot water

Blend the ingredients to make a smooth, fairly stiff but spreadable paste.

MAKES 125 ML (½ C).

Creamy lemon drop icing

15 ml (1 T) butter, at room temperature
250 ml (1 c) icing sugar, sifted
30 ml (2 T) lemon or lime juice

Beat the butter and icing sugar together until the well blended.
Gradually add the juice, stirring until the icing is smooth but runny enough to spread over the cake.

MAKES ABOUT 125 ML (½ C).

Cream icing or filling

Give stiffly whipped cream extra taste and interest by adding fresh fruit, lemon curd or crushed meringues. We added a little plain yoghurt to make it less rich.

250 ml (1 c) cream, chilled
30 ml (2 T) caster sugar
30–60 ml (2–4 T) plain yoghurt
a few dollops lemon curd, fresh berries
  or a few crushed meringues

Whip the cream and caster sugar together until stiff. Fold in enough of the yoghurt to make a spreadable mixture. Fold in the lemon curd (delicious with yoghurt cakes), berries (excellent with sandwich cakes) or meringues (perfect for oven-pan cakes).

MAKES 300 ML.

Butter icing

This is the most commonly used icing. It can also be used to sandwich cakes together.

125 g butter, softened
250 g icing sugar
about 15–25 ml (3–5 t) milk
5 ml (1 t) vanilla essence

Cream the butter until smooth. Gradually add the icing sugar, beating until the mixture is light and fluffy. Add a little milk to give the mixture a thick, spreadable consistency. Beat in the essence.

MAKES ENOUGH FOR 1 STANDARD CAKE.

VARIATIONS

Chocolate: Add 30 ml (2 T) cocoa to the icing sugar or 2 squares melted chocolate to the butter.
Coffee: Add about 30 ml (2 T) strong black coffee instead of the milk.
Mocha: Add 15 ml (1 T) cocoa to the icing sugar and use 30 ml (2 T) strong black coffee instead of the milk.
Orange or lemon: Substitute orange or lemon juice for the milk.

Cream cheese icing

The cream cheese icing is delicious with vegetable cakes such as carrot cake, while the chocolate variation is excellent with chocolate cakes.

500 g icing sugar, sifted
150 g creamed cottage cheese
30 ml (2 T) butter, softened
5 ml (1 t) vanilla essence

Mix the sifted icing sugar, cream cheese, butter and essence together.
Beat until creamy.

MAKES ENOUGH FOR 1 LARGE CAKE.

CHOCOLATE CREAM CHEESE ICING

Prepare the cream cheese icing as described, but add 60 ml (¼ c) cocoa and 100 g melted dark chocolate to the mixture.

COOKED ICINGS

Caramel cream icing

This yummy caramel icing is delicious with any cake but goes especially well with nutty cakes. Cream and brown sugar are heated to make a thick caramel paste that can be used as an icing or filling.

250 ml (1 c) cream
125 ml (½ c) soft brown sugar
2 ml (½ t) vanilla essence

Bring the cream and sugar to the boil in a saucepan. Stir continuously. Reduce the heat and simmer the mixture for 10 minutes. Add the vanilla essence and pour the mixture into a large mixing bowl. Chill for at last 3 hours or until very cold. Whip until stiff and spread the icing over the cake.

MAKES ABOUT 180 ML (¾ c)

> Carmen says
> To make a more runny icing gently whip the mixture with a wire beater.

7-minute icing (meringue icing)

The meringue mixture is whisked over boiling water until thick and glossy. Use it to decorate fruitcakes or fresh vegetable cakes such as carrot cake. It takes only 7 minutes to make this icing, which is why it's also called 7-minute icing.

375 ml (1½ c) caster sugar
1 ml (¼ t) cream of tartar
80 ml (⅓ c) cold water
pinch salt
2 egg whites
5 ml (1 t) vanilla essence

Put all the ingredients in a glass bowl over a saucepan with boiling water. Beat with an electric beater for 7–10 minutes or until the mixture is thick and glossy. Leave the icing to cool for a few minutes before using it to decorate a cake.

MAKES ABOUT 500 ML.

UNCOOKED ICINGS

Royal icing

This icing is traditionally used to decorate fruitcakes.

2 egg whites
15 ml (1 T) lemon juice
500 g icing sugar

Whisk the egg whites and lemon juice together until stiff peaks form. Sift over the icing sugar and beat with an electric beater for about 7 minutes or until stiff.
To decorate: Spread apricot jam over the entire cake. Roll out marzipan (see p. 206) and put it on top of the cake. Cover with the icing and leave it to harden.

MAKES 500–750 ML (2–3 C).

Marzipan

Fruitcakes are covered with this almond paste before being covered with royal or plastic icing.

500 g ground almonds
500 g icing sugar
1–2 egg yolks
5 ml (1 t) vanilla essence
    or rose-water
1 ml (¼ t) salt
15 ml (1 T) lemon juice or brandy

Mix the almonds and icing sugar. Lightly whisk the egg yolks, mix in the remaining ingredients and add the mixture to the almond mixture. Mix to make a stiff paste. Knead until the paste is elastic and can be rolled out easily. Wrap the marzipan in clingfilm and store in a cool place.

MAKES ABOUT 500 G.

Orange curd

This variation on lemon curd is made with orange juice. It makes a delicious filling for cakes, tarts and meringues. Alternatively serve it with freshly baked warm scones.

zest and juice of 3 large oranges
zest and juice of 1 lemon
500 ml (2 c) sugar
125 g butter, diced
10 ml (2 t) cornflour, dissolved in a
    little water to make a stiff paste
5 extra-large eggs, lightly whisked

Heat the zest, juice and sugar over medium heat. Add the butter and stir until the sugar has dissolved and the butter has melted. Leave the mixture to cool and beat in the cornflour and eggs. Return the mixture to the heat and, stirring continuously, simmer slowly over low heat for 20 minutes.
Pour the curd into a clean, sterilised jar or container and cover the surface with clingfilm to prevent the mixture forming a skin.

MAKES ABOUT 500 ML (2 C).

VARIATION
Lemon curd: Substitute lemon zest and juice for the orange zest and juice.

Carmen says
Lemon curd is usually made in a glass dish over boiling water but this easy recipe is made in a saucepan directly on a stove plate. The cornflour prevents the egg separating.

Lemon chiffon filling

This lighter variation on lemon curd is ideal to use as a filling for sandwich cakes and mini pastry shells.

4 extra-large eggs, separated
200 ml sugar
125 ml (½ c) lemon juice
2 ml (½ t) grated lemon zest
pinch salt
15 ml (1 T) gelatine, soaked
    in 50 ml cold water

Whisk the egg yolks lightly. Add half the sugar, lemon juice and zest and salt.
Whisk the mixture in a bowl over boiling water until the mixture is thick and pale.
Melt the soaked gelatine in the microwave oven, taking care it doesn't boil. Beat the gelatine into the egg yolk mixture.
Whisk the egg whites lightly. Add the remaining sugar and beat until stiff.
Fold the warm egg yolk mixture into the egg whites.

MAKES 500 ML (2 C).

Orange curd

Mock cream

A much lighter alternative to fresh cream, perfect for filling and decorating cakes.

250 ml (1 c) evaporated milk, chilled
15 ml (1 T) icing sugar
pinch salt
3 ml (generous ½ t) vanilla essence
5 ml (1 t) gelatine, soaked in
    15 ml (1 T) cold water
25 ml (5 t) boiling water

Whisk the evaporated milk until stiff and beat in the sugar, salt and vanilla essence.
Dissolve the gelatine in the boiling water, leave it to cool and whisk it into the evaporated milk mixture. Use like cream.

MAKES ABOUT 500 ML (2 C).

CHOCOLATE ICINGS
Boiled chocolate icing

If you don't like rich icings try this delicious chocolate icing.

400 ml boiling water or Rooibos tea
250 ml (1 c) sugar
50 ml butter
50 ml cocoa
50 ml cornflour
7 ml (1½ t) vanilla essence

Mix the boiling water or tea, sugar and butter and heat until the sugar has dissolved. Mix the cocoa and cornflour with a little of the sugar syrup to make a smooth paste. Add the paste to the remaining sugar syrup and, stirring continuously, heat until the sugar syrup comes to the boil and thickens. Add the vanilla essence. Leave the icing to cool for a few minutes then put it in the fridge to chill. Use as needed with chocolate sandwich cakes (the icing will be fairly slack).

MAKES 400 ML.

Chocolate ganache

Rich, creamy and decadent — this chocolate cream will transform the most basic chocolate cake into sheer heaven.

300 g dark chocolate, broken
    into squares
300 ml cream

Heat the chocolate and cream in a glass bowl over a saucepan with boiling water or in the microwave oven at 75 per cent power. Heat until the mixture has melted, stirring occasionally.
Pour the mixture into a bowl and chill it. Using a wire beater, beat the mixture at 5–10-minute intervals until it has a spreadable consistency.

MAKES ABOUT 300 ML.

Yoghurt ganache

To make a lighter ganache, mix the melted chocolate with plain yoghurt instead of cream.

200 g dark chocolate, broken
    into squares
1 container (175 ml) plain yoghurt

Melt the chocolate and mix it with the plain yoghurt. Chill the mixture until it thickens slightly, beating it occasionally. Pour the ganache over the cake.

MAKES ABOUT 250 ML (1 C).

CHOCOLATE DECORATIONS

Decorations made from chocolate give cakes an extra air of elegance, especially if casually piled on top of the cake.

Chocolate curls

Melt 100 g dark chocolate and, using a spatula, spread it on a cold surface – marble works well. Leave the chocolate to cool and become firm but not rock-hard.
Using a knife with a large blade, scrape the blade over the chocolate at a 45° angle. Holding the knife at both ends, press it down slightly. As the knife moves along it will form curls. If the chocolate is too hard the curls will break into pieces.

> **Carmen says**
> Store the curls in an airtight container in the fridge.

Chocolate shavings

Using a potato peeler, scrape shavings off a slab of chocolate. The chocolate should preferably be chilled.

Chocolate decadent

Spoon a little melted chocolate into a plastic bag and snip off a corner to make a piping bag. Hold the piping bag about 2.5 cm above a clean sheet of baking paper and, applying gentle pressure, make a lacy pattern using fairly rapid circular movements.

> **Carmen says**
> A plastic sleeve used for filing sheets of paper makes a sturdy piping bag.

Chocolate leaves

Wash rose petals or mint leaves well and pat them dry. Using a small brush, spread a fairly thick layer of melted chocolate over the back of the petals or leaves. Leave the chocolate to dry. Carefully loosen the tip of each leaf and peel away the chocolate leaf from the real leaf. Store the chocolate leaves in an airtight container.

NUTTY DECORATIONS

Caramelised nuts

Delicious on all cakes, from health to chocolate cakes.

100 ml sugar
60 ml (¼ c) water
250 ml (1 c) pecan, Brazil or hazelnuts or almonds

Heat the sugar and water in a small saucepan over low heat until the sugar has dissolved. Increase the heat and, without stirring, simmer the syrup for about 10 minutes or until it turns a caramel colour. Add the nuts and stir to coat them with the syrup.
Turn the nut mixture out onto an oiled baking sheet and separate the nuts with a wooden spoon.
Leave the caramelised nuts until cold and use to decorate cakes.

> **Carmen says**
> - **To make praline:** Prepare the caramel syrup as described. Add the nuts, mix gently and pour the mixture onto a greased baking sheet. Leave it to cool. When hardened, break the praline into rough chunks or give it a quick blitz it in a food processor. Sprinkle the praline over icing.
> - Sprinkle finely chopped pistachio nuts over an iced caked.

FRESH DECORATIONS

The latest trend is to adorn cakes with fresh decorations rather than spend time making complicated trimmings.

Fresh fruit

Berries such as youngberries and strawberries, fresh figs, granadilla pulp and pomegranate seeds can all be used to adorn cakes. Pile plenty of fruit on top of a cake to give it a lovely fresh look. Fresh lime, lemon and orange slices or lightly char-grilled pineapple slices also add to a cake's visual appeal.

Fresh orange peel

Make citrus peel curls by soaking long strips of orange, lemon or lime zest in iced water.

Crystallised orange peel

Using a canelle knife or a zester cut long, thin strips of orange peel. Roll each strip in caster sugar and leave them on a sheet of wax paper to dry.

> **Carmen says**
> A zester is ideal for making thin strips of citrus zest while a canelle knife is used to remove longer, thicker strips of peel or to carve designs in the peel of oranges.

Grilled citrus zest

Using a zester remove thin strips of zest from 3–4 oranges. Put the zest in a small dish, pour over boiling water and leave the zest to soak for a few minutes. Drain and repeat the process twice more.
Pat zest dry with paper towels and sprinkle generously with caster sugar. Using your hands, mix the zest and caster sugar, ensuring the zest is well coated. Lift the zest with your fingers and shake gently to remove any excess sugar.
Spread the zest on a baking sheet lined with baking paper and put it under the heated oven grill until crisp, taking care the zest doesn't burn. Leave to cool before using. Store the zest in airtight containers until needed.

> **Carmen says**
> Thin orange slices can be grilled similarly except the slices don't need to be blanched in hot water.

Citrus peel in syrup

Remove the peel of a large grapefruit without cutting into the pith. Put the strips of peel on top of each other and cut them into thinner strips. Put the strips in a saucepan, cover with cold water and bring to the boil. Simmer for 10 minutes and drain. Heat 180 ml (¾ c) water, 125 ml (½ c) sugar and 1 star anise, stirring until the sugar has dissolved. Add the peel and simmer for 15–20 minutes or until the sauce thickens and the peel is transparent. Remove with a slotted spoon and dry them on a wire rack. Use the strips to decorate desserts or serve them as is with other sweet treats.

> **Carmen says**
> Dip the strips halfway into melted chocolate.

Glacé orange slices

The tang of the orange slices is delicious with cheese-, orange and fruitcakes.

250 ml (1 c) water
250 ml (1 c) sugar
2 small oranges, cut crossways into 3 mm thick slices

Bring the water and sugar to the boil in a saucepan and simmer for about 5 minutes. Add enough orange slices to make a single layer in the bottom of the saucepan. Simmer for 20–40 minutes or until the slices are transparent. Turn them occasionally. Drain the slices and put them in a bowl. Repeat with the remaining orange slices.
Pour the remaining syrup over the orange slices and leave them to cool.

Van der Hum glacé fruit

I was given this recipe years ago by the late Trudie Taljaard. She used to spoon the fruit over Cambrieni cheese for dessert. Delicious! The fruit is also ideal for adorning fruitcakes that have been covered with royal or meringue icing.

500 g selection of glacé fruit
500 ml (2 c) Van der Hum liqueur

Slowly simmer the fruit and liqueur until nearly all the liquid has been absorbed by the fruit and the fruit is syrupy. Spoon the fruit and syrup on top of the cake, allowing the syrup to run down the sides of the cake.

Ginger strawberries

These spicy strawberries are delicious with gingerbread or ginger ring cake — spoon the berries into the hollow.

3 cm piece fresh ginger
160 ml (⅔ c) water
125 ml (½ c) sugar
10 ml (2 t) lemon juice
8 x 250 ml (8 c) fresh strawberries, quartered
fresh mint (optional)

Bring the ginger, water, sugar and lemon juice to the boil and simmer until reduced to about 250 ml (1 c) syrup. Pour the syrup over the strawberries and leave to cool. Decorate with fresh mint, if desired.

Citrus vanilla compote

Pile citrus segments and peel on top of fridge tarts. Also delicious with unbaked cheesecakes.

1 pink grapefruit
1 orange
60 ml (¼ c) water
60 ml (¼ c) sugar
5 ml (1 t) vanilla essence or ½ vanilla pod
pinch salt

Peel the grapefruit and orange and cut the peel into very thin strips. Boil the peel in the water for 1 minute, drain and set it aside.
Cut the fruit into segments, working over a bowl to catch the juice. Squeeze the juice from the membranes. Bring the water, sugar and vanilla to the boil, stirring until the sugar has dissolved. Reduce the heat and add the peel, salt and 60 ml (¼ c) of the juice. Simmer for 2 minutes. Add the fruit segments to the syrup and leave to cool.

MAKES ABOUT 250 ML (1 C).

Carmen says
If using a vanilla pod, cut it open and remove the seeds. Add the seeds to the egg yolks and sugar and proceed with the recipe as described.

Spicy fruit compote

This fruit compote makes an excellent filling for pancakes.

250 ml (1 c) fresh orange juice
250 ml (1 c) water
250 ml (1 c) caster sugar
juice of 1 lemon
1 vanilla pod
1 cinnamon stick
5 cm piece fresh ginger
500 g fruit in season, such as oranges, berries, peaches, plums, pineapple and mango

Bring everything except the fruit to the boil and simmer for 15 minutes. Add the fruit to the syrup and leave it to cool.

MAKES 750 ML (3 C).

Carmen says
Mix a can of granadilla pulp with the mixture.

Fresh fruit compote

This fruit compote transforms the most basic cake, such as a sponge or Victorian sandwich cake or Swiss roll, into something special.

2 oranges, peeled and cut into segments
3 granadillas
250 ml (1 c) mango cubes
125 ml (½ c) pineapple cubes
15–30 ml (1–2 T) sugar
15 ml (1 T) chopped fresh mint
pinch salt

Mix the ingredients and chill the mixture.

MAKES 375 ML (1½ C).

Spicy clementine marmalade

This marmalade complements blue-cheese cake (see p. 79) or any orange cake.

10 small clementines, washed
375 ml (1½ c) sugar
500 ml (2 c) Rooibos tea
3 star anise
1 clove
1 cinnamon stick

Prick the clementines all over with a needle (do not peel them) and halve or slice the clementines into wedges.

Bring the sugar, rooibos tea and spices to the boil in a large saucepan, stirring until the sugar has dissolved. Simmer for about 10 minutes. Add the clementines and simmer until the fruit is soft and glossy but still whole and a fairly thick syrup has formed.

Spoon the marmalade into sterilised jars and seal.

MAKES ABOUT 750 ML (3 C).

```
Carmen says
```
To prevent the peel from being too chewy, cook the clementines in advance until the peel is soft enough to be pierced with a cocktail stick. Drain the clementines and proceed with cooking them in the syrup.

Poached fruit

Serve the fruit with a flat cake such as a polenta or semolina cake.

1 litre (4 c) water
zest and juice of 1 lemon
1 vanilla pod
375–500 ml (1½–2 c) sugar
2 pears, halved
3 plums, halved
handful seedless grapes

Bring the water, lemon zest and juice, vanilla pod and sugar to the boil. Add the fruit and poach for about 10 minutes or until the fruit is just soft but still firm and whole. Remove the fruit from the syrup and leave it to cool.

Blueberry sauce

Pour the sauce over iced cupcakes or an iced sandwich or flat cake, such as a polenta cake, to create a striking effect.

750 ml (3 c) blueberries
160 ml (⅔ c) light brown sugar
30 ml (2 T) lemon juice
capful brandy

Bring the blueberries, brown sugar and lemon juice to the boil in a saucepan and simmer for about 7 minutes or until a fragrant sauce forms. Add the brandy. **Serve** hot or cold.

Carmen says
Substitute any other berries such as strawberries or mulberries.

Dried fruit slices

Thinly slice fruit such as apples and pears (do not peel or core the fruit).
Dip the fruit slices in lemon water to prevent discoloration and put them on a baking sheet.
Dry in a 100 °C oven.
Store the dried fruit slices in an airtight container.

Crystallised flowers and fruit

Edible flowers such as pansies, rosebuds or rose petals, lavender flowers, mint sprigs and leaves, grapes and even small bunches of grapes give cakes a festive look. Dip the fruit or flowers into lightly whisked egg whites and roll them in caster sugar. Leave to dry.
Dip the edges of rosebuds quickly into melted chocolate for a pretty effect.
Arrange bunches of the fruit and flowers on a cake.
Pile rose petals on top of a cake and pipe over thin strands of melted chocolate.

Index

Conversion charts

Weight-volume equivalents

INGREDIENTS	ML	GRAM
Almonds	250	150
Cake flour	250	120 – 135
Cocoa	250	100
Coconut	250	80
Cornflour	250	120
Custard powder	250	130
Pecan nuts	250	100
Polenta	250	70
Sugar:		
Brown and white sugar	250	200
Castor sugar	250	210
Icing sugar	250	130
Walnuts	250	100

Substitutes

250 ml self-raising flour	250 ml (1 c) cake flour + 7,5 ml (½ T) baking powder
5 ml baking powder	1 ml (¼ t) bicarbonate of soda + 2,5 ml (½ t) cream of tartar

Oven temperatures

	°C	°F	GAS MARK
Very cool	90 – 100	180 – 200	Low
Cool	140	275	1
Moderately cool	150 – 160	300 – 325	2
Moderate	180	350	3
Moderately hot	190	375	4
Hot	200 – 220	400 – 425	5 – 6
Very hot	230 – 260	450 – 500	7 – 9